"In these captivating stories Roger G
still be a powerful way to engage with
ing dilemmas. You will learn more philosophy by reading this one
enjoyable and illuminating journey through contemporary morality, politics, and spirituality than you would by taking any ten philosophy courses at most universities."

—Rabbi Michael Lerner, editor of *Tikkun Magazine*,
chair of the interfaith Network of Spiritual Progressives,
and author of *The Left Hand of God: Taking Back
Our Country from the Religious Right*

"Heart-opening and beautifully written. *Engaging Voices* invites us to
experience how opening ourselves to what others have to say—especially those we fundamentally disagree with—tests our moral courage in ways that accelerate inner growth, and provides pathways for
improving our collective lives."

—Paul Wapner, Director of the Global Environmental
Politics Program, American University, and author of *Living
through the End of Nature: The Future of American Environmentalism*

D0051944

Cover Design by Jeremy Reiss, J. Reiss Creative

Library of Congress Cataloging-in-Publication Data

Gottlieb, Roger S.
  Engaging voices : tales of morality and meaning in an age of global
warming / Roger S. Gottlieb.
     p. cm.
  Includes bibliographical references (p.   ).
  ISBN 978-1-60258-260-6 (pbk. : alk. paper)
  1. Environmental ethics. 2. Dialogues. I. Title.
  GF80.G68 2011
  179'.1--dc22
                              2010031665

Printed in the United States of America on acid-free paper with a
minimum of 30% pcw recycled content.

Engaging Voices

Tales of Morality and Meaning in an

Age of Global Warming

Roger S. Gottlieb

BAYLOR UNIVERSITY PRESS

For
The Earth
Without whom this book could never have been written

CONTENTS

There is no one living without failings; no person that is so happy as never to give offense; no person without a load of trouble; no person so sufficient as never to need assistance . . . therefore we should think ourselves under the strongest engagements to comfort, and relieve, and instruct, and admonish and bear with one another.

—Thomas à Kempis

THE STORIES OF SAMUEL PRANA

I met Samuel Prana some years ago. I had been giving lectures— at universities, churches, civic groups—about religion and the environmental crisis. I'd begin by describing some ecological problems: not just in abstract terms that people could shrug off, but in ways that would make it real. For example, I would talk about "body burden"—the hundreds of toxic chemicals you can find in the blood of newborn babies; or the Great Pacific Garbage Patch, which is a kind of thick stew of plastic waste that ocean currents have drawn together—it's now bigger than the United States. What do such things mean, I would ask, for a life of faith and morality? Then I would show how religious thinkers, leaders, and lay people were all changing their traditions, coming into a new understanding of our responsibilities to the earth, and becoming environmental activists. Along the way I would look at some moral questions that affect us all, religious or not: How much consumption is justified? Can a capitalist society ever be sustainable? and Is the hope that we could truly respect other species—like the hope that we could live by the Golden Rule—just an impossible ideal? Then I would end with a plea that we face our grief and fear, not give in to despair, since we couldn't really say what the future would bring, and choose to be the kind of people who honored and respected all of life—even if we didn't know whether we would be successful in ending the madness of the way we were living.

It was a pretty good talk, if I say so myself: passionate, informative, inspiring. With the odd joke to keep people listening.

It was after I did one of these at a local university—something to do with Earth Day, I think—that Samuel came up and introduced himself.

He was a tall man, very thin, in a clean but much-worn black suit, white shirt, and gray tie. He had the largest eyes I had ever seen—a blue so dark they were nearly black, rarely blinking, and fixed on my face with a concentration that was almost frightening. His face had enormously deep lines, around his eyes and mouth, across his forehead. Whatever else was true about him, he hadn't had an easy life.

He talked so low I had to strain to hear him. And I thought he had a foreign accent, perhaps from somewhere in eastern Europe, but it was hard to tell. Something about him was odd. He didn't have the "let's talk about this like colleagues" attitude of a professor, and with his gray hair and wrinkles he certainly wasn't a student. Somehow I knew he wasn't a typical ordinary-citizen-interested-in-the-topic either. There was none of the "please enlighten me" look that I sometimes get after a talk, nor the one that says, "I've got a bee in my bonnet about" (global warming, why religion should be abolished, my daughter who teaches recycling in elementary school . . .) "and I'm going to tell you all about it."

Maybe it was the way he looked at me that made me pay close attention, rather than go into my usual "the brilliant but very approachable professor will now answer all your questions" routine.

The look in Samuel's eyes was one of—well, it's not easy to say, exactly. Perhaps *generosity* is the word. He was here, those intensely focused eyes said, to help me. To help me see something I'd missed and learn something I needed to learn. At the same time there was nothing fanatical or obsessed about him. He was totally self-confident in a relaxed way that led me to suspect that whatever he believed he had thought about very carefully, very intelligently, for a very long time.

So instead of running off back home, I invited him to go out for a cup of tea, something I never do after lectures.

As I settled down with a large ginger mint tea from the coffee house, Samuel, who had accepted without hesitation my offer to pay, sipped his hazelnut latte. We began to talk. Or, rather, he started to talk, and I to listen.

"There's no doubt you're a bright fellow, Gottlieb," he began, using just my last name in the way eastern Europeans often do, "but you're missing something. Maybe the most important thing. Certainly you care about what you are saying, maybe too much. But yes, it is important that you care. Except . . . in the end there is a big hole in what you do."

"And what's that?" I asked, with a tolerant smile. After all, I prided myself on having thought of just about everything. Not every detail, of course—there were countless facts about environmental problems, and church resolutions, and international environmental agreements, that I didn't know. And never would. And there were some tough ethical issues that would stay open as well: how much consumerist consumption was reasonable, and how much was, well, too much? How to choose between preserving an old-growth forest and helping people into decent jobs? That sort of thing. But I had always prided myself on being a "big picture" kind of guy, and I was pretty sure I knew what large-scale perspectives were out there. I had a handle on how various religions and different political groups understood the world in general and environmental problems in particular. I could tell you about the conservative opposition to global warming policies, the religious critique of liberalism, and the five ways economic globalization destroyed both community and ecology. I knew who was right, who was wrong, and who was inconsistent. Who avoided reality in favor of cheap spiritual clichés, and who used political correctness to justify violence, who forgot the economy when thinking about God, or God when thinking about technology, or differences between owners and workers, or people in the U.S. and people in Bangladesh. I had my reasons, lots of them, all lined up and ready to go.

"What you are missing," declared Samuel slowly, reaching out with a long, bony finger to tap at my arm, "is that it really does not make so much difference who is right."

"What?" I demanded, incredulous, pulling back from him. Maybe this gentleman wasn't so smart after all.

"No," he answered, "what is really important is not being right, it is how we can live together even if some of us are right and some are wrong, and others are half right and half wrong, and the rest have not made up their minds. How will we do that?"

By the bewildered expression on my face he probably realized I hadn't a clue what he was talking about.

"Look here," I replied (being a bit confused, I got a bit more pretentious, and I figured I'd take the easy examples first). "Wasn't it 'right' that democracy should replace inherited political power? That the slaves should have been freed? That women got the vote and the right not to be abused by men? When people take *moral* stands, as opposed to just acting out of habit, or because they think something feels nice, aren't they saying at the same time, 'This is right, this is the way things should be'?"

"All well and good," he replied, clearly unimpressed. "And also painfully obvious. This is what philosophers have always done. Looked for the right answer. It started with Socrates, who did so well in Plato's dialogues that the people he argued with always seem not to know what is going on. Most of the time all they can say is, 'I see, Socrates.' And Plato set the stage for what followed. Thinker after thinker telling us that *he*—unlike all the ones who had preceded him, of course—had the real truth. He would give us the only rational way to think, the only sure morality, the ultimate meaning of human existence. And so on. And for our religious people it was even worse. The biblical God tells the Jews, 'Do it this way, no argument!' And so we also will be like God—we will tell you what is right and wrong, what is the blessing and what is the curse.

"So everyone does this: the preachers, political activists, and talk show hosts; every newspaper editorial and presidential press conference. My position over yours, my values to dominate society, my view of God and heaven and ethics."

His voice had risen a bit, and he paused to cough, and then take a breath. "So," I asked gently, "what's wrong with that?"

"What is wrong is that it does not answer the question I just asked you: how are we to live together, talk together, when we do not agree? How can we speak to one another in a way that realizes there will always be differences and recognizes and learns from our differences? How do we do that, if the main thing on our minds is always, 'I am right, you are wrong'?"

I stroked my beard and pressed my lips together, the professor being thoughtful. "But Samuel," I answered, shifting unconsciously into my calm, teacherly tone, since I thought this was just a common undergraduate error that needed an expert corrective, "don't you realize that certain differences simply *can't* be accepted? For me it is fine for people to worship in different buildings using different prayer books. But if someone wants to force everyone else to worship in his building using *his* prayer book, how are we to accept *that* difference? If the religious conservative refuses to have his daughter educated, and we have a law saying *all* children must be educated equally, what can we do?

"We can disagree on where the universe came from: created by a God, product of a big bang, woven out of the entrails of a spider. You have your myths and I'll have mine. But what if someone has a myth that says some group—say, the Jews—are responsible for all the problems his country faces, that Jews are immoral monsters with the ethical status of germs, and must all be killed? How am I to coexist with the man who wants to kill me? You see, the lion and the lamb can accept each other's differences, but if they lay down together, only one of them is going to get up afterward, and it won't be the lamb."

I paused, pleased with my clever turn of phrase about lions and lambs, and smiled encouragingly at him. It was a common mistake, after all.

"Really," replied Samuel, and he sighed heavily. "I would have expected better. This is just the standard philosophical refutation of relativism and false tolerance. And like most standards, it is true—but only as far as it goes. We have to have certain agreed-upon values and laws. Certain kinds of rules make others impossible. Certain views are very lethal. Believe me," his intense eyes got even more intense, and he rubbed the back of his neck as if thinking of some old pain, "I know all about the stories that would kill a person for being different, better than you do.

"But all this is beside the point. It is not what I'm talking about.

"So sometimes all we can do is fight the other side, or make laws against them." He reached over to tap me on the arm again. "But what *else* can we do? If we are not to go to war with them, Gottlieb, if we are not going to put them in jail—and always remember, if it is possible to put them in jail, it is possible that you, too, would end up there! If we are not to *compel* them, then what are we to do? How can we talk to them? What kind of people do we have to be to do that?"

He sipped some more of his coffee, got his breath back, and began again.

"Please do not talk to me about all the unreasonable, crazy, violent people. For always remember this: wherever you draw the line, and put some people outside it—call them Nazis, fundamentalists, al-Qaeda, imperialists, the ruling class, global corporations, military dictators, communists, radicals, tree huggers, meat eaters—wherever you draw the line there will be some people still on *your* side of the line.

"Tell me: how will you talk to *them* when you disagree? The more frightened you get that the people on your side maybe are really on the other side, the more you will want to prove them wrong. All of a sudden these people also will be people who must be controlled, overcome, shut out, coerced. You will draw your line closer and closer until it is just you and seven other people who think exactly like you.

"So no matter how much you tell me that 'Some people can't be talked to, it's foolish to try, you just have to defeat them,' the problems I'm talking about will return again and again. What will you have if you don't learn something else? Endless war—with guns, with words, with what is in your heart—is that the way you want to live?

"And the other thing you have forgotten is this: unless we learn how to talk to people we think are wrong, we cannot be right ourselves. After all, we learn morality as we learn science—from other people who teach us ways to think about what we think, to question our beliefs, to test our conclusions. That is what all this moral reasoning is, no? We feel strongly about something—homosexual marriage, war in Iraq, global warming, free enterprise—and then we try to evaluate what we feel: Are we consistent? Have we looked at the facts? Are we forgetting the consequences on *other* people of what we think is such a great plan? Are we demanding too much of people . . . or too little? Are we privileging the way we do things in our little corner, or the world, or our time, and forgetting that it could be different somewhere else—or that it was not always like this?

"If we do not hear such questions, put to us by people who are very different from ourselves, how are we to be as sure that actually we are right—and not just continuing some mistaken prejudice? Those stories you love to tell about political progress—how wonderful it was to end slavery or give women the vote—every time you tell that story you are saying, 'Those people on the wrong side did not think, did not listen, and ended up living lives of cruelty, selfishness, oppression.'

"How can you know you are not doing it yourself, right now, if you do not listen? Did not every one of those oppressors fail to listen? Could you be doing the same thing?

"Look at it this way, Gottlieb: of course we can *end up* with new laws, with violent revolutions, with assassinations even. We can mock the politically incorrect, or the foolishly liberal, or the narrowly religious, or the orthodox seculars. We can end up there, certainly.

"But that is not where we should *start*. So I ask you—what do you know about what you do first, before you stop the conversation and make the people on the other side obey?"

He stopped, so out of breath I wondered if he had a lung problem. He gave me another intense look, daring me to offer another facile philosophical retort.

But I couldn't. I was stumped. I drank some tea to give myself time to think.

Oh, there were some pretty trite answers I could have given, more of the "standard" philosophy sort of thing. Let's all be rational, avoid self-contradiction, take established facts into account. If we are talking about morality, we need to think about how our actions affect other people; and we need to find some way to think ourselves out of the naturally self-centered perspective that people naturally take. We have to distinguish between scientific claims, which can be tested, and religious claims, which cannot, at least not in the same way. We have to think about principles to direct our actions, and the effects on human happiness of what we do, and what virtues make sense for human beings. When we talk about justice, we have to be careful about gender bias, racial bias, cultural bias, and—well, you get the idea.

But having said all that, and even having taken it seriously to some extent, well, then we could get down to what really mattered: showing that our beliefs and values were correct.

Samuel was saying something different. For him, openness was not just another move in the game, openness *was* the game, because without openness we couldn't be changed by other people, and couldn't really live with them. We would just try to make sure they came around to our side. And ultimately we couldn't even really learn about how ethical we were, how committed to a real justice or just all the time falling back on some knee-jerk, self-congratulatory story about our own moral correctness.

Of course, to get Samuel off your back you could invoke all the people who just wouldn't be part of a conversation. You might want to talk, but they would put a machine gun on the table and tell you what to do. Over all this, you might say, was the shadow of Hitler—the one we *cannot* talk to.

"Again," answered Samuel, a little impatience in his voice, "you miss the point. Do not go rushing to Hitler, for God's sake. Is Hitler right around the corner, breathing down your neck? No, Hitler is in the past, Hitler is finished and known.

"Are you finished? Have you nothing to learn? Are you willing to respect other people to the point where you find some truth in what they say? If you cannot, how will you be in a community with them? And how will you learn what you need to learn about yourself?

"The key to moral conversation is that you and the other people are *not* finished. You are in the process of becoming. That is why you talk. Not just to pound out the same old ideas over and over, but to change, to grow. *That* is what makes a moral community. That is what you do *before* you turn to the laws and guns and the shaming of all the ones you despise."

I was silent. And silence is perhaps the greatest acknowledgment a professional argument maker like me can make of a superior . . . argument? Well, Samuel hadn't really made an argument, but what he had done was cast the whole process of moral conversation in a new light, a goal not of finding the truth, but of mutual understanding. And to have that understanding, we had to have a certain kind of relationship. And therefore the relationship, not the elusive truth, was the key. How can I be committed to my moral values and stay in touch with people with very different ones? How can I think not just for myself but for the relationship as well? In a way, it was simple, painfully simple. How had I missed it all these years?

"Realize," said Samuel, putting on his coat and getting ready to leave, "I am surely not the first person to think like this. Women philosophers have been talking for years about empathy—really trying to understand what other people feel as a basis for knowing how to act. There's the idea that democracy is about citizens communicating with each other, and not just people voting as separate individuals. Gandhi began from a position of moral humility. It is not for me to judge others, he would say, because I am so morally weak myself. The whole civil rights movement in your country used to talk about something they called the 'beloved community'—a time when love and respect shaped all our relationships with others. Buddhist teachers have warned us against being attached to our beliefs, as if these verbal formulas were some kind of immovable mooring spot for a windblown selfhood. The Talmud recorded the wrong positions as well as the right ones. Truth and reconciliation commissions ask us to listen to each other's stories, even if those stories are about terrible violence against our families. Professional peacemakers do the same.

"All I am suggesting is that you take those values and put them to work here, in all these encounters you have when you think about morality, about what life means, in this terrible time."

Over the next few years we met once in a while. He always came without warning—at a public lecture, during my office hours, even a few times after sitting, quietly, without taking off his coat, in the back row of one of my classes. We would go over this idea of his, this idea of moral conversation in a moral community, over and over again. It was attractive in so many ways, but so alien. I still wanted to win the argument, to be right. No matter how much I tried to think in a "spiritual, nonviolent" way (as I'd come to describe it) about moral conversation, I'd slip back into the old style. Samuel would point this out to me, over and over again, tapping me on the forearm for emphasis, sipping his coffee, sighing over what a blockhead I was. And I'd agree, and go back to where I started.

At times I would wonder how you could be open and still have a serious moral position. Wasn't Samuel just asking me to be wishy-washy—weak and unprincipled? What good was that to anyone—especially in a time of global environmental crisis, ethnic violence, vast inequalities of wealth, and a population so miserable that its members took endless quantities of legal and illegal drugs just to get through the day? We desperately needed answers, a correct analysis, and unshakable moral values.

And then I remembered something from my youth, something I still think about with embarrassment. For a time in the late 1970s

I was part of a tiny political group—fifteen of us actually—called Jews for Justice. We were a collection of left-wing Jews who both supported Israel's right to exist and condemned its occupation of Palestinian land. We opposed anti-Semitism as well as colonialism, suicide bombing by terrorists as much as Israeli militarism. The established Jewish community hated us for supporting a two-state solution and criticizing Israel. And the left hated us for supporting Israel's right to exist and for criticizing anti-Semitism. We were dedicated, passionate, concerned, highly educated, and very emotionally immature. Eventually differences within the group started to become our whole focus. One side placed too much emphasis on anti-Semitism, one side not enough. One side thought too much about the occupation, one side only thought about terrorism. And on and on it went—more anger, more distrust, less and less listening, everyone sure they were right and the other side wrong. No wishy-washy types here, never fear. And then it got so bad we split up—into one group of eight and one of seven. We were going to solve the endless, intractable conflict between the Arabs and Israel—and we couldn't even get along with each other.

Wasn't that just what Samuel was talking about?

For a long time I didn't see him. He and his ideas faded from my mind as I occupied myself with teaching and writing, political arguments and moral judgments. I worried about the environmental problems that kept getting worse and a kind of religious and political insanity that had erupted everywhere. I was frightened for the future of life on the planet, appalled by all the crazies, and mad at the people who wouldn't face the truth. I knew it wasn't much, but I had to prove them all wrong—at least to my students and the small readership of my books and articles. Being right was my defense against fear and a lurking sense of helplessness. If I wasn't right, what good was I?

One morning I got, for the first time, a phone call from Samuel. He asked after me, and while I was very glad to hear from him, I was concerned about how weak and throaty his voice sounded. "Are you all right?" I asked. He laughed, then coughed badly, then laughed again. "I am what I am, just like God."

He told me to meet him in the same coffee place we'd first talked, in the late afternoon of the next day.

When I got there he was nowhere to be seen. So I got some tea and waited. Time passed. My mind wandered to our many meetings, and Samuel's ideas of a spiritual, nonviolent moral conversation to sustain a moral community. As I was going over his ideas once more, a tap on the shoulder brought me out of myself.

"You Professor Gottlieb?" asked a slender, teenage girl in a black sweater.

"Yes," I told her.

"You look just like he said you would—like a teacher whose mind is a million miles away from where he is." She smiled, not in a mocking way, but not particularly friendly either. "This is for you." She smiled again, and left.

It was a package wrapped in plain brown paper, with a small note on top, in a shaky, spidery longhand. "Gottlieb, this is for you. I don't need them anymore, not where I'm going. You are having such a tough time moving to the next level. Maybe this will help. Don't be afraid to change. Goodbye."

I tore open the package to find a manuscript, page after handwritten page in the same spidery script, called *Engaging Voices*. It was the stories that follow.

1

WHY AM I ALIVE?

"Why are you alive? Why are you alive?"

The strange phrase kept repeating itself in Kate's head, and she had a hard time getting her mind around it. What kind of a question was this? But it was, after all, what she was supposed to ask them.

"Remember," her brother Ned had told her, "these are not your ordinary students. There are murderers, rapists, people inside for political violence or massive white-collar fraud that cost thousands of people their pensions. They are angry, bitter, well defended. You've got to hit them right between the eyes with simple, hard questions, or they will just stare at you."

Ned spoke from experience, she knew. He had been teaching this philosophy course at Smithfield Maximum-Security Prison for over a year. But he had hurt his back, pretty badly this time ("Pushing too hard in yoga class," he laughed, and then grunted with pain as the chortles brought on a spasm in his left hip) and had begged her to take his place for today's sessions.

"Most people don't like to think about these questions, and if I let one class go, they might not come to the next one. They would just go back to being in prison, without thinking about why they are there or what it means."

Kate wasn't altogether sure it was better to think about it. If they'd still be in jail no matter what they thought, what difference did it make?

"All the difference in the world," Ned had replied, a little impatiently. "It's all about what it means. Is it a prison? Is it a kind of monastery? Is it a punishment for your moral failings and a chance to make amends, or the effect of a racist justice system in a racist society? What you think determines how you feel, how you survive, what you can hope for. If they are going to move on from being thieves, drug dealers, or murderers, they have to develop some awareness. And then The Movement will really need them. What they've been though and how they've changed could teach us all a lot."

He had spoken with such force that Kate knew he really needed to believe it—that doing this sort of thing, after all, was why he thought he was alive. He was her fundamentally decent but usually self-preoccupied older brother, who always had one politically correct cause or another at the forefront of his mind—health care reform, end the war (whichever war it was), or raise the minimum wage. For the last two years it had been the fate of prisoners in what he called, scathingly, the "prison-industrial complex," referring to the joint effort of law enforcement, prison operators, and surveillance technology producers to manage, and at times exploit the labor of, mostly nonwhite American citizens for upwards of a hundred billion dollars a year. Ned didn't handle disagreement too well, and certainly not from the younger sister he loved dearly but to whom he still needed to condescend.

So Kate didn't tell him that she suspected doing philosophy in a prison—or maybe anywhere else—was just a way to pass the time. People, she felt, did what they wanted and looked for justifications later. If they wanted to be kind, they would choose a kind philosophy; if they thought their wives should serve them, they would find a handy patriarchal religion to tell them this was what the Father (or Allah, or Adonai) had in mind. Kate trusted her intuitions, her gut feelings, more than she trusted Ned's endless political rants. She could sense what was going on, and didn't need philosophy, which just covered up people's fear and greed.

But here she was, settling into a hard wooden chair outside the Warden's office, holding tight to her oversized REI bag and hoping the thin cardboard container inside wouldn't spill, about to lead a philosophy discussion in a prison. "Warden likes to talk to everyone who comes in here," the massive prison guard had said, looking her over appreciatively. It probably wasn't too often that they got a visit from a nice-looking young woman, and Kate sensed this guy, whom she dubbed "Big Guard" in her mind, would be more than happy to talk philosophy with her. She smoothed the nonexistent crease out of her black slacks, adjusted the collar of her gray tunic, fidgeted with her small amethyst crystal necklace, and wondered if she had dressed too fancy or too plain. She was about to tighten the barrette on the simple ponytail that held her thick brown hair off her pretty, oval face, when the Warden appeared.

"Welcome, welcome to our facility," beamed the Warden, as he came through his office door to greet her, his completely insincere smile a jarring contrast with his eyes, which told you that since he'd seen everything already, no matter what you had, he wasn't impressed. "So nice of you to take Ned's place. Our guests do so enjoy the little chats he has with them."

Kate eyed him skeptically: was all this a joke to him? Did he think there was something funny about people, even inmates at a maximum-security prison, thinking about what their lives meant?

The Warden looked her over, just as Big Guard had. Kate had not felt so much like a piece of meat on display in a butcher shop for a long time. Perhaps the women's revolution hadn't quite made it past the chain-link fence, the barbed wire corners, the four massive doors it took to get in, or the guards with high-powered rifles on the towers. Twenty years ago she had signed up for Feminism 1A and never looked back. It had saved her life, she was sure. Here it didn't even exist.

Trying to be polite, she said she would do her best but she was sure she wouldn't be as good at this as Ned, who had done graduate work in philosophy. She was just a social worker specializing in homeless mothers.

"Never fear, never fear," murmured the Warden, with the same mix of reassurance and slight mockery. "Just ask a few questions and let them talk. It doesn't make any difference, really, does it? No matter what they say the prison walls will still be there. And they will be inside. There will be guards in the room, so don't worry about a thing. Just don't get too close to them."

Steep flights of stairs led her down into the prison's poorly lit basement, and then a long dark corridor ended at a large iron door. Big Guard was now joined by a second—a small, sullen middle-aged man whom Kate immediately thought of as Little Guard, her mind racing around to placate her nerves. Kate gave him a quick half smile and walked into a small bare room filled with a dozen metal chairs. She tried to move one to make the arrangement more circular but found that they were bolted to the floor. Big Guard tapped one of the chairs with his nightstick. "Sometimes the conversations get a little, you could say, heated. So to keep the brothers from making a really good point by smashing each other over the head, the chairs can't be moved."

"Stand back now," Little Guard warned her, "they're coming in."

They were tall and short, black and white and Hispanic, old and young, wearing faded dungarees, blue work shirts, and prison name tags. Many had the bulging muscles of inmates who, lacking any other control of their lives, had shaped their bodies with intense weight training. Others looked pale and weak, tufts of gray hair sticking up from nearly bald heads, scruffy day-old beards on wrinkled faces, hands that moved this way and that for no discernible reason.

They stared at her with a mixture of surprise, hostility, and thinly veiled lust. "My name is Kate. I'm Ned's sister," she explained. "Ned can't come today so he asked me to fill in."

"What's his problem, he don't love us no more?" This from Raoul, a broad-shouldered, powerfully built, very short Hispanic who grinned at her with an insolent challenge.

Kate decided to try the light touch. "He loves you plenty. He just hurt his back doing yoga."

"Yoga?" Raoul crossed his arms in front of a massive chest. "What a waste of time. Supposed to make you strong and he messes himself up."

"Well," said Kate, trying to get things underway, "it's not just for strength like weight lifting or running. . . ." She paused, embarrassed. Not too much long-distance running for prisoners, she realized. "It helps center you, make you calmer and happier."

"Happy! Ha!" snorted Raoul, "I'll take a woman, a Colt 45, and some rock. I don't want to be centered, whatever that is. Let some lady make me happy, let the pipe take my mind somewhere else." He high-fived a tall, thin inmate next to him, and a few unenthusiastic "yeahs" echoed in the room.

"Well," Kate pushed on, "I can imagine a few minutes of that feels pretty good. But is that why you're alive? That's today's topic, by the way. Is that really the best thing you can be doing with your life?"

"You got anything better?" Raoul countered, stretching an arm rippling with muscles and pointing his finger at her. "It's what everybody wants, ain't it? The white guy in the suburbs, he's doin' it with an SUV and a big house. I'm from the hood, and I do it my way. You lady, what do you do?"

"Do you really think everyone is just after pleasure of one kind or another? Is it all the same?" Kate answered, hoping they wouldn't notice that she hadn't answered his question.

"He probably thinks so, but he's wrong," declared a small, painfully clean-shaven white man in the back row who, Kate saw, carried a Bible. His name tag listed him as David. He had large brown eyes, short brown hair meticulously combed, and he spoke slowly, with intense conviction. "The sinners live for sex and drugs and money. And I'll tell you this, Raoul is right that it's the same for the poor folks in the ghetto and the rich ones in their fancy houses. But all their pleasure and vanity will turn to loneliness and despair. If you haven't been saved by Jesus, you are on a dark road."

"That's just what I'm tellin' you," Raoul shot back, pointing at him. "You want your happiness just like I do. Only yours comes from that book you're always carrying on about, and mine comes from what I said. Everybody is just out for themselves, trying to get high on something."

"I know you feel like that," answered David, his voice low and serious, moving his Bible to rest over his heart. "And I understand, because I used to live like that myself. It wasn't drugs for me. It was money. And good times. I had a Caddy dealership outside Utica. I sold them new and I sold them used. I cheated buyers in ways you couldn't imagine—hustled my employees, lied on my accounts, and bribed the city government to give me breaks on my property taxes. The money rolled in, and I drank some, gambled some, and cheated on my wife with good looking younger women I could get because I always had a fat bankroll in my pocket."

"Is that why you're here," asked Kate, "for cheating your customers?"

"Not at all. No, I got sick, really sick. Some kind of pretty rare bone cancer. I lay in that hospital bed, day after day, night after night, scared and lonely. My wife would barely come to see me, my kids neither. Can't blame them, I was a lousy husband and father. To the doctors and nurses I was just a slab of meat on a bed. They went through the motions, treated me like a collection of X-rays and test results, doled out their chemicals and radiation and kept tabs on whether I was alive or dead. And then . . . I started to feel lost—not just sick and hurting but like I'd missed something really important. I started to see that all the time I thought I had been going up—lots of money, big house, wife, mistresses, fanciest car in town—I was going down. I was completely alone, alone and unloved, and it was all my own fault. I began to wonder if there wasn't more to life than money and good times. And I started to think: even if I get better, is that what I want to go back to?

"Then the hospital preacher came to see me. I'd heard about Jesus since I was a little kid—went to church and recited the prayers like everyone else. But it never meant anything. Just seemed a sucker game for people to get theirs in heaven rather than on earth. Well, I wanted mine now, not later.

"But it turned out I hadn't really gotten anything. I'd lost all love and respect for myself, so I couldn't get it from other people. And anyway other people were just suckers to be hustled. The world was a place to make a sharp deal, get a little drunk and laid, and buy something fancy and expensive. But after a while I didn't really enjoy what I had, I just wanted the next thing down the line. I was just running from one thing to the next. None of it gave me any real pleasure anymore, but I couldn't stop."

Kate was quiet, waiting for someone to respond to the powerful narrative. But the silence just built and no one responded. Except . . . was that some kind of sadness in Raoul's eyes, which a moment before had been so arrogant and hostile?

"Tell you the truth," David went on, "I'm glad I got sick, or I would have run forever, 'til the day I died. Anyway, the preacher told me about God's perfect love and forgiveness. About a God who so loved us, so loved *me*, that he let his only Son come into this terrible world and get spit on, to show us what perfect love is. And he told me that I could have that love any time I wanted. I didn't have to a better person, I didn't have to be brave or honest or kind. Not right away at least. I just had to let Jesus into my heart. So I did—I let Jesus in, and Jesus brought me love and contentment I'd never thought possible.

"I got better and left the hospital. My wife divorced me—with plenty good reason—sold the dealership, and took the kids to Europe on my money. I was broke and my family was gone. But that was all right, because I was saved. Born again. And that's what I am today."

"I don't understand." Kate was taken aback by David's long, moving story. She had her problems with Christianity, to be sure, especially the Evangelical, all-you-need-is-Jesus, the-Bible-is-the-word-of-God, everyone-else-is-a-sinner variety. But it certainly seemed to have taken David from a meaningless life to a meaningful one. "If you became a Christian, and stopped cheating people, and lying, what are you doing here?"

"I did the Lord's work. And here I am."

"The Lord's work?" Kate repeated, completely puzzled, thinking of missionaries in Africa, nuns working in hospitals, preachers in tents at revivals. "Why should they put you in jail for that?"

David was silent, his lips pressing tightly together.

"You want to know what kind of *Lord's work* this brother did?" drawled Jamaal, a middle-aged African American with a round red hat on his head and a heavy beard. His brown eyes were so glittery they seemed to be lit from the inside by a fever. "You want to know?" he repeated, stretching long, muscular legs and making silent clapping motions with huge hands. "He shot a doctor. Dead."

"I took God's vengeance on a murderer," David hissed through his rigid lips. "And defended the unborn."

Kate was stunned into silence, her mind in turmoil. This was not what she had expected, not at all. She had been ready to be distantly sympathetic to people born into poverty who had turned to drugs and violence; to be properly outraged at selfish swindlers from the upper classes; or even to be threatened by men who in a fit of jealousy had murdered their wives.

But this was violence for a good reason, *religious* violence. God's work. What could she say? She desperately fought through her "ums" and "uh-huhs" to remember Ned's advice: "Just ask them to explain what they mean, to make *other* people understand why it seems reasonable. That's the whole trick of philosophy." How could anyone make sense of murdering a doctor because you didn't like what he did to a fetus? She would never accept this. Never.

"I don't think I understand, David," she said quietly, forcing her voice into an imitation of neutrality. "How do you get from the love of God and how peaceful and contented you felt to murder?"

David sighed, as if he'd heard this a million times before but would explain it yet again. He held up his open palm toward her, as if keeping her away.

"People like you," he said, with just a hint of contempt, "have no idea how to live. You think life is about pleasure, and convenience, and" (his voice raised into a shrill parody of a female tone) "*my choices*. And the more you choose what *you* want, the further you get from God. You want sex without children, so you take a pill or get an abortion. Kids don't fit into your plan, so you hire strangers to take care of them." His voice rose, his head turned from side to side as if the room were filled with immoral women and he could convince them all. "Limiting yourself to one man is too confining, so you sleep around, until you feel like a piece of meat. You want to explore your *options*, so you want everyone free to be queers. *You*," almost shouting, he shook his finger at Kate, "have no business talking to me like this, questioning me. You are a woman, and women are commanded by God to obey their husbands."

"I don't understand," said Kate, even more confused. "We're not married."

"The Lord's word tells women to be silent in church."

"We are not in church."

"Are you stupid?" He slammed his fists down into his thighs in frustration. "The Bible is telling you to be quiet when men are present, to serve, to obey. I am to you like God is to me. If you don't like that, it is simply because you have rejected God's word."

"I will try this one more time, stupid female that I am," Kate continued, smiling now, torn between thinking what a sick fool he was and being angry at his primitive sexism. "What has all this got to do with killing a doctor?"

"It has *everything* to do with it!" He stood up, leaned forward toward her, his eyes darting back and forth in a frenzy of righteous rage. "You, emancipated woman, with your big mouth and your tight pants, you would rather follow your own selfish desires than the will of the Lord. But to please God we must obey him. And when God tells us to protect the innocent then we have to do God's work on earth."

Suddenly his voice softened, and the maniacal aggression in his voice changed to sorrow. "I didn't want to kill that doctor. I didn't want to kill anyone. I've never even been in a fistfight. Jesus put love in my heart, not hate. But," he looked at Kate pleadingly, "the unborn are alive, they are human, they have a right to live.

I was killing him, yes, but I was saving them. Trying to stop this terrible new holocaust. And maybe scaring some other doctor not to do abortions. Really, more than anything, I just wanted God to love me, and forgive me all my sins." He stopped suddenly, looked around almost surprised that he'd gotten up, sat down quickly, and held his head in his hands.

"Take it easy, brother," said Jamaal, patting David's shoulder, adding to Kate, "He gets excited. But you know, he's got the right idea. Life is about submission to God, to Allah, not self-indulgence, personal pleasure, and the kind of decadence we in the U.S. seem to have perfected."

Well, thought Kate, maybe this one would be more polite. "So, how do you know it's God you're serving, and not just an inflated version of your male ego," she wanted to say . . . but didn't. "Really?" she asked. "How do you know you and David are serving God?"

"In truth," said Jamaal, "I am, and he's not. He does have the right idea about what's important, he's just doing it wrong. Only Islam is God's plan for the world."

"And how do you know that?"

"Because Allah has told his prophet, Muhammad, peace be upon him, in his holy book. There is no need to look further; all the truth is there, in the Qu'ran. You would find it, if you bothered to look." He tilted his head to one side, gave a small smile, and asked, "Have you?"

As a matter of fact, Kate hadn't. She really did not care to read a book when those who followed it had such a bleak view of women. Jamaal and the Qu'ran, David and the Bible. From where she sat, they were all the same. Whatever they thought about God, they all wanted their women to be servants.

But Ned had warned her about this too: "Look, some of these guys, well, to put it mildly, they are kind of sexist pigs. All that women's lib that is so important to you means nothing to them. But try to leave that aside and draw them out. If we get them talking, if they see us listening and learn to do some listening themselves, they might change, or maybe lighten up a bit." Kate hadn't paid too much attention, knowing that she wouldn't find a lot of enlightened men behind the walls of a prison. Yet hearing it now she was surprised at how much anger was welling up inside. She did her best to keep it hidden.

"You've got me there, Jamaal," she finally replied, keeping her voice as even as she could. "So why don't you tell us what is in there."

Jamaal shifted in his chair, closed his eyes as if asking for guidance from an unseen source. His voice took on a hushed, reverent tone. "It takes a whole lifetime to even begin to understand God's word, but here is what you must know. God made the universe, he made us. And he made us for a purpose: to follow his law, study his ways, obey his teachings. Each day we pray that Allah should bless us, and we give alms for the poor. Once in our lives we must go to Mecca. For the rest we have detailed laws, Sharia, which tell us about business, family, how to eat, how to be married. This is the natural law for all peoples, the only way for human beings to be happy. This is why we are alive."

At least he got to the point, Kate thought. Then Charles, the oldest man in the room—thin, with very white skin, delicate features, and dark rings under pale blue eyes—broke in, "So Islam makes you happy?"

"There is no peace like the peace of Allah," Jamaal replied softly. "The only thing worth living for is obeying God."

"I can see how *terribly* happy you Muslims are," Charles answered, his voice dripping with scorn. "I'm sure flying planes into buildings, cutting people's heads off for television cameras—that obscene video of what they did to the reporter—and screaming 'Death to America' is just a *delightful*" (he minced out the word like a gossip reporter) "way to pass the time."

Jamaal's eyes narrowed, and as he leaned forward in his chair, his mouth curled downward in contempt. "You think we are terrorists because we kill what you call the innocent, right?"

"That's right," said Charles. "And all your rhetoric is about death and blood and killing. It seems to be what you live for."

"And you don't? The American government with its war on Iraq—when you drop bombs on cities, cut off electricity to hospitals, make mistakes by hitting civilians—who do you think dies then?"

"Yes, people die, but that's a war."

"Exactly," said Jamaal. "And we too are at war. You have occupied our lands, undermined our culture, threaten us with drugs and pornography, pollute the holy soil of Arabia with your troops and Internet. So we resist. And you call us terrorists."

"Your religion is just one big excuse for violence—a crazy excuse," Charles replied with unveiled disdain.

Kate was silently cheering Charles. She wanted to see the religious fanatics put in their place.

Jamaal looked up and smiled, which surprised her. She was sure Charles' hostility would cause another rant. Jamaal just leaned back in his chair in an exaggerated imitation of relaxation.

"Let me just ask you this, *brother*," he drawled, with a mocking familiarity. "Is it our ideas that bother you, or the fact that we fight for them? You whites would really prefer that all the people of color would be strung out on drugs, lining up at methadone clinics, or wailing to Jesus. You don't like us proud and strong, do you? And you don't like my Arabian brothers proud and strong either. So you call it terrorism.

"I grew up on the South Side of Chicago. My mother went to church all the time, praying to Jesus to save her soul and her family, and to be patient and kind, a good Christian woman. Meanwhile two of her kids—my brothers—got into drugs. She didn't fight for them, just kept praying. The pastor didn't fight either—he just kept calling out to Jesus and making sure the collection plate was filled on Sunday. I was the youngest, and I saw my brother die because the dealer—some piece of garbage like Raoul—sold him some bad dope." He looked over at Raoul, daring him to say anything. Raoul smiled a cold, angry smile but kept silent.

"Nobody told me how to fight back—until some Black Muslims came to town. Everything they said made sense to me—how the whites wanted us drugged out, how the dealers and the cops worked together, how Jesus was a blonde-haired, blue-eyed God of lying down and taking it, no matter what. So I joined up, changed my name, learned the prayers. I went to see the dealer who'd killed my brother. I told him to stop. I warned him. And when he didn't listen I blew him away. And I'd do it again, even though I'm in here for it."

Again Kate was shocked at the violence. But then she wondered what she would do if somebody had hurt her family. She'd go to the cops, of course. But what if the cops didn't do anything? What if somebody had paid them off? What then?

Charles' mouth had hardened in distaste, as if someone had offered him rotten meat. "You want to be a Muslim? Be a Muslim," he almost hissed. "Just leave me alone. You and him," pointing at David, "keep your goddamn religions to yourselves."

"Live and let live, is that the way you want it?" demanded Jamaal.

"You bet."

"So why do you impose your values, your culture, your system, on Iraq and Afghanistan?"

"So the people can have the freedom to choose, to have rights."

"But that is not who we are," shouted Jamaal, perhaps no longer sure who "they" and "we" were. "Our religion is a religion of complete submission to God, it is not about choice. When you threaten that with your alien ways you threaten everything of value in our lives. We will not allow you to destroy our faith." Suddenly he shouted, "*We will win the war.*"

"Some faith," murmured Charles. "Tell me again about how your *faith* said it was just dandy to saw somebody's head off and put the video on the Internet."

Jamaal, his voice now an accusing snarl, shouted, "This horrifies you so much, this video of Pearl's head being cut off? Tell that to the people who died from American bombs. We've got a long way to go before we match what you've done, *without* religion, a very long way."

"We aren't proud of it, not like you," Charles shouted back.

"Oh, well, so I guess how you *feel* is what is crucial. Well, guess what, you hypocrite; in the end people are just as dead. At least *we* are honest. *You* hide behind lies about democracy and freedom."

They glared at each other, each protected by the truth.

"Let's take a short break," Kate said brightly, wincing at how phony her false cheerfulness must have seemed. "I brought a little something." She reached into her bag, opened the flimsy cardboard box she'd carried in past the guards, and passed out some chocolate donuts.

As Kate watched the box go around, she realized that she had wanted to shout back at Jamaal: You think it's so glorious to die or kill or make a war. And you so love to oppress women. But then, when she looked closer, she saw the fear behind the rage. How hurt they'd all been. Nobody starts out like this. But what was the difference between explaining these guys—and explaining them away? Was it really respectful to make excuses, to think about their pain, and not to engage with what they were actually saying?

Kate had worried the men would be insulted by the snack, or think the donuts were ridiculous. But they all reached eagerly for the sugar treat, and chewed with intense concentration and clear delight. How like little boys they were, Kate thought to herself. All the anger, the certainty, the attachment to God or drugs or whatever. Just give them a donut and they're happy. Damn, she corrected herself quickly, there I go again. They are not little boys, and they deserve to be taken seriously. Don't they?

Charles wiped the last crumb from the corner of his mouth, looking slightly ashamed that he'd fallen so low as to be eating cheap chocolate donuts with the low-class types around him. Then he turned to Kate, as if the others were beneath him, talking almost painfully slowly, like he was explaining all this to children. "We have a system in the United States; it's called capitalist democracy. In the system we have rights—to believe what we want and be who we want. As long as we don't interfere with other people, we get to decide what we want to live for. We can be Christians or Buddhists or Muslims or atheists as we want. And we get to buy and sell, to create new products and new companies. And it works. That's why we are so much richer than all those hundreds of millions of

Muslims, who sit on the oil wealth and go no place. We don't owe our lives to God, unless we think we do. We don't owe our lives to our neighbors, except to pay our fair share for the army and the police and the roads. Since everybody is going to have a lot of different ideas about why we are alive, we leave it all up to the," he slowed down even more and pronounced each syllable with great emphasis, "*in-di-vi-dual*," then turned to Jamaal. "You think you're alive to follow the Qu'ran, David loves his Bible, Raoul wants his good times, I wanted to make money and run a great corporation, somebody else wants to play the guitar or write a book. Well, here we can do whatever we want. And that's why *this*," he raised his hand up suddenly, extended his arm, and spread out his fingers, "is the greatest country on earth, and people from everywhere else risk dying to get here."

Kate wondered if Charles' gesture to the great country included the inmates, the guards, and the sharpshooters, or if it started somewhere else.

"And you," Charles kept at it, pointing his finger at Jamaal and David, "you'd take all that away. You call it faith, I call it mindless slavery."

Kate looked over at David and Jamaal, wondering how they would take this last jibe. How much they had in common, she thought. A kind of brute, mindless certainty; and a willingness to kill for that certainty.

"Mindless slavery? You think that is the life of faithful Christians?" David actually laughed. He seemed completely unbothered by Charles' condescension. "Why don't you take a look at all these free," he stopped for a moment, then imitated Charles' drawn-out pronunciation, "*in-di-vi-duals* of whom you are so proud. Are they not slaves to money, greed, and being better off than their neighbor? To sex, alcohol, status, and petty pleasures they can't put down? Their freedom makes them so happy that they are on all these new drugs to keep them from being miserable—first the antidepressants for the grownups, then the college kids, then high school, and middle school, and now elementary school. A plague of heroin and meth and OxyContin and booze is sweeping through the teenagers of the middle class, a plague of divorce through the parents, and nobody is taking care of the elderly."

Kate's mind raced. There were things coming out of the mouth of this religious nut that . . . she agreed with! Was it possible? No! *Nothing* that a fanatical killer, a sexist pig like this said could be true.

"This is your secular freedom? No thanks. I admit it." David tapped his chest. "I am a slave . . . to Jesus. What were you a slave to?"

"I helped run a major energy company," countered Charles, who had clearly not been prepared for a dumb fundamentalist to answer back so forcefully. "I started with nothing, *nothing*," he yelled over at Jamaal, as if to say that he too knew what hard times were all about. "I worked nights to get through college, started at the bottom, pulled myself up. I was making $4 million a year, plus stock options. We created 42,000 jobs in the U.S., India, Canada, and the Philippines. We did business with everyone from the U.S. government to Zimbabwe."

Wait a minute, thought Kate, this sounds a little familiar.

"Benron? Is that why you're here?"

"Yes," admitted Charles, his tone suddenly not so self-assured. "I admit, things got a little out of hand. We made some promises we couldn't keep, tried to keep the value of the stock up by pretending we were in better shape than we were, and then it all fell apart."

"Ah, the blessings of capitalist democracy," Jamaal jeered. "You call it freedom, I call it theft, and no fear of God, who saw what you were doing even when other people didn't. Too bad about all your workers' pensions, wasn't it?"

"Oh," shot back Charles. "Somehow all those devout Saudi princes don't seem to mind money so much."

"The Saudis? They are Westernizers, imposters, no true Muslims." They glared at each other. Another standoff.

"And I suppose," said a medium-sized man sitting cross-legged on a chair in the back row, who'd perked up when Charles had mentioned Buddhists, "that someone will tell us that Benron is no true capitalist democracy—that it has to be Ben and Jerry's, or some other glorious example of free enterprise." He laughed, but gently. Kate saw that his name was Arthur, and he had, she thought, a remarkably kind face, with light brown eyes that seemed to see everything about you. While he didn't have the huge muscles of some of the other inmates, he held himself with a kind of wiry grace that suggested great physical strength.

Arthur unfolded his legs, nodded smilingly to David, Jamaal, and Charles, and then turned to Kate. "Those of us who are not Christians or Muslims, or capitalists or communists for that matter, who are simply human, how are we supposed to keep up with all this?" He turned in his seat. "Some Christians are pro-choice, and would think what you did was a great sin, David. Some Muslims think Islam preaches tolerance of other faiths, Jamaal."

"I told you," Jamaal answered, the contempt rising in his voice again, "they are no true Muslims."

"No doubt, no doubt," nodded Arthur. "But that is what they say about you. How am I supposed to know who is right? What I can see is that *all* the true believers—all the Orthodox Jews, and the Saudi princes, and al-Qaeda, the red-white-and-blue patriots and the ones that despise America, all have plenty of anger, even hatred, to go around—and sometimes you seem angriest at people who are closest to you. Is that the way you want to live? Filled with that rage, that desire to kill?"

"You got a better idea?" asked Raoul.

"I think I do. Before I came here, I was as violent as any of you. My father was black, my mother white, and where we lived no one accepted me. I was 'nigger' to half of them, and 'honky' to the others. All the kids picked on me for years. So I made myself tougher than any of them. After nine years of karate I could split boards with two fingers and I knew three ways to break a guy's nose. I got stronger and stronger, won match after match. And it still made me crazy that people would look at me and just lump me into some group that they hated. So one day as I was walking home from work four teenagers jumped me. They had bats and knives, and they started calling me 'nigger' and 'faggot' and all the other things nasty kids do. I would have ignored them." He paused for a moment, looking around the room, his eyes flickering from face to face. "I wanted to. Really. But they threatened me with the bat, and one of them grabbed me from behind. I snapped. In thirty seconds two of them were paralyzed because I broke their spines, one lost an eye, and one—who fell hard when I kicked him in the sternum—hit his head on the edge of the curb, went into a coma, and never woke up.

"I'm in here for life. 'Unreasonable response,' the judge called it. Hatred, rage, out of control, I call it. But I know better now."

Kate felt a little like crying. Another killer—another victim. Her instincts had been to like this guy—the calm voice, the gentle way he had pointed out to Jamaal and David and Charles that anyone outside their little circle wouldn't go along with their ranting. But then she saw the rough kids who'd jumped him. They also knew what they wanted, why they were alive. And look where it had all ended up.

"What do you know?" she asked him, hoping against hope for a little sanity.

Arthur sat up very straight in his chair and started to count out points on his fingers. "I know that I was living in a prison of my own making. That I was totally out of touch with my emotions, so I just acted them out. That I created a reality of hatred and revenge." He stopped counting and held both palms up. "Look where it took me." Back to counting. "I know that the more I want things I don't have, the more miserable I am. That when I accept all the things I cannot control, when I'm moderate in my habits, and most of all when I make sure that I am aware of what is going on in my mind, that I can be peaceful in myself and feel compassion for others— even here." He raised his palms up again, and looked around at everyone with a sweet smile.

"How did you get to all this?" asked Kate.

"Five years ago some Buddhists came to teach here. It was a way to get out of cleaning the toilets for a few hours each week, so I went." He slowly folded his legs back into a meditation posture on the hard metal chair. "They taught us to meditate, to see how attachments to our desires were making us unhappy, and that compassion for everyone, including ourselves, is the only way to happiness."

"So Buddhism is right and Christianity is wrong?" asked Charles. "Another nutty religious type. Just keep adding them in." He smiled scornfully, looking to Kate for agreement and not getting it.

"Not at all," Arthur answered, smiling warmly back at Charles. Kate really liked his smile. "I've learned so much from Buddhism, it's true. But you could probably learn all this other ways—from any religion or no religion. Really, it's about mindfulness. Knowing what you are doing with your mind. Seeing how unhappy you make yourself and others when you compulsively back away from someone, or move with anger, or let fear make you crazy. It's not easy, don't get me wrong. I'll be working on this for my whole life."

"Well, if you don't care about anything, why are you alive?" This from Raoul, who had, Kate realized, a knack for hitting the essential point in few words.

"Life is reason enough. I am alive to breathe, to observe my emotions, to find my way to a place of peace. There is a part of myself which is constantly separating myself off from pain and discomfort and disappointment—as that part recedes, something else arises. A calm, compassionate center of awareness."

"So," Raoul asked, "if I was to walk up to you," he stood and moved in front of Arthur, raising his hand into a fist, "and if I was to smack you, what would happen then?"

"Watch it, Raoul," warned Big Guard, pulling out his nightstick.

"Easy, man," Raoul grinned in response. "Just making a point, a philosophy point. Right, teach?" And he sat back down.

Kate didn't know how seriously to take any of this. Was it a performance for her benefit, meant to frighten her? Would Raoul really have punched Arthur? What in God's name was she doing here? Everyone seemed locked in their own worlds, how was she supposed to connect with them? She tried to assert her position as teacher again.

"So tell us, Arthur, how does a Buddhist respond to violence?"

"Look, Raoul," Arthur began, turning to face him, "don't get me wrong. I haven't forgotten what I know, and if I wanted" (had his tone changed—a sudden hardness coming into it?) "I could put you in the infirmary—or the morgue—in about five seconds." Raoul flinched, but then leaned forward. *I'm not afraid of you*, his body language said, but his eyes said something else.

"But, really," Arthur continued, his tone returning to gentleness, "it's about looking at my own response. The sense of threat is a tightening in my stomach, a tingling in my hands. My mind races around in fear, and then my thoughts turn to hate: 'I'll get this guy if he makes one more move, I'll kill the son of a bitch.' Now I can be aware of all that, calm my mind, slow down my breathing, realize that my anger is a bigger poison, a bigger threat to me, than anything Raoul could ever do. Nobody can make me afraid, or angry, or violent. Only I can do that. And I can stop it."

"So," Kate asked, "the key is your own state of mind?"

"Exactly."

There was a long pause. None of the other prisoners had ever thought of such a thing. Who would have imagined that this was what life was all about? And while Kate had heard some of these ideas about mindfulness and meditation before, it had always seemed like self-indulgence for uptight middle-class types, not something you could use in real life.

The silence was broken when Richard, a tall, thin white man with long black hair pulled into a ponytail, a bony face, and large, awkward hands, coughed with theatrical loudness. Faces turned toward him. "That's it," he said loudly, with unveiled hostility, "concentrate on your own state of mind. Your own feelings. Your breath, your emotions, your latest bowel movement. By all means. What could possibly be more important?"

Kate had noticed him making angry faces while the others had talked, especially Charles. Was he another crazy? And she didn't like it that sarcasm should follow something so positive. "What's your point?"

"Just this." He stood up and took a theatrical pause. "All of you," extending a bony finger at Raoul, David, Jamaal, Charles, Arthur, and then Kate, "are living in some kind of dream. Don't you know what is going on? We are destroying the world acre by acre, species by species. From the fished-out oceans to a hundred toxic chemicals in the blood of every new baby."

"Ah, the environmentalist speaks . . . again," smiled Jamaal.

"Have faith in the Lord, brother, not Sierra Club," laughed David.

"You idiots," Richard was almost yelling now, and Kate recalled once more what the guard had said about these guys not having much tolerance for disagreement. "How long do you think that your holy books and churches are going to last if things keep on like this? What will you do when the earth stops being a home for human beings? You believe your religions can outlast the *earth*?

"Don't your faiths teach that the earth is a gift from God? Then why are we treating it like some cheap, throwaway toy that can be replaced real easy next Christmas? David, where is the Golden Rule when our smokestacks kill the forests of Norway, or our energy use creates monstrous floods in Bangladesh?"

Kate reflected that these particular men of faith were rotting in prison, and not likely to do much about acid rain or global warming. But she didn't think anyone would appreciate that insight at the moment. Anyway, Richard had clearly given this rap before, so she might as well see where it led.

Richard turned to Charles, whose mouth was already curled in contempt. "And you, Mr. Benron, maybe you're so selfish you didn't care about the people getting screwed by the sweetheart deals you bribed your way into with foreign governments, but did you ever think what kind of world you were creating for your grandchildren? What will you say to your granddaughter when she asks, 'Grandpa, why didn't you stop it?' 'Sorry, I was too busy making money, that's what I was alive for.'

"Don't you get it? Your God, and your capitalism, and your," he jerked his chin toward Raoul, then Arthur, "endless self-pre-occupation with pleasure or personal peace or mindfulness or whatever, are useless now. Either we realize that or we will choke on our own wastes."

Well, well, thought Kate, approvingly. She had been a passionate environmentalist for years and always wondered why, with everything that was going on, people could act as if nothing was happening. But Richard, even though there was something a little off in the way he yelled at everyone, clearly knew what was up. How in God's name had he gotten *here*?

"Our tradition is steadfast. Everything we need to know, we know already. God gave us our holy book, and faith in that is all that we need."

Kate had been lost in thought. Was that David or Jamaal? And did it make any difference?

"We'll take care of it with technology. Machines made the mess, machines will clean it up. The market at work." Was Charles really as confident as he sounded?

"It's nice to see I've brought the secular and the religious together," Richard said, with more than a touch of irony. "You see? You really do have something in common—a refusal to look at the truth. Oh, I understand where you are coming from. It took me some time to face it. I was too scared, because I knew deep inside that it was bad, really bad. And I didn't want to think about it.

"But then I found out that the land under my house had been a shoe factory seventy years ago and that the little pond outside my backyard still had leftovers from the chemicals they used to cure the hides. *That* was why my sister was the way she was—cleft palate, learning disabilities, asthma. My sister was gentle, innocent, sweet. She loved me, even though I'm, well, not the most lovable guy around." He made a self-deprecating face, then shook his head as if warning himself to stop it. "The two of us used to go out to that pond, listen to the birds, catch frogs. Just sit together. Pretty much, all we had was each other. She never had a harsh word for anybody, but she used to cry herself to sleep at night.

"I started to study everything I could about environmental problems. What we're doing to all the little ponds, and the big lakes, and everything else. And to people too. And yeah, David, I joined Sierra Club. And worked for them on a bunch of campuses. But they were too careful, too damn *moderate*," he sneered, as if referring to a mortal sin. "Then I found Earth First!—'No compromise in defense of Mother Earth,' we said. We sabotaged some bulldozers building roads in wilderness areas; set a few fires in new houses to stop suburban sprawl. Some people got hurt. Not that much, really. Not as much as my sister and the kids with leukemia from the PCBs in the drinking water. But they caught me, and the corporate polluters and the builders pressured the government to put me away for a long time. And they have."

"So you see," observed Arthur quietly, using his palms-up gesture again, "in the end, what do anger and violence do? You're angry about what happened to your sister. And you want to protect the earth. But before you can change the world, *you* must change. You must be the peace, the sustainability, *yourself*, or you will get nowhere—but here, which is, I guess, a kind of nowhere."

"You know," retorted Richard, his eyes narrowing with focused fury, "you phony spiritual types are the *worst*. 'Be calm, watch your breathing, purify your mind.' By the time you get all that together, New York will be underwater. We don't have *time* to become enlightened. We're on the Titanic, you idiot, do you want to sit around meditating or try to save the ship?"

Arthur closed his eyes and took a long breath. "Ah . . . the savage joy you take in the faults of others. Most all, I think, you love your self-righteous rage. Do you really think a person has to be furious to be effective, to do something in the world?"

Richard stared at him, then, surprisingly, answered in a much quieter tone. "So you are going to be calm and peaceful, not like me. You're going to make some changes in the world with—how do you guys put it? A loving and compassionate heart? Well, tell me, give me the word, set me straight: how much are people like you actually doing? You say it's possible, and maybe it is. But how actual is it?"

"Hey man," Raoul broke in with a phony friendly grin, "sounds like this brother" (pointing at Richard) "is maybe really the selfless one—he's willin' to go to jail to protect a tree. And this one" (at

Arthur) "just wants to make sure he's chillin' all the time. Most important thing for him is, don't get bent out of shape. Course this brother" (back to Richard) "is crazy, for sure. But so what?"

"I'm not sure he's crazy," Kate spoke carefully, noticing once again how very clever Raoul was. Was that street talk of his an act?

"This is very interesting," she added. Then remembered how much she had hated pretentious professors saying, "Very interesting," as if anyone gave a damn whether they thought it was interesting or not.

"Or not, lady," said Big Guard. Kate hadn't realized he'd been listening. "But right now time's up."

"Well," Kate tried once more, "I hope this was at least a little fun," then cursed herself silently for a silly turn of phrase. Did these guys look like they ever had fun?

They all just stared at her, each one locked up in his own world again.

Of course Kate didn't have a clue about the doubts and fears they never shared. Charles would toss and turn every night, asking himself over and over how it had gotten so bad. Would some government regulators have made things better, even though as a good conservative he knew that governments only made things worse? And what was wrong with him, that he had gotten carried away in the insanity and lost any shred of decency? He would never forgive himself. But still he was sure that only the free market would make it possible for people to have a good life.

In their private movements Jamaal and David both got a little sick of all the angry self-righteousness they thought they were supposed to show everyone else. They had turned to God out of despair, and found love and a peace so deep there were no words for it. But then it always seemed to get down to my way against your way, the saved and the damned. Why couldn't it all be love and peace?

Richard hated himself sometimes for how much he consumed. He ate steak in secret, even though he knew how bad meat eating was for the environment. Sometimes he felt like the biggest hypocrite on earth.

And Raoul, wrapped so tight in his sharp tongue and untutored smarts, had nightmares about crack—the feel of the pipe in his hand, the huge, desperate inhalations, the mind-numbing rush that followed. And then he would wake up, sweating, clutching the blankets, missing it desperately. He would remember being strung out, promising himself he'd find some way not to give in to his cravings, and then running back to the pipe as soon as he could. He had built up a little dealership for himself, just selling to a few people so that he could afford his own habit. But every bit of profit he'd turned had gone up in smoke. Then he'd tried to make one really big deal, and ended up buying from the cops. He'd be here for awhile, telling everyone how much he missed the street. But a small part of him was glad he was here, because he didn't think he could control himself outside. He really didn't have anything else to live for but crack, and he knew that was death.

Kate gathered up her things and stood up, making one last attempt to reach them. "Thank you for having me. I really enjoyed this and I hope you did."

"Passed the time," mumbled a skinny white man who hadn't said a word.

"Would have passed anyway," Raoul laughed.

The prisoners filed out first, not one of them so much as glancing at her. As she was leaving, Big Guard reached out and grabbed her, gently, by the wrist.

"You should know something."

"What?"

"Richard, that great environmental guy, he's not in here for messing up a bulldozer or setting a few fires."

"Why is he here?"

"He killed his wife. She was cheating on him with a corporate lawyer. He brained her with a can of organic, fair-trade coffee, and she never got off the kitchen floor. Got a temper, that one, love of nature and all." He winked at her and laughed.

Kate ducked her head and hurried along the long, dark corridor, up the flights of stairs, through the enormous, clanging doors, past the towers with the sharpshooters, and, thankfully, thankfully, across the parking lot to her car.

Could that have been true, she wondered? Or just a kind of sick joke from Big Guard? Could someone so moved by what we have done to the earth also be a jealous murderer? Could you tell nothing about what a person was from what they said they believed?

She thought about their violence—she who hesitated to kill mosquitoes—and she thought about how hard it was for them to listen to each other. Except for Arthur, they just wanted to be right. A little bit like everyone else in the world these days, really. Maybe there was some connection, some tie, between the way they were so quick to hate and sometimes even to kill, and the fact that they couldn't listen to each other. Had everybody locked themselves into a prison—so scared to let anyone in that they couldn't let themselves out? Could that be it? Then she heard Ned's voice, "It's the system, the damn political and economic system, it messes people up."

And then she thought of herself: she wasn't violent; she tried to be open, to listen to others, to be tolerant. But certain things she stood for would *never* change: women's rights, the environment, nature, compassion. Was she really more open than Jamaal or David or Charles or Raoul? Or was she just closed in a different way?

Back at the prison, Big Guard turned to his partner. "God, I'm glad that's over. What a waste of time. All those guys yelling at each other, saying nothing." He just wanted to get home and be with his wife. They'd been married seven years, and there still wasn't anything in the world he loved more than her face. Maybe she had put on a few pounds since the kids, or maybe more than a few, he smiled to himself, but it didn't matter. She was his reason for living. And the kids . . . running around their small living room, giggling, getting into mischief, stopping to give him a kiss, and then running off again. Coming home to that after a day with these savages, well, it was worth it if he could give them a house and a car and some good times. Did any of those guys have families? If they did, would they be so crazy?

Little Guard didn't answer. He had another four hours on his shift and he would have killed for a cup of coffee. Sometimes he felt so tired he didn't know if he could keep working. This place, he thought, this place would make anyone nuts. He felt as if the grayness of the walls, and the darkness of the prisoners, had spread though the rest of his life. Nothing was fun anymore. He didn't really have any friends. He'd stopped caring about the playoffs, and since the incident, his doctor had put him on an antidepressant, so he couldn't even get drunk. "Things will look up with the medication," the doctor had assured him. "Your mood is dark because you lack certain chemicals in your brain. Once the medicine starts to work, and brings more of the chemicals in, everything will be better."

God, he hoped so. Otherwise, what was the point in being alive?

2

CHOOSE

The room was shabby, but Richard was used to it—and a dozen rooms just like it. Old wooden chairs, political posters on paint-peeling walls ("Save the Bay," "Universal Health Care," "End the Occupation," "Eat the Rich"), scuffed linoleum floor, and, this was a definite plus, a large blackboard covering one wall. Why, he wondered, do we always have the crappy rooms, and the people we are fighting have carpets, beautiful desks, and the latest computer-DVD-Internet-TV consoles with recessed push-button controlled track lighting and a seven-foot screen? Oh well, if we had them, we'd be the people we were fighting.

Despite the room, he was, for the most part at least, thoroughly happy. The sudden, unexpected pardon from the governor after the new evidence had surfaced had been a joyful shock. The day he left Smithfield, smelling the late April flowers and feeling the sun on his face, was one of the happiest he had ever known. To walk out of that place, to never see any of those horrible people again.

41

And now he was back to work. The local National Environmental Coalition organizer had left to go to law school. The job didn't pay much, but this was, after all, what he lived for. He had gotten right into it—contacting several people who had experience in progressive politics, setting up tonight's meeting. He had the perfect issue. And if things went right, in a few hours there would be a functioning coalition of activists under his direction. He just had to handle it, and watch his temper.

He took a large piece of red chalk and wrote on the board: *National Environmental Coalition, Binghamtown Chapter, Possible Issues.* He would list a bunch of things, but he knew which one he wanted them to choose. A little preliminary organizing had gotten him, he believed, some allies. They would all support the same thing, it would seem spontaneous, and then the group would be moving in the right direction.

Over the next twenty minutes, people straggled into the room. Richard was thankful that there were several women and at least a few people of color. It wouldn't do to be all male, and it *really* wouldn't do to be all white—even if black people often didn't get the importance of environmental issues.

"Welcome, folks, welcome," he began, speaking loudly to get their attention. As they quieted, he softened his tone and smiled— he'd learned to handle people at meetings years ago, and this sort of thing always worked. "My name is Richard, and I'm the local organizer for the N.E.C." He gestured to the board so they'd see what it meant. "Thanks to all of you for coming. We're here to start a new campaign, something we can all support and hopefully put some real muscle behind." He paused and looked them over, broadening his smile. With any luck, these would be his comrades for some time. Not forever, that was for sure. He'd done enough political organizing to know that every group would fall apart after a while. People burned out, or disagreed too much, or nothing worked. Or something worked for a time, and then stopped working. But this was the start, and the start could be beautiful.

He took a deep breath, calming his nerves. "Let's begin by introducing ourselves. Who are you, and why are you here? I'm Richard, and I'm here because I love the earth, and want to save it from the disaster people have been creating for the last hundred years. I want to save the wetlands and the rain forests and the polar bears—and in doing that, we'll be saving people too." He stopped and nodded at a short, stocky young woman with a red bandana wrapped around her close-cropped black hair, wearing faded jeans and an oversize sweatshirt with a "Fair Trade NOW" logo on it.

"I'm Wendy. I saw an e-mail about a new political group here, and this campus has been politically dead for so long, I thought I'd check it out. I've been an activist for a while—did some things in my high school, helped organize for better wages for nursing home workers, mostly immigrant Haitian women. And I worked to set up the Women's Center here. Environment? Yeah, of course. But it's what we're doing to people I care about, people here, not in some wilderness someplace else." Richard smiled and nodded, making a mental note to show her how the two went together.

"My name is Fred," said the man next to Wendy. He was in early middle age, ramrod straight, clear skin, blue eyes, short brown hair in perfect order—looking like he might have come from playing squash at the club. "I'm minister at the local Congregational church and Protestant chaplain on the campus. We've had a study group all this year about faith and nature. We've seen that God gave us the world and, as it says in Genesis, it's up to us to protect his gift of," he paused before the next word, almost caressing it with his tone, *"creation.* So I'm ready to do some protecting." He smiled at Richard, knowing how organizers think. "I might even be able to bring several of our members on board."

"Great, great," Richard smiled back. Now here was a find, he thought. Liberal Protestants—quiet, hard workers, and didn't like to argue. Perfect.

An overweight older man followed. He was straight out of central casting's model of a left-wing college professor: wire rim glasses; salt-and-pepper beard; thinning, unkempt hair; poorly matched, wrinkled clothes; and an air of confident authority. "I'm

Roger. I teach sociology here. Hell, I'm so far to the left I fall off the planet every once in a while. But I'm with Wendy. I'd like to see something, *anything*, happen."

An African American woman in her forties in a bright gold shirt and a flamboyant scarf, with tight jeans and a full head of intensely curly black hair, spoke after the professor. She had a loud, confident voice, neither aggressive nor friendly, just a large presence in a small room. "I'm Erica, here in the law school doing a special course on community environmental litigation. The way I see it, black folks are taking the hit on this, just like they always do on everything else. So I'd like to work on environmental racism. The rain forest and the polar bears," she shook her head and chuckled, as if thinking about them was a bit funny, "not so much."

Richard nodded encouragingly. This could be a dynamite group.

"Excuse me," said a thin, younger woman, with a long brown ponytail that went almost to her waist. She wore a dark blue crystal on a leather thong around her neck, patched jeans, and a black T-shirt with a picture of a redwood tree on it. Her large green eyes were kind, but there was a kind of tentative fear in the way she held her mouth. "I'm kind of new to all this. What's environmental racism?"

Richard started to explain, but Roger broke in. "Simple—people of color are more likely to be exposed to pollution, less likely to have it cleaned up, and the people who pollute them are less likely to be punished. The idea's been around since the early '90s. Helped take environmentalism out of the realm of saving the wilderness for rich white men to hunt in, and put it in terms that ordinary people could understand. When you talk about environmental racism, the environment isn't somewhere else—like the rain forest or the polar bears—it's your kids' schools, the water coming out of your kitchen tap, the land your house is built on. And *you* are the endangered species."

Richard had to admire how slickly Roger answered the question. The damn professors, they sure knew how to talk, he thought. We'll see down the line if he can do anything else.

"Well," said the woman hesitantly, obviously unsure of her-self. "That all makes sense, I guess. And I want to be supportive to everyone. Oh," she paused, and the fear in her mouth showed up stronger as she looked down at her lap for a moment, then back up. "My name is Lily. I'm here because of my mother—Mother Nature, I mean." She looked around hopefully to see if anyone smiled; no one did. "I feel most myself when I'm in the woods, or in a kayak on a river. But before long the woods will be clear-cut and all the rivers will dammed up or too dirty to boat in. I want to do my small part, like the Reverend said, to protect."

"We're here for everybody," Richard tried to reassure her. "People, nature. Same struggle, same fight."

"Oh lord," Roger broke in, with the casual self-assurance of someone who had been controlling classrooms for thirty years and was sure that he could speak any time he wanted. "Maybe we could skip the slogans. An awful lot of the time people don't get along because somebody's interests get met and others get forgotten."

Richard could feel his temper rising. He started an angry comeback, and then held his tongue. Who was this old guy to tell him how to talk? Everybody's interests would be taken seriously in his coalition. They just had to learn to see their interests the way he did.

"I hope you don't mind my asking," Fred turned to Erica. "Are you saying that poor people, or people of color, don't need to care about wilderness?"

"Tell you the truth, Reverend," answered Erica, "there isn't a whole lot of wilderness in the inner city. African Americans used to connect to nature plenty—but that was in the South, when we were sharecropping the land. Now we're in ghettos in the North, or crummy little suburbs that got walled in by the big interstates built in the '50s. It's what's coming at us from the lead smelters down the street that matters to us, not the redwoods."

"Great discussion, folks, just great," interrupted Richard. "But maybe we can finish our introductions first?"

The rest of the people went around in turn, and Richard saw them as the usual suspects. A few grad students, a few undergrads.

Concerned with pollution, fired up about global warming. The typical types you'd find in a shabby basement room in any more or less liberal college town. Except for one guy, Benjamin, who announced he had come to see what their strategy would be. He was small, with a tight, focused face and eyes that took everything in without giving anything away. Who was he?

"Great, just great," Richard repeated, and then made a mental note not to keep saying it. "So let's see, what do we want to work on? From what I've heard already we can list," writing on the board now, "*Pollution, species loss, saving nature, environmental racism.*" Now the tricky part. He knew the most important issue, the best one to organize around here and now, but he had to let people feel they had had their say. "Does anyone have an idea about how we could bring a lot of these things together?"

"I need to be clear on something," said Erica, looking back and forth at Fred and Lily while she adjusted her bright scarf, a tight note in her voice. "Why you care so much about," she semi-imitated Lily's hushed tone, "*Mother Nature* or," now she did the same thing with Fred's ministerial style, "*creation* while *people* are getting treated like dirt." Wendy nodded in clear agreement. "It's too bad if some tree goes extinct, or the last polar bear drowns. But where I come from, a black community has three incinerators and is fighting off a fourth. The white suburb nearby has nothing—no fumes, no trucks rumbling down the roads day and night, no problems with the drinking water. *We're* the ones who get sick from it all, and no one will buy our houses, so we can't move. We've been demanding the EPA to do something, but the corporation we're fighting gave a lot to the current administration, and the whole thing has been tied up in court for years. So many people are out of work that some people *want* the new facility, so they can get a few more jobs. 'I'll think about cancer later,' a friend of mine told me. 'Right now, I'd like to earn enough money to take care of my kids.' So what do you say we deal with the polar bears *after* we take care of the humans?"

She ended with a cold stare, an aggrieved and self-righteous tone. Wendy tried to catch Erica's eye so that the black woman would know she had an ally.

"I don't understand. Why do we have to choose?" Lily asked in a small voice, first looking up and then back down at her hands. A newbie, thought Roger, who doesn't realize that every group that tries to makes the world better spends half the time fighting itself.

"I feel bad for all the people who are suffering," Lily continued, "but the trees are dying too." She looked imploringly at Erica, who avoided her gaze.

"Trees? *Trees?*" Leaning forward in her seat like she was about to stand up and lead a march somewhere, Wendy didn't bother to conceal her scorn. She had some bad memories of people like Lily from her high school—the ones with the dreamy looks in their eyes, who talked about *The Earth* in reverent tones, as if they were praying to the mud, and who never had time to do anything for another person. She knew people like Lily couldn't be trusted. "Look, *people* have rights. *People* deserve justice. People have culture, family, history, politics, art, technology," nodding at Fred, "and religion. And people can act on moral values—that's why we deserve moral respect. So we don't have to think about taking care of a goddamn tree, but we do have to think about black people being screwed by some polluting company."

Well, well, thought Richard. No doubt a little philosophy major, along with her activism. I'll just have to let this one play out.

"Very good," offered Roger, a little pretentiously. "Not much of a basis for the politics of the," he pointed to the board, "National Environmental Coalition, but certainly a pretty good summary of the usual reasons why we live in a people-first—the fancy name is anthropocentric—culture. I mean, the reasons are not very good, if you think about them, but the summary was."

"What's the problem?" Wendy answered breezily. "I'll work with the Coalition to clean up the mess that's poisoning people. If it's good for the trees, that's fine. But that's not why I'm doing it. Because I don't owe trees *anything*! I owe people, and that's all."

"So only people have moral value?" asked Roger.

"That's it. The rest is for the New Agey types who want to worship the *cirrrrcle of liiiiife*," she said in a bad imitation of *The Lion King*.

"I believe in the circle of life, and I don't think it's silly." Lily spoke up again, this time more firmly. There was still some fear in her eyes, but something else as well. "Maybe I don't belong here." Her loneliness rose up in her, and she made a half movement to collect her things to go. Why did people have to be so mean? Why was it always, always, easier to be by herself out in the woods?

Uh-oh, thought Richard. This is getting messy.

"Of course you do, of course you do." He offered his warmest, most reassuring look. "There's no reason we can't do the same thing for different reasons, right? If you want to save the trees, that's great. If Wendy and Erica want to lessen pollution for people, that's great too."

"Did you notice that the trees are all dying, but we've got more people all the time? Maybe the trees need help more than the people," Roger broke in, with an "aren't I clever" look on his face. Watch it, Roger thought to himself, she's just a kid. But he remembered all the other people who had wasted his time in meetings like this, and he felt like he was just too old to deal with it. Maybe if I put her in her place, we could get down to doing some real work. That's what she said she wanted anyway.

"Trees—people. Yeah, they are *just* the same." Wendy obviously didn't think Roger was so clever. "Look, man, I don't care what you say here, but if you had to choose between ants and your mother, or saving a rat and saving some kid somewhere, which would you choose? You really telling me that's a hard choice? People just are worth more than nature."

Erica nodded. She also wasn't too fond of the wilderness lovers—especially the ones who ignored what happened to people of color. They were all for nature preserves, even if it meant that the natives who lived off the land got moved somewhere else. And they were doing that all over the world. But then a sudden doubt struck her. Hadn't people said things like this about blacks too—about how they weren't rational, or cultured, and that was why they didn't deserve rights, why they weren't worth much? And women too—the same thing. Could there be something in common here? She gave her head a tiny, unnoticeable shake, as if to clear away the doubt. She knew what she was doing—protecting her community. Let nature take care of itself.

"I'm not so sure you can tell the two apart." Fred spoke slowly and carefully—a minister used to making his points but always trying to alienate as few people as possible. "I believe that God created us all. And after the sixth day he looked at creation and said, 'This is *all* very good.' Not just people, but everything. Our Muslim friends say that 'every species is a nation—just like humans.' We are all God's children.

"If you are not a person of faith, there are lots of other reasons. Think of how it took millions and millions of years to get to humans—and we came along just like everything else did. Generation after generation, trial and error, genetic mistakes and genetic successes. Each species is like an incredible work of art."

"And don't forget," Richard added, thinking if they could get over this nature-people split things would go much easier, "without nature all of us would be dead as a doornail. The sun's energy, fresh water, the bacteria in the soil that make everything grow. And the air—every time we breathe we are connected to something outside ourselves, something nonhuman. No breath, no connection—no life."

"No connection . . . no life. I like that very much," nodded Fred, jotting it down in a little notebook. Richard had a feeling he might show up in next Sunday's sermon.

"Sure we *need* air and plants. We need shovels and computers, too." Erica was ignoring her doubts. "But just because we need something doesn't mean that it has *rights*."

Fred closed his eyes, folded his hands in front of his chest, said a brief silent prayer, and put on his most earnest tone, hoping he could reach her. He had come to see how terribly important it was to act, *now*, and wanted them all to act together. He almost reached out to put his hand on her arm, but held himself back. "If you are my sister or my wife or my daughter, it's not a matter of indifference to me whether you live or die, whether you are happy or unhappy. I *want* you to be alive and happy. That's a value for me. And it matters to you as well, right? You want to be healthy, to have love in your life, to have a good job and a supportive community. You need certain things to be yourself, your best self. Those are *your* values. And *you* have value just because certain things are valuable to you. And that's how I value you as well.

"Now, trees don't talk about their values, but surely it is better for trees to be healthy than sick, to have clean water rather than acid rain, to have the climate stay in the same range it has been in. Those are values . . . for the tree. And you can go up the line from the individual tree, to the species, to everything that lives on the earth. We all have ways to be healthy or sick, balanced or unbalanced, in tune with each other or falling to pieces. In that way, humans are no different than anything else in nature. To be alive is to have values. And value."

"Hmm," answered Wendy, and Richard could see the little philosophy major about to strike. She looked up at Fred with a fair imitation of innocence. "So certain things are better for us and certain ones worse, and that's what our values are, and since certain things are better or worse for the maple tree, it has values too, and that's why we should be good to the tree. Is that it?"

"That's it."

"Well . . ." and now the innocence was replaced by something less friendly, "I'm no expert in evolution or ecology, but I know this much. In the forest and the ocean and the swamp, it's all eat or be eaten. Big fish get the little ones, lions get the gazelles. Even more, there have been a lot of changes around here over the last few million years. Things get cooler and warmer, the land changes, whole ecosystems come and go. Hell, Tibet used to be underwater. What was good for one group of species gets replaced with something that's good for some others."

"Yes, yes," Roger asked impatiently. "Life is change. So?"

"Soooo," answered Wendy, dragging out the word for emphasis, then nodding her head with each example, "when one person tries to kill another, we call it murder. When a factory pollutes a river and poisons a tribe downstream, we call it a violation of their human rights. When our civilization seems hell-bent on changing the climate of the whole damn planet, we—or at least you guys"— she gestured at Richard and Lily—"call it a planetary *emergency*. Yet when the lion eats the gazelle, or an ice age wipes out the dinosaurs, or one kind of tree species replaces another in the forest— we just call it *nature*, and think it's fine.

"Even more," she looked around triumphantly, "I've heard that in a few billion years the sun will explode and that will be bye-bye for the earth. So what difference does it make if we are changing the climate or wiping out some species? They are all doomed anyway. In the meantime, let's take care of our fellow humans—or at least stop ripping them off." She stared hard at Fred and Lily, hoping this would shut them up. She was so tired of this argument. There was so much injustice to fight, and these people wanted to waste time on this hippie nonsense. People were being abused everywhere—it broke her heart.

This was going too far afield, thought Richard, getting more nervous. All this abstract talk about valuing people or valuing nature was a waste of time. Let's get to work, he wanted to yell, but stopped himself.

Meanwhile, Roger was holding forth again, just a hint of irritation in his tone. He'd heard this sophomoric argument a million times. Did people have to be simpleminded to be political activists? "Suppose, Wendy, that you found out that your mother, God forbid, had developed lung cancer. And suppose one cause of that cancer was the secondhand smoke from *your* cigarettes. Would you then say, 'Oh well, she will die eventually anyway, it doesn't make any difference if I gave her cancer'? I doubt it. You would be horrified by what you had done. In the same way, we don't have to believe that the earth is going to last forever, or that the earth's ecosystems won't change, to want to find some way to live that doesn't hurt them, *especially* if the reason we are hurting them is often just greed, mindless aggression, or incredible moral sloppiness."

"Moral sloppiness? Nice phrase, what the heck does it mean?" asked Fred.

"The waste, the waste," Roger repeated, a kind of despair edging into his tone. "Appliances like TVs that suck power all the time, wasted food, billions of pounds of packaging. Junk mail, junk food, junk cars . . . junk."

Erica made an impatient face. "Yeah, some of it is junk. But you know, try living without the technology that makes it." White professors, especially the men, she thought, they know so much they don't know anything. "Humans used to be at the mercy of nature *all the time*. Insects would eat half the crop and we'd starve. Bad winters would freeze us. Babies and mothers would die in childbirth. Well, technology changed all that: indoor plumbing, sanitation, medicine, refrigerated food—on and on. You," she turned to Lily, "think nature is a darling mother only because all these other people figured out how to tame the bitch."

"So," answered Wendy, holding both hands out in a palms-up "Isn't it obvious?" gesture, "our job is to take care of each other. If that means cleaning up a bit, fine. But the reason we clean is us, not trees or bugs or fish."

Erica nodded in agreement. Fred and Lily seemed distinctly uncomfortable. Roger looked bored—he'd heard it all before and probably written an article on it. Richard was desperately trying to think of a way to bring people together. Did all this arguing mean they couldn't do something together? That would be terrible.

"You're right, Wendy," Lily said, after the long silence. She really liked Wendy—the way she spoke her mind, even to a professor. She hoped the other woman didn't think she was stupid.

That's good, thought Richard. "You're right," even though she doesn't really think so. "There is a lot of death in nature," Lily went on in a quiet voice. "Evolution, accident, everyday death. But is it really the same, do you think?" Ask a question, Richard noticed. Don't just lay it on them.

"Is what the same?" Wendy was lost, you could see it in her face, but she also suspected something was coming.

"Is what human beings do the same? Is there any other species that multiplies without limits? That takes over so much of the earth?"

"You build house to house, until there is room for no one but you," murmured Fred to himself. Then he looked up: "Sorry, that's from Isaiah."

Lily continued, a soft pleading tone in her voice: "That moves plants and animals around so that you have strange new species in places that can't handle them, that creates poisonous garbage that will kill for thousands of years? And now . . . and now we know how to create new life forms. I once saw—this is so horrible I never forgot it—a picture of a fly they had messed around with: it had eyes all over its legs and wings and back, eyes everywhere."

That stopped them all. There were a few minutes of silence—was it a horrified silence, or an embarrassed one?

"You're right, you're right, you're right," Erica almost whispered, her harshness replaced by a sudden vulnerability. "I know what we're doing is . . . well, it's really unthinkable, isn't it? But I can't deal with everything. I've seen so many of my people ripped apart, I just feel sick about it. As for the trees and the frogs? It's probably too late for nature, it really is. If I can help clean up the places people of color live, that's what I'm going to do."

"I understand," responded Lily, "really I do." Erica's open look turned to a sudden glare that said, how does a rich white girl like you have the nerve to think you understand me?

"Not about being treated badly by the world. People have treated me OK, or better." Lily offered an apologetic smile. "No, I mean when I think about what we are doing to the planet, I get that same sick feeling. I know I have to do something, and I know I can't do much, so a lot of other things that I know are important"—she looked beseechingly at Wendy and Erica—"won't get done. But there are so many people—six billion, and more all the time. We're not in any danger, except from ourselves, that is. And

every ten minutes another species . . . gone. Habitat . . . gone."
Were there tears in her voice? "How can we continue like this?
How can we?"

"Is this the way to treat God's creation?" Fred asked, getting
no answer.

The mention of God made Richard nervous. Secular types got
uncomfortable and lapsed Catholics went ballistic. He'd have to
step in now.

"Right, right," he said cheerfully. "This is great, fascinating.
But we have gone on for awhile on these, uh, *philosophical* questions. How about something practical?" He smiled broadly. No one
said no, so he took that as agreement.

"About eight miles from here, where Route 26 meets the Vestal
Parkway, there's a wetland. It's only about 77 acres, but it's important. It takes in overflow from the river after heavy rains, and it
cleans and filters the water that passes through it. There are some
muskrats, an endangered species of butterfly nests there. Audubon
Society has an overlook to watch a whole bunch of waterfowl, and
the songbirds are incredible in spring. The land is private, even
though people have treated it as a kind of reserve for years. The
owner died two months ago, and his heirs, who live in Denver,
want to sell it. There's a buyer lined up, a company that builds
malls all over the East. They want to put a big one in there—with
all the usual stores. It's illegal to just drain a wetland, but somehow
they got an exception. They'll pave it over, make flooding more
likely, take away about the last tiny bit of wild around here, add to
the traffic snarls with new roads, and probably pollute the groundwater." He looked over at Erica hopefully.

He stood up, trying to communicate his excitement to them. "I
say—we should stop it. We could work with the Audubon folks—
they'd hate to lose the birds; and the Clean Water Coalition should
support us as well. Let's make it into a nature preserve. People are
just waiting for somebody to take the lead on this one. Who better
than us?" He looked around encouragingly.

"Hate to lose the birds, would they?" asked Erica quietly.

"Absolutely."

"Well, why don't you ask those lovely Audubon folks if they care a damn about all the black people who have lost jobs in this terrible economy?" Her tone had turned harsh again. "Any good jobs in this mall? Some affirmative action slots for black contractors? If there are, I'd say let's go for it, and let the birds take care of themselves."

Wendy nodded, clearly in agreement. Lily and Fred frowned—they were nice, but this didn't sit well with them at all.

Roger cleared his throat, waiting for maximum attention as people turned toward him. "Even if it's only people we are talking about, there are conflicts. Support the farmers or the ranchers, build the new school here or there, build a school for kids or a nursing home for the elderly or a hospital for the sick. Resources are always limited, people always want for themselves—and why shouldn't they? That's why this kind of conflict isn't a stranger in morality and politics, it's the host.

"And here Wendy was quite clear: if the cleanup helps the animals, fine. But we don't do it for the animals, we only do it for the people. Only people count. Is that the way we all feel?"

Richard could hear the impatience in Erica's voice. "This ain't your seminar, Doc, so don't start with questions for everybody else. What do you think?"

"Me? Oh I don't know," he sighed heavily, as if he couldn't carry a heavy weight any further. "I try to love the oak trees and my neighbor both. In a way, the oak tree is my neighbor as much as old Mr. Taubman who lives next door, or that gorgeous widow Sarah Griffith who lives across the street. I don't see why we can't *all* get along.

"Mostly I hate the waste, the stupidity. *Why* do we have to choose between cleaning up the ghetto and saving the polar bears? Who says that's the choice? *Who*? Maybe we could do both and skip the new bombers or the new makeup or a whole season of *American Idol*." He opened his eyes wide in mock horror.

"Because, I ask you—*what are we doing with all this*?" Surprising everyone, he raised his voice almost to a shout and waved at the world, his carefully scripted professor's manner replaced with a mixture of despair and rage, his eyes narrowing as if holding back tears. "Eating meat filled with antibiotics, driving huge cars with a single person inside, using cell phones that take pictures and play music and are made with toxic heavy metals." He turned to Erica, his voice almost a shriek: "Is this what we have tamed nature for? For poison and trivia?" To Wendy, angrily, "Forget who you're doing it *for*. Who deserves rights and who doesn't. Just ask yourself: 'How do I want to live?' For waste? Waste for people, for the planet, for Fred's miracle." His voice dropped, almost a whisper now. "What a waste." He stopped suddenly, gave a brief, embarrassed grimace, and then stared at the floor. I can't stand it, he thought, I just can't stand it.

"Nice, Doc, nice," Erica smiled approvingly. "Didn't think you had it in you." She paused, adjusted her scarf, then held up one finger and shook it at the professor almost playfully. "But one little thing you forgot."

Roger looked up, intrigued, slamming down his despair. He liked to be challenged. It got boring being right all the time.

Erica spoke slowly; was she mocking his professorial style? "It isn't people in general doing all this. People in general didn't pollute the ghetto, factory owners and politicians—almost all white—did. Humans didn't kill the Native Americans, white settlers did. This isn't about the human condition. This is about one group of people taking advantage of—*oppressing*—" she added a heavily academic tone, "some other group. If these two," she pointed at Fred and Lily, "want to add in flowers and bugs to the ones getting oppressed, OK, I'm not so sure, but OK. But even if you add in all the bugs and flowers you want, it's not 'us' doing it. It's some particular group."

"Which group is that?" Roger asked quietly.

"The rich, the capitalists, the politicians, men, sometimes whites. Call 'em what you will. You get the idea."

"Indeed I do," Roger kept on. "And you, you're not part of this evil group, I take it?"

"Do I look rich, white, or male to you?"

"Not at all. However, I imagine you drove here. That you live in a house or apartment with indoor plumbing, that you buy," he gestured at her bright scarf, her slightly stylish jeans, "a fair range of clothes, that your food, like everyone else's, travels an average of fifteen hundred miles before you eat it. That you own a computer and a cell phone. That's for a start. Am I wrong?"

"Guilty as charged. So what?"

"Well, then *you* are part of *them*. Even the lower classes in this country consume huge amounts of energy and put out huge amounts of waste."

"All of us are part of the problem," Lily jumped in. "We all take more than we need."

"I don't take more than my share. I barely get by as it is," Erica bristled.

"How much do you think is your share?" Roger was poking back at her. She glared at him.

"Really, how much is enough, and how much is too much?"

"Who are you to ask me that question, you . . . you privileged white man," she sputtered in a sudden rage. "You've taken *every-thing* there is to take, and you're going to ask me about my ratty old Honda? Or how many shirts I buy in a year? And you, Miss Lily . . . *white*." She poked a finger at Lily. "One look at you and I can tell that you were born with a silver spoon shoved up somewhere comfortable."

Lily hung her head. It wasn't clear if she was scared, embarrassed for Erica's rudeness, or suffering an attack of upper-class white guilt.

Roger just shook his head. *If she knew where I was born, she'd sing a different tune.* But suddenly he was too depressed to correct her.

Damn, thought Richard, *we'll never get anywhere.*

"Look," he said quietly, trying to imitate Lily's friendly, non-threatening tone. "This is not about individuals. Sure it's great to recycle and drive a Prius (if you can afford one, I sure can't) and eat organic and no meat. But really it's about the big picture—the laws, the giant corporations, the governments. It's about what *they* do—whether you want to save nature or people. It's only when we can fight back, *together*" (trying to be inspirational now) "that we stand a chance. One struggle, one fight." He saw Roger roll his eyes. "Oh, I know it's kind of a dumb cliché, Roger, but it's still true. So, everyone, what do you say? Save the wetlands? Protect the endangered species? Keep the traffic and the pollution down? Curb global warming? It's right here, in front of us, we can do it."

No one answered. He'd have to try something else. "Let's take a break," he suggested. He was getting pretty nervous now. Between all these abstractions, and all this hostility, the whole thing might go nowhere.

During the break Lily shyly approached Wendy, put a hand on her shoulder, and whispered something in her ear. Wendy narrowed her eyes in instant distrust, but then burst out laughing and whispered something back. Then Erica came over, and soon the three of them were chuckling together.

Meanwhile, Roger, Fred, and Richard tried, and failed, to make small talk.

After Richard started them up again, Erica turned to Lily. "OK, I'm not so pissed off anymore, at least not at you. But I'm still not sure that we can work together."

"No, no, there's got to be some way to understand each other, to support each other." Richard was getting frantic.

"Let's try this," Fred said, calmly ministerial again. "Maybe . . . tell just" (glancing at his watch) "a few of our stories. What led us to what we care about? Maybe if we think of each other as *people* and not just *positions*, something can come unstuck—since right now it all seems pretty stuck."

"I'll tell you my story, if you think it will help," Erica offered. Her eyes softened as if she remembered something sweet, but there was sadness in the curve of her mouth. "I grew up without a father. He was killed in the first Gulf War, blown up by a land mine nobody had noticed. So I was raised by my mom—but just for a while, because she died of pancreatic cancer. That kills you fast, and young too. Then my aunt took over. She worked two jobs for years to put food on the table, get me decent clothes, keep me out of trouble. I wanted nothing more than to succeed to make her happy. 'Erica,' she used to say to me, 'you're my shining star. You can do anything.' Then she got it too—pancreatic cancer. And soon she was gone."

The softness disappeared from Erica's eyes, replaced by a cold stare. "I started asking questions, and after awhile the answers were pretty clear. It was the water—what we drank, what we cooked with, what we used in the shower. Two electronics firms had factories nearby. They used a particular solvent to clean the parts they were using. When it was too dirty to use anymore, they dumped it—into the ground, and into the water supply. We tried to bring a case. They fought us with big-time lawyers: delay, delay, delay. Then the company that owned the company that owned those companies went bankrupt and dissolved, and there was no one left to sue.

"So if I come across a little angry," Lily nodded her head in a "well, just a bit" gesture, "now you know why. I'll never forgive the people who did this, and I'll try to keep it from happening somewhere else."

After a long moment Lily looked up and started talking, so softly everyone stopped moving, coughing, and shuffling the way people do when they're tired and it's late and they've just heard something upsetting.

"I was a very lonely child. Very. Another cliché, for sure— little rich girl (you had me there, Erica) that nobody paid attention to. My father was into global finance, always jetting off to Saudi Arabia or South Africa or Japan. My mother, my beautiful mother, was the star of the New York art scene. She owned galleries and cultivated young artists and chaired trustee committees for the symphony. And me? I had nannies and tutors and private schools. And a huge mansion with beautiful grounds. And no friends. So I went out to those beautiful grounds. To one particular tree, that I used to climb on and sit with for hours, listening to birds in spring, watching the leaves change colors in the fall, hearing the squirrels chatter. I belonged up there, in my tree. I was safe, and cared for. The tree was always there for me—after my parents had a fight, after I went to bed crying because no one loved me. The tree was always there.

She shifted in her seat, folded her hands together, then put them back at her sides. "Until one day it wasn't. I came home late from school and there was just bare earth where my tree had been, and all the other trees around it had been torn out as well. 'We're putting in another tennis court,' my father told me when I called him, pretty hysterical. 'What difference does it make to you? There are still plenty of other trees.'

"'But this one was my *friend*,' I screamed at him. I didn't say what I really meant, that the tree had loved me more than he had.

"'Friend, is it?' he just said. And hung up."

Then Lily looked at everyone in the room in turn. Her shyness gone, she suddenly seemed to be getting energy and confidence from somewhere else. "I *loved* that tree—like a friend or a parent or a sister. I knew what it smelled like in every season, when the buds would come out in spring, what the rain sounded like on its leaves, how cool it kept me in August.

"They killed it. For a stupid tennis court. Which they didn't even build. I never forgave them.

"And that's why I'm here."

Richard didn't know what to say, he really didn't. For a moment his need to control them all, to make sure they went where he wanted them to go, just faded away. These were all good people, dammit, why couldn't they agree? Or even make contact? He sensed that sinking feeling his therapist said was depression, where it all seemed impossible. He had to save the earth, and he wasn't able to even get a half-dozen people in a scruffy basement room to work together. If only there was some plan that would make them all happy: save the marsh and get jobs for minorities in the new nature reserve? Have ecology taught at the school in the black neighborhood—to help get the kids into college, or at least out of gangs? He just knew that black kids needed wilderness as much as white kids, even if they were poorer and didn't get to go to

$1000-a-week summer camps. And if people like Erica didn't real-
ize that, they were wrong. And he didn't mind saying that, even if
he was white. But that wouldn't help. People would just tell him he
was a paternalistic racist, which he wasn't. He knew that for sure
as well.

From the back of the room one of the people who hadn't opened
his mouth stood up. He was, Richard realized, much older than
your usual political volunteer. This wasn't even one of your newly-
retired-lots-of-volunteer-time-on-your-hands-60ish type. This guy
was *old*. Richard had hoped he'd be one of the people who didn't
talk, showed up at all the meetings, and cooperated. Guess not.

The old man, who'd come in late and hadn't introduced himself, turned slowly to the room. "You and you," indicating Erica
and Wendy, "you love people. You and you," to Lily, Richard, and
Fred, "you love the trees and the animals and what keeps them
going." "You," he pointed to Roger, "not sure what you love, at all."

"Me neither," responded Roger, a little sadly.

"So, we all love something. Isn't that enough?" Slowly he sat
down.

Thank God, thought Richard. Maybe this will do it.

Suddenly a security guard poked his head in.

"Hey folks, time's up, way up. Gotta close the building. Don't
worry though," he laughed a little. Had he been listening to them?
"You can come back tomorrow and do it again."

"Until when?" someone thought. "Until we get it right? And
when will that be?"

WHAT IS TO BE DONE?

Lily knew she couldn't go on anymore. Still, she was scared about how they would respond. Maybe she should leave without telling anyone, just not show up. But she couldn't do that. She would have to go to the meeting and tell them she was leaving the group, leaving the university in fact, to go live on The Farm.

Somehow Richard had managed to convince them to try to save the wetland. They had been joined by some Audubon Society people, some from Fred's church, and even a few representatives of the black community, interested in having a tie-in for minorities in the environmental education center they had hoped to put at the refuge. It seemed like it would work—the birds and butterflies would survive, the swamp would help the local ecology, people would get to enjoy nature, and residents from the poor community would get jobs at the nature center. And things were going well. Some city counselors had supported their efforts. A few high school classes had visited. An article was written in the local paper.

But The Developer had other ideas, and (she hadn't really expected this) so did people who wanted more local jobs—building the mall, working in the stores. Then there were the taxes that would help repair the terribly run-down high school and the city hospital. A lot of people didn't think that "saving nature" was such a terrific idea, not if it meant lousy schools and a crummy hospital and your neighbors out of work. The Developer had much better connections with the zoning board, and had promised not to develop some other parcel of land, somewhere else, in exchange for rights to pave over this one. That was good enough for the city and state. Several of the key players were up for reappointment or reelection this year, and to many of them The Developer had always been a "real friend." Others just saw things his way, not the way the group did.

So it had turned into a struggle, and a big one. Lily hated struggle. Just as the disagreements at the first meeting of the group had almost led her to leave, the shouting matches at the last demonstration, and the way Richard had ripped a sign out of that man's hand, had scared her much too much. What good was all this fighting? How could they save nature, and make the world safer for people, with anger? Where she grew up, people hardly ever raised their voices. It just wasn't done. She would never understand how people could stand there and scream at each other the way they had at that last city council meeting. It was worse than anything.

She would be sorry to leave. People had worked really hard and gotten close to each other. Erica and Fred would talk about religion, Fred asking Erica a lot of questions about the Baptist church and the "African American community," as Fred always called it. And she and Wendy had done some talking too. About where they came from and what they wanted. She tried to understand Wendy's style—which was almost as aggressive and abrasive as Richard's. "You know," she'd once told Wendy, "when you raise your voice and start to criticize people, even people I'm against too, I get a little scared. I keep thinking, 'What if *I* say something she doesn't like? Will she turn on me like that?'"

Wendy had laughed, even put her arm around Lily's shoulders. "Hey Lily, omelet . . . eggs . . . can't get the first without breaking the second, right? The tone in my voice isn't important. Getting yelled at, *not important.* Angry, schmangry, not important. What's important is changing this god-awful society for the better. This is politics, my friend, not a tea party."

Lily had smiled back, but hadn't been at all sure. She wondered about all the other people who would be scared by hostile put-downs, and an absolute certainty that *we* are right and *they* are wrong. Would people who got turned off by that sort of thing come to a meeting to begin with? Or come to a second one? And what about people who thought, "I agree with the Coalition about A and B, but with The Developer on C, and maybe on D I'm thinking something no one else is." How could people like that join in The Movement (the way Richard and Wendy said it, it always seemed to have capital letters), if The Movement was just about being right?

Still, she could hear Wendy or Richard in her head. "You may have a point, and we certainly should be welcoming to new members. But the important thing is the struggle, and the *struggle* is important because we are *right.*"

Lily could see what they meant, but then she wondered about Martin Luther King Jr., and Gandhi. They had principles, stood up for them, had even been to jail. But their meetings had prayers in them, and they talked about their opponents respectfully. They admitted their own limitations. When people in the Coalition disagreed with Richard, he just tried to argue them out of it, sometimes a little meanly. When people disagreed with Gandhi, and offered to go along with him even though they disagreed, he said, "No, do what *you* think is right. You must listen to your own inner voice." Or something like that, she couldn't remember exactly.

If King and Gandhi could do what they did without anger and put-downs, why can't we? she wondered.

But whatever other people wanted, *she* couldn't do this anymore. She would move to The Farm—where people were doing absolutely organic and biodynamic farming, trying to give back to the land as they worked it. And had no animals to exploit, except a fat old black cat and bouncy half-lab, half-pit bull rescue dog that liked to lick everybody and chase the cat. They prayed in the morning before chores, and they meditated in the evening. Rachel, who sort of ran things, said over and over again that "Love is the answer, the only answer." Lily wasn't completely sure what Rachel meant, but she had never seen Rachel raise her voice, or argue with anyone. She just said what she believed, and then would tilt her head and look at you with a lot of focused attention and ask you what you thought. And that would be that. No yelling, no arguments. Lily liked that a lot. It made her feel so much safer.

"If we expect to be able to change the world," Rachel always said with complete confidence, "we have to *be* the change we want to see take place. Don't want people eating animals? Stop eating them yourself. Don't want people to destroy the earth with chemical farming? Farm a different way. Don't want people to be mean and selfish? Learn to be kind. Don't like big corporations? Stop dealing with them. Can't do anything big? Do something small. Get your own head together before you start telling other people where *their* heads should be. Politics? Fine, when you can do it without rage, power trips, and all the rest. Can't do it without that? Then get yourself together until you can. Live in your own community, with others who are on the same trip you are. Then, maybe, you'll bring some sanity into the world."

That's where Lily was heading. Where it was pure and safe.

Just thinking about Rachel and The Farm gave her courage. She would go to the Coalition meeting, explain why she was leaving, wish them the best—and they would all part friends.

Several miles away, Roger was trying to get off the couch. Right now it just seemed too much effort. His house, a small ranch with a big deck surrounded by woods, a twenty-minute drive from the university, was a mess—books, magazines, and papers scattered everywhere; dishes overflowing the sink; laundry piled on the floor. He just didn't seem to be able to function very well anymore.

Oh, he taught his courses, and managed to write a few articles a year. He still felt at least a little bit of pleasure when some editor asked him for an opinion or he got invited to give a talk. But all of it had gotten pretty bleak lately. The thrill, to say the least, was gone.

It wasn't hard to figure out why he felt so bad—he knew what was going on. The rain forest—disappearing. The glaciers—melting. People in the third world—starving, murdering each other in ethnic wars, or getting killed by their own governments. Underground storage tanks of gasoline—leaking into the groundwater. Sales of weapons around the world—going up. Condition of the air in China's cities—going down, way down. He couldn't put his mind on anything else. Sitting on his deck and looking at the maple and oak trees that stretched in back of his house, he would think of nothing but how many were dying from acid rain. A colorful bouquet of flowers on the department secretary's desk—blue irises and white roses in a lovely arrangement—would just remind him of how many pesticides were used to grow them, and how many of the underage workers who processed them were going to get cancer.

He knew that people were fighting back, just as he had for years. But wasn't it always too little, too late? Didn't the polluters and the developers always come back next week, next month, or next year? Or just change their tactics? Make something illegal here, and they would start producing it there; talk about global warming, and they would scare everyone with high oil prices and demand to "drill, baby, drill." Talk about the dying polar bears, and they would make fun of you as an environmentalist wacko. Or the media would make a big fuss about something—climate change, cancer, whatever—and there would be TV shows and breathless reporters and hearings. Everyone would think, "The people in charge, they really are going to take care of this. I don't have to think about it anymore." Then they would go back to worrying about the kids and their jobs and who won the big game. And nothing would change. The few victories were sweet. But they couldn't stack up against all the losses

His therapist said he was depressed, and, unlike the times when he'd had long arguments with her, he'd agreed. His wife had been clear, painfully clear, as she walked out the door the last time. "I love you Roger, I always will. But I can't live with you, not the way you are now. I just can't listen to any more stories about the dying coral reefs, or mountaintop removal mining in Appalachia. *Enough.* If you want to live your life thinking of nothing else, go ahead. Not me. Maybe I will get cancer, or die of acid rain. Maybe. But in the meantime I want to live and have some joy even. If all your political knowledge makes you miserable, what good does it do the planet?"

She was right, and he knew it. But that didn't mean he could do anything about it. After all, the latest issue of Sierra Club's magazine had just come in, with a study of toxins being dumped into rivers. And there was the story in the *Times* about the disastrous effects of mining for the heavy metals used in cell phones. And new information from the Environmental News Service on his e-mail about—what was it about, anyway? He'd have to go look at it again. It was important, he knew that, at least.

Grunting with effort, he hauled himself up, grabbed a jacket, and headed for his car, cursing himself for not riding his bike, and then mocking that tiny concern when it was big changes that were really important.

Fred put down his Bible. When things were difficult, he always turned to Psalms. And things were difficult now. He would have to leave the Coalition, and he felt terribly guilty about it. "Give me strength, O Lord," he prayed. "And a little less guilt," he added, more to himself than to God.

Fred was sure that love of God and love of people and love of nature all went together. He was blessed that his congregation and the higher-ups in his denomination felt the same way. And he never felt so much himself as when he was on the front line and fighting for an important cause. That was when he knew he was truly serving God. It was action, action in a spirit of love, that was really where it was at.

And now he knew he would have to stop. His family needed him. His wife's cancer had returned, after they all had thought it was gone for good. But a new lump had been found, and a new round of chemo arranged. She would end up exhausted and miserable because she couldn't function the way she wanted to. And they would all live with the unspoken fear of her death.

Which left him to take over what his wife did and keep on doing his part as well. Sylvie and Tom needed him to drive to the soccer games, go to Tom's medical appointments, help with homework, and talk about their problems. Because they had problems too, for sure. Sylvie was fourteen, and the whole boy-girl thing at school made her nuts. And Tom, who had big-time learning issues and needed a lot of physical therapy for his back, always felt left out and clung to his parents as his only real friends—and then just hated himself because he didn't fit in with anyone at school.

It wasn't fair, Fred thought, uselessly. Not fair at all. Not cancer *and* Tom's special needs.

But he knew it was worse, much worse, in other places. Kids weren't just a little unhappy or lonely, unable to play sports or uptight about boyfriends and clothes. Kids were living on one meal a day, bathing in sewage, breathing fumes from refineries. That wasn't fair either. What was God thinking?

Benjamin looked over his notes once again, his dark brown eyes narrowed in concentration, his small, round face with the small brown mustache a study in focus. Yes, all of his points were in order, and if they didn't convince the Coalition where it should go now, well, it wasn't his fault. They had tried this sort of ad hoc, "let's find an issue and run with it" style, and look where it got them—no place. They got shot down by The Developer and his pals. He could smell the hopeless resignation coming from the group, which wouldn't last very long unless he gave it a new direction. A long-term direction. Very long-term. They had to see that the point wasn't to win one struggle. Winning or losing one struggle meant *nothing*. Whatever they saved could be taken away in a minute—change the laws, cancel a government program, whatever. The only protection was The Party—something tightly organized, with enough people in it to stand up to politicians, corporations, and all the other ruling-class interests.

That's what he was about—building The Party. It would be focused, well run. Able to mobilize tens of thousands of people for direct action, millions of voters. It would have a democratic structure, representatives from local groups, and a central committee to respond to events on a day-to-day basis and make long-term strategic decisions. The tactics would vary from place to place: win some elections, organize some big demonstrations, maybe some civil disobedience from time to time. They would make sure to get footholds in other groups—unions, environmental organizations, women's centers, minority churches, all across the board. Only The Party could take the long view, bring together all the different interest groups: women, blacks, gays, unions, environmentalists. Only The Party would stand for real unity among the oppressed. It wouldn't come next week or next year. It might be twenty years before it was really together. But it would come. He knew it.

Multinational corporations laughed at little groups like Richard's. State and city politicians smiled, shook their hands, and went on taking money from the local fat cats. Corrupt black leaders, self-serving big-wig feminists, up-and-coming Hispanics—they all just protected themselves and their friends. The Party would be different. It would stand for a sane, decent, sustainable society in which women and all minorities were respected, where the earth was cared for, where the economy worked for human needs and not profit for a tiny crowd of owners. And where democracy wasn't a sham, like here, with a lot of lying phonies pretending to care for the country and just lining their pockets after they got elected. The leadership of The Party would be devoted and filled with integrity, honed like a fine carving knife by decades of study, work, and struggle. Hundreds of meetings, dozens of campaigns, coalitions, negotiations, small successes leading to bigger ones, and some failures too. He knew they wouldn't win every battle. But they would win the war—they would make their society sane and just.

The Party would be different from the short-lived movements, the isolated little groups, the people who wanted a better world but didn't have a clue how to get there. He knew The Party would be different. Otherwise, he almost never let himself admit it, there wasn't any hope.

Richard was on the edge. It was a dangerous place to be, but he was almost beyond caring. They had been *so* close to a victory last week. Support from the community, clear goals from the group, good publicity. And then the tide had turned. The damn zoning board had given its permission for a preliminary environmental impact statement. And the statement, *duh*, had already been prepared, and whizzed through the environmental board at a hearing no one had been told about. "Terrible irregularity," the mayor had said as Richard buttonholed him in the hallway. "We'll definitely look into it. At some point. So much going on in the city right now, hard to get such things underway." Then Richard had made a mistake. He *knew* it was wrong, but he was so mad he started yelling at the mayor, telling him what a crooked windbag he was. The mayor just looked at him, raising his eyebrows with a knowing stare as if to say, "You are nobody." Then the mayor smiled and said out loud, "I take it I won't be getting your vote in the next election?" The smile faded. "And now get out, before I have you thrown out." So much for Richard's carefully cultivated connection with the mayor's office.

And the last city council meeting had been worse, if worse was possible. Richard had made a thoughtful, reasonable statement. He'd offered signed support for the nature center from Fred's group of local ministers, Erica's supporters among minorities, and Wendy, who claimed to represent SAP—Students Against Pollution. Terrible name, but they all thought it was funny. The council members smiled encouragingly when he began to talk, but soon were looking at their cell phones, consulting their notes, whispering comments to each other. When he started to talk about humanity's need for the natural world, about how we were all going a little crazy because we had lost touch with other life forms, one of them had looked up sharply, rudely interrupted, and said, "Young man, the first thing a good citizen with a family needs is a job, not a tree, a swamp, or a butterfly. If you had a family, perhaps you'd understand that." That had gotten him so mad he lost his place in the statement. He stopped for a moment, then looked up to try to make eye contact with them like he knew he was supposed to, but he saw by the looks on their faces that it was in the bag for The Developer. So he put down the statement and started in on them. Warning. Threatening. Telling them that the people would rise up in defense of nature, that they were just *part* of nature defending itself against the chain saws and the cement and the poisons. His voice got louder and louder, until the chairman banged his gavel and told him his time was up. But he wouldn't stop until the cop grabbed him roughly by the arm and dragged him out of the room, telling him, his voice gentler than his steely grip, to get it together.

He'd seen the horrified looks from other members of the Coalition—Lily seemed like she might faint; Fred was about to reach for his Bible, no doubt; Roger had a kind of offended distaste written all over him. Erica and Wendy, only they might have understood. Maybe.

Well, tonight he would tell them: it was time to get serious. The Developer put down some survey stakes. They would rip them out of the ground. When the bulldozers came, they could trash them overnight. Any signs advertising the mall would be torn down or, better, burned. "No compromise in defense of Mother Earth" had been his slogan before, and it would work again. He had *tried* it the other way, he really had. Long meetings, listening to everyone's damn opinions, trying to find common ground. Playing by the rules in the farce they called democracy. He'd done all that, and look where it had gotten him.

Tonight would be the test. Were they in or out? Lily wouldn't be able to handle this, Fred kept looking at his watch every time the meeting went two minutes over. Roger was too negative about everything. The rest? He'd just have to see. If he had to, he'd do it himself. And if he got caught and had to go back to jail, it was worth it. No compromise. None.

Erica wasn't really looking forward to the meeting of the Coalition that evening. They'd had some disappointments recently, and she could see that people were, to say the least, not happy. But one setback was hardly the end of the world. You won some, and you lost some, and that's just the way it was. The deep ache she carried for her family had taught her about loss early, very early. She had never expected to have a life free from pain, not after those funerals. And as a black woman from a poor neighborhood, she never expected to be able to change the world all that much either. They would do what they could and leave the rest, as Fred would probably say, to God. What else was there?

Men, thought Wendy, they could be such *babies* sometimes. Don't get what you want and you start screaming. Yeah, it had been a disappointment when the city council and the planning board and the mayor had sold them out. But there were still things they could do. And even if they didn't save this piece of earth, that didn't mean they'd wasted their time. They'd involved a bunch of people, gotten their point across to the community. If it didn't work this time, maybe it would work next time.

There was never any way to know the effects of what you did. She'd learned that from her mother, who worked for years as a lawyer representing workers in health and safety cases, and recently natives when the corporations went after their land. "You will lose an awful lot of battles, my dear. But it's the fight that counts, and remember—each victory is as precious as diamonds. To win, though, you've probably got to lose an awful lot of times first." Then she'd hugged her, and stroked her hair. It was kind of a weird thing to say to a precocious thirteen-year-old girl going through a big-time rebellious phase: smoking dope and messing around with boys, and thinking her mother's political trip was a waste of time. Thank God she'd outgrown that crap in a few years, her pointless rebellion done in by the pointless boredom of living for cheap thrills. When her favorite teacher, a femmey gay male English instructor, was fired for choosing the wrong poets for his students to read, she got into organizing big-time. She'd rallied the students, and some parents, and brought in the ACLU. They hadn't totally won, but they hadn't totally lost either. After that she was hooked—she'd be an organizer for life. Win or lose, what else was so much fun?

The shabby basement room where they'd first met was crowded. People knew that something was going to go down tonight, one way or another. Richard had written "FUTURE DIRECTIONS" on the blackboard, followed by a half dozen question marks. As Roger came in, he almost turned around to leave. Why all those question marks? he thought, wouldn't one do? Lily and Fred, not knowing of the other's plans, each felt a pang of guilt. Whatever those directions are, they each thought, I won't be part of it. Wendy, Erica, and Benjamin were geared up. All right, each of them thought to themselves, let's get to work.

"Well," Richard began, trying to start the meeting with a light touch, "I guess things haven't gone *completely* smooth." A few nervous laughs echoed, but most people weren't amused. "So it doesn't look as if our original plan is going to work. What now?"

A few moments of silence followed. No one was eager to make the next move. Fred made a short prayer for help, and forgiveness, and raised his hand.

"I really appreciate everything we've done here. And I really love you all." People smiled—they liked Fred, and they didn't mind his ministerial overstatements. "So it is with great sadness that I have to tell you I'm leaving the group. There are some serious health problems in my family now, and they need my help. I just won't have the time or energy to save the world anymore." He gave a slight, sad smile. "I'll be too busy trying to save my kids and my wife." Murmured responses of disappointment, along with sympathy and support, ran through the room. Richard was a little more direct.

"But we need you, Fred." He'd counted on Fred to step up his involvement. The minister had always talked about King and

Gandhi. Maybe they could do some kind of civil disobedience at the construction site. It would be great to have a minister leading it. The press loved that kind of thing. And Fred had brought in a lot of church people. Would they leave if he did? "And doesn't your family need a cleaner earth and some nature to grow up in?"

"I'm sorry, Richard, really I am." This is what Fred had been afraid of. "I guess because it's *my* family, I believe I owe them more. They have to come first."

"Why is that, Fred?" asked Roger, surprised at his own coldness. "Don't they already live much better lives than three-quarters of the rest of humanity? I mean, I'm sorry about the illness. But you're not the doctor, and you have health care coverage. So why can't you come to a few meetings, and still take part in whatever else we do?"

"I just don't have the emotional energy for it," Fred replied. "And you know something? I'd also like a little bit of time for myself—to take a slow walk with my old dog, or just hang out in the evening with my kids doing . . . nothing."

"My friend Rachel says we have to care for ourselves, whatever else we are doing." Lily thought if there was room for Fred to leave for personal reasons, there would be room for her as well. "Want to care for the environment? You have to care for the environmentalist as well. So I understand, Fred, and I support you."

"Great, just great," grumbled Wendy. "Let's all take care of ourselves. That's surely the most important thing. By the time we get ourselves all nice and taken care of we'll all be sick as dogs from pollution."

"But Wendy," Lily said pleadingly, feeling like it would slip away in a minute, "how can we do anything if we aren't in good shape ourselves?"

"Good shape? What a lot of crap." Wendy's impatience twisted her mouth and cheeks in knots. "We eat processed food; live in nuclear families so overloaded emotionally half of them end in divorce and the other half are getting by on drinking, adultery, and Prozac. We leap at anything to escape—TV, Twitter, a maxed-out credit card. You think you can take care of *yourself*? You can't. Only if we change society can we change our heads. The rest is a fantasy, an escape hatch to nowhere."

"So what's your plan?" countered Roger. He felt angry at everybody. "You really think we can work nonstop until the revolution solves all our problems? What kind of revolution do you think we will make if we are all so burnt out we can't think straight? I saw all those people who never cared for themselves in the '60s and '70s, in all the little groups I was in."

Oh Lord, thought Richard, not another one of Roger's back-in-the-day raps.

"'Stop the war,' 'End racism,' 'Smash the state.' Meeting after meeting, group after group, countless demonstrations, eight-hour discussions about how to live and what to believe. We ended up exhausted, emotionally drained, too uptight and tired to think straight—until one by one we peeled away and no one was left but the complete crazies."

"Maybe you did. I won't." Wendy didn't buy it. The old guys, she thought, that was their world. This is mine.

Benjamin saw his opening and leapt into it. "Maybe we could get a little perspective here?"

Roger turned on him with a cold stare. He thought he had plenty of perspective already and wasn't going to get any more from this quiet little guy who had come to all the meetings, said very little, but always seemed to be taking mental notes on everything people did. Was he an agent?

"Try this on for size. Nothing, *nothing*, this group," he gestured with his hand at the room, "can do will have any lasting effect. Only as part of something bigger, stronger, and more organized can we hope to change anything."

"We *are* part of something," Richard countered. "There are thousands of environmental groups in the world. Every country has something like our EPA. We may have lost this swamp, but the global environmental movement is on its way."

"Nonsense," said Benjamin dismissively. He adjusted his glasses with one hand and starting poking at the air with the other, talking faster all the time. "Look at what Roger went through. Antiwar movement? The U.S. got out of Vietnam, but how many wars have we been in since then? Disarmament? We spend more on war than we ever did. Smash the state? It's bigger than ever, and even more in the service of the powerful—retired generals work for the munitions makers and lobby Congress; the heads of the Fed and the economic advisors come from Wall Street, the energy companies write the energy policies."

"Let's not overdo the gloom," said Roger, on the attack once again. "Think of women's rights and the struggle against racism. We've got a black president, a woman Speaker of the House, and we've had three women secretaries of state. Half the damn Ivy League have female presidents."

"Oh sure," countered Benjamin, shaking his head as if this was so obvious. "They've created a space for women and blacks, and soon Hispanics, to join the elite. But check the statistics on black poverty, and crimes against women. And look at how sexist culture is crippling women around body image and cheap sexuality that starts for eight-year-olds. The system ate the movements of the '60s and '70s and didn't even burp. It just changed the rules a bit. But those in power stayed in power."

"I'm getting a little lost here," Erica said. "This is an environmental organization. What are you talking about?"

"I'm talking about a *system*," Benjamin said slowly, emphasizing the last word as if everyone else was a little slow. "Corporate power; militaristic, repressive governments; the exploitation of women; poverty for racial minorities; endless pollution; destruction of wilderness. Global, impersonal institutions and rules. I call it capitalism—you can call it what you want: patriarchy, industrialization, rule by social elites, entrenched selfishness and greed. Whatever you call it, all the parts work together. Because capitalism needs to expand, it has to produce more and more, and destroy the earth more and more. Because it has to sell all the crap it produces, it needs everybody to consume like crazy, and it has to hook people on fashion, toys, and junk. Because men are trained to be on top, they have to be militaristic just to prove their manhood. Because we need to justify the wars, we have to hate "them," whether they

are Muslims or communists here, or Jews and Americans somewhere else. Because a serious environmental policy would interfere
with growth, we have to pretend it isn't necessary, or claim we
are doing something when we aren't, or tell everyone that serious
environmentalists are *extremists*, God forbid, when the *real* extremists are the ones who are driving us to the brink of disaster and
supporting a vicious, destructive culture."

He paused. He had them in the palm of his hand. Now was the
moment.

"Because it's a system," he said very quietly, looking around the
room at each of them, "we need a systematic answer."

"And just what would that be?" Roger asked, his tone riddled
with sarcasm.

"The answer is The Party. Focused, clear, in it for the long-
term, knowing that the enemy is organized and works together so
we have to be organized and work together as well. The Party of the
New World Order, I like to call it. Other people might have other
names. We will build it slowly and carefully, training cadre, gain-
ing experience, fighting on a thousand fronts: wetlands here, battered women there, mountaintop removal in West Virginia, lead
smelters in Dallas, stronger unions in New York, gay marriage in
California. And all the time, I mean *all* the time, stressing how
these things work together."

"A Party. A *Party*." Roger laughed out loud. "I'm sorry, Benjamin, really I am, but you have got to be joking."

Benjamin's cold stare indicated, quite clearly, that he wasn't.
He'd expected disagreements, doubts, arguments. But not ridicule.

"Exactly what will this Party be like?" Roger went on quickly.
He would take care of this little guy in about two minutes. Didn't
anyone ever learn from the past? "Let's just see what our options
are: There were the large Socialist parties in western Europe and
the U.S. at the end of the nineteenth century and the beginning
of the twentieth. They had millions of members, seats in parlia-
ments, seventy mayors in the eastern U.S., summer camps and coffee houses. They had it made, right? Except that when war loomed
in 1914 they almost all betrayed their countless resolutions *not* to

support another capitalist war. The ones that didn't go back on their promises got repressed by the state, abandoned by their so-called allies. Patriotism and war fever won the day. It seems the leaders of *The Party* were more interested in preserving *The Party*—and their own positions of power and status—than in the principles they had said they stood for. In a few years the whole movement collapsed.

"Then we have the Communist parties of the '30s and '40s and '50s. Controlled by a rigid hierarchy that demanded mindless obedience. Their leaders turned into a new ruling class that treated the masses just as badly, maybe worse, than the old one.

"Get the point? Well, here it is: *every* mass organization in this society, *every single one*, is dominated by an elite. Elites work for the good of the elite, not the masses. It's a simple, iron law.

"Then you've got the tiny little left parties of the last thirty years. The Green Party of Germany accomplished some good things, no doubt, until it self-destructed in internal conflict. In the U.S. the Greens haven't gotten that far, they just self-destruct on internal conflict before they even get to do anything at all.

"So you've got internally conflicted and impotent—or united, powerful, and corrupt. Great choice."

"I'm with you," Wendy agreed. "The last thing we need is another big-time, male-dominated institution. The women's movement worked because it was *un*organized. A thousand little organizations, ten thousand consciousness-raising groups where women shared their personal experiences and learned to think politically, dozens of issues in different places, dozens of important thinkers, many different ways of looking at the issues. That's what made it powerful. That's why Hillary could run for president thirty years later, and the Muslim world is scared to death that women might rise up, and conservative Christians" (Richard thought of David from prison) "hate feminists more than anything.

"And that's what the environmental movement should be. Ten thousand organizations—clean the water, bikes not bombs, outlaw dangerous chemicals, increase fuel efficiency, eat local food, and one for you, Lily," she smiled, which was nice, because Wendy didn't smile too much at meetings, "save the damn whales."

"Do you really think the women's movement worked?" Benjamin asked. This was too easy. "There were a few gains, I grant you that. More women professionals, a little more awareness of things like rape and violence against women. But long-term? Women are poorer than ever. Women of color at the bottom of every social measure you can think of. The system just took the cream off the top and gave it some crumbs—just like it did with blacks in the late 1960s. And all those gains for the middle-class women? Watch them get wiped out in this huge recession we're having."

"A few gains?" Wendy broke in. "You're nuts. Ask any woman who can call the cops on the husband who beats her if that's a small thing. Ask a lesbian, who can get *married* now, what the difference is between being gay now and gay forty years ago. Somehow this all got done without a party."

"The system doesn't care about gay marriage, or who beats whom," said Benjamin with an almost scary intensity. What was under the quiet, controlled face he wore? "The system just wants to keep its power and privilege. Let gay people have expensive weddings. Let women work for Exxon. It's all the same. And in the meantime everybody can talk about 'progress' while the war machine and the pollution machine keep chugging along. A half a million people lost their jobs last month, but defense spending is, guess what, up. The system wants the oil, and they will bankrupt the country to keep it. Think gay marriage will stop that?" Why didn't they see this? It was so obvious.

"*Enough*," said Erica firmly. "We all know that trying to make the world a better place has its ups and downs. Life does too. Going over all our disappointments just brings everybody down. Don't we know anything?"

After a long wait Roger answered, fighting through his irritation and hopelessness. "Here's what I know, and God knows it isn't much. Try to build something that will bring all the groups together. In the '60s we just spit on the working class because they supported the war. Or maybe just because they didn't dress like us or use the same slang and they had short hair. And they hated us as well. The environmental movement won't get anywhere unless it makes common cause with a lot of people—minorities, unions, even progressive businessmen. It's just. . . ."

"Just what?" Benjamin jumped in. Roger was making his case for him.

"Look at us. *Look*!" He raised his voice in frustration, staring at each of them in turn. "We couldn't possibly do it. This country, this world, is divided into splinters that can't work together for more than a few minutes. Everybody wants what's best for *them*, right now, and they aren't willing to sacrifice, to compromise even, for the sake of the whole. We *need* to reduce consumption. But can you imagine some political party trying to get elected on *that* slogan—*Vote for me, I promise you'll have less*? Your Party might be the best thing, Benjamin, and we might never win without it. But it's just not possible." He slumped back in his chair, energy drained. "No wonder my therapist says I'm depressed."

"Your therapist isn't the only one," said a voice from the back of the room. Everyone laughed, even Roger.

Lily saw her chance. "We all have these . . . problems . . . which make it so hard to do this work. Look at me. I'm scared of conflict, makes me so upset I can't think. So I need to work on myself so that I'm emotionally strong enough to deal with the real differences people have. I can't be a delicate little pushover and save the world, can I? And other people want power, or they are so angry they cause fights in the group, or they want to be the big star. We don't know how to be the kind of people who can make a peaceful world. No one teaches us to respect each other, honor our leaders, and support people learning how to be stronger. We learn just the opposite.

"So I'm going somewhere to learn how to do those things. I'm going to live on The Farm. This is my last meeting."

Richard visibly flinched. Between Roger's depression, Fred's family problems, Benjamin's fantasy of the Grand New Party, and now this, the group might fall apart tonight.

"But Lily," he implored, "we need all the folks we have. I know we had a setback, but we made some progress, and we can make some more."

"Everything we do can be swept away. I want something that lasts, that isn't so fragile." She turned to Benjamin, a soft smile lighting up her thin face. "In a way, I agree with you. We need people who see the *whole* picture—I just think only people committed to spiritual self-transformation can see it." She looked at Wendy. "You're right. We need to be strong, to resist. There is nothing, *nothing*," a surprisingly steely note sounded in her usually timid voice, "stronger than spiritual truth. At The Farm each person has a spiritual focus for their lives—dealing with anger, or fear, or insecurity, or their need to dominate. We will change the world like that—one person at a time. It's the only sure way."

Roger had his usual impulse to tell Lily all the reasons why this sort of thing never worked. But then he thought about praying and meditating each day—would that help him hold the pain he saw everywhere?

Erica broke in, shaking her head side to side in an angry gesture that reminded Lily of a dog shaking a bone. "You're just abandoning the poor and the weak"—yet a small, unacknowledged corner of her mind envied Lily a little—"while you go off to be nice to yourself."

"Ah, Lily," Wendy added, with a sad smile, hurt that Lily hadn't talked this over with her first, "you still don't get it. Change comes in bits and pieces. Made by weak imperfect people who screw up constantly. All these groups that Roger put down actually did some really good things. The Communist Party helped give us the labor movement, the Socialist parties cut into the pure capitalist power that was exploiting people without limit. The Social Democratic parties in western Europe put in socialized medicine, made education easy to get, supported day care for working mothers. The New Left got all these causes on the table—sex, race, gay rights, disabled rights, animal rights. Sounds silly in a long list like that, I know, but what a difference this has made! Did we create something that can't be swept away? Will it all be perfect forever? *Is it heaven!* No, but it's better. Dammit, it's better."

She raised her open hands over her head and shook them for emphasis. "And who were the people who did all this? Ego-tripping, confused, arrogant, whatever. So what? If the guy who fixes your plumbing isn't so nice, do you care? Or are you just glad your toilet works? It's the same with political change. It's messy, temporary, partial, and sometimes the people who do it are a real drag. But it's the best we can hope for."

"If you hold out for perfection, you'll end with nothing," said Erica, her tone even more strident because of her own doubts. "*You* can do that because you're privileged. Black folks are used to getting less, and half of it is broken when we get it anyway. So we don't expect perfect. Okay is the best we hope for." She pointed an accusing finger at each one in turn. "Not your perfect Party that will make us feel like Jesus is back on earth, Benjamin. Not your circle of spiritual perfection, Lily. People like you, you're willing to sacrifice a little bit in the present for something that isn't real in the future. And not your endless put-downs of everybody else because you're so miserable, Roger. Just ordinary, messed up folks, putting one foot ahead of the next, making tiny little improvements."

Wendy and Erica glared at Lily, who hung her head. She felt like crying, and she didn't know that part of them did too.

For a while, nobody had anything to say.

This is my chance, thought Richard, or the whole thing will go up in smoke anyway. "We really do want to make it better, right Erica?"

"Right," said Erica. Wendy nodded. "So we have to make a statement, one they can't ignore. Remember Malcolm X, Erica, do what needs to be done 'by any means possible'?"

"Where is this headed?" asked Roger impatiently. He hated it when white radicals started quoting Malcolm.

"We don't *allow* them to build the mall. They start building, we tear it down. They put up billboards, we burn them. They bring in bulldozers, we break them. 'No compromise in defense of Mother Earth.'"

"Violence? *Violence?*" Lily put her hand to her mouth, aghast. Her eyes went wide with shock. Yelling at people was bad enough. Now this? "You want to build a peaceful world by breaking things? And what if someone gets hurt?"

"No one will get hurt, I'll make sure of that. And peaceful? Well, a graveyard is peaceful, but that's only because everyone's dead. I'm for justice, and protecting the earth."

"But violence *never* works, it just makes things worse."

"Really?" Roger put on a pseudosmile and his voice had a kind of phony inquisitiveness. Lily cringed, afraid of what would come next. "And have you studied *all* the times violence has been used in social movements? And made an exhaustive catalog of *all* the effects it's had?"

"But," Lily sputtered. It seemed so obvious when Rachel said it. And Gandhi and King. "Are you saying it's good to be violent? That we should just blow things up and shoot people?"

"I'm saying I don't know," he answered, his depression once again masked by irritation, "and I don't think you do either. Look at Richard's idea: if the plans for the mall go ahead, we strike back. Now, there are all sorts of reasons why this is a bad idea." Richard bit his lip but held his tongue. Roger ticked off his fingers: "First, *they* have the police, the FBI, and, if it ever came to that, the army. Second, the more violent people are to the enemy, the more violent they tend to be to their friends when disagreement happens. I like you, Richard, but you get pretty scary when you think someone is crossing you. Third, and maybe most important, violence discredits the movement as a whole. People look at the Earth First! types and think environmentalists are a bunch of terrorists. Mild-mannered folks are scared off, environmental issues lose at election time, and politicians shun us."

"That's right," Lily said, nodding at each point.

"Sure it's right, but now let's reverse it. 'We're not powerful enough?' That's for sure, but it's not about winning some grand battle, it's about showing the people in charge how committed we are and making these little development projects a *lot* more expensive. After all, the antiwar movement didn't beat the police or the FBI, but it made the Vietnam War just too much trouble. The ghetto riots didn't defeat the National Guard, but they scared white politicians so much they passed a whole War on Poverty to placate the blacks. Think that would have happened if the blacks had just asked nicely? And finally, maybe violent environmentalism turns people off. And maybe it legitimizes the more moderate groups. Maybe people say, 'All environmentalists are crazy,' but maybe they say, 'Gee, these Sierra Club types aren't so bad compared to those other guys.' Maybe. Maybe. We just don't know."

Richard was about to chime in, supporting Roger's arguments in favor of violence, challenging the ones against. But a sudden thought struck him, and he couldn't speak until he turned it over in his mind. "We just don't know. We just don't know." Is that what was driving everybody a little crazy? Lily and Benjamin, him and Erica and Wendy, *none of them knew what had to be done to save the planet and protect people.* Everyone here was a good person, spending time in these boring, frustrating meetings because they wanted to make things better. But they didn't know how. They just had some ideas, ideas that usually went along with the prejudices they walked in with, or their personalities, or whatever.

Suddenly he remembered their first meeting, when the old guy had talked about love. But along with the love there was the terrible fear for everything and everyone that was being hurt and lost. For him it was the earth, and the people getting poisoned. For Erica it was her neighbors, the other people of color. For Lily, it was the trees and the river. And he could see, suddenly, that probably almost everybody, everywhere, had that same fear these days. Even people on the other side, who were scared that environmentalism would cost them their jobs or take away the things that gave them the little pleasures of life. And the real problem was, nobody knew what to do. But seeing that, well that was just *too* scary. It's the fear, the fear, he realized. Was there any way to love without being afraid for what you loved? And was there any way to be frightened without getting angry at the people who thought differently than you?

He tried to hold on to the thought, but he couldn't. Then the desperation took him, digging in claws so hard he could hardly breathe. He fought back with what he knew best.

"You're all aware of what's happening to the earth. I say, resist, protect life. Let's add something to your list of maybes, Roger: maybe if we had a million really angry activists, something would change."

"A million angry activists would just be a million angry people, doing what angry people always do—fight with each other, do dumb things, and sooner or later—probably sooner—self-destruct."

This came from a tall, heavyset women with dark frizzy hair and green overalls, a mud-spattered brown sweater draped over powerful arms.

"Who the hell are you," sputtered Richard. The woman was a complete stranger.

"I'm Rachel, I run The Farm. I came to pick up Lily and make sure you guys didn't gang up on her for splitting from your little group."

"I'm fine, Rachel, just fine." Lily's head was down, embarrassed. "We should just go."

"Oh, we'll go, all right, but not before I add one little thing to this lovely exchange of views." Lily was surprised at Rachel's tone. Rachel had never sounded this sarcastic and abrasive before.

She stood among them, hands on her hips, a deep certainty in her eyes and voice. "None of you, none of *us*, are ready to really make things better. We're just too emotionally immature, selfish, and addicted to a lot of crap that's making us sick. Until we are ready, things will just stay the same. The capitalists will be replaced by the communists, the Democrats by the Republicans, and back again. One gang of lying thieves will give way to another. Find a safe place, like The Farm, and work on yourselves. Maybe in ten years you'll be ready. Maybe you'll never be ready and only your kids will. There's no other way."

Wendy jumped in, angered by the women's know-it-all tone. "Everything you stand for could be swept away in a second. Change the zoning, up the property taxes, whatever—and your precious safe place would be gone in a heartbeat. *There are no safe places—* not The Farm," she turned around to Benjamin and Richard, "not The Party, not the great noble deed of violent resistance, Richard. Nothing is safe, so we just have to work as best we can *without* safety."

"You can be safe if your mind is at peace," Rachel responded with quiet firmness, unmoved by Wendy's rebuff.

"You think you're going to get a peaceful mind by living in some rural cocoon? Where you only talk to people who are just like you? That's a great way to learn, isn't it?" She laughed, not pleasantly. "No, not there, not on the meditation cushion or the yoga mat either, lady. That's like saying you're going to get big muscles by lying in bed until you get stronger just by thinking about it. No, a peaceful mind comes by struggling and trying to be peaceful *in the struggle*. Only that."

There it is again, thought Richard. "The only way," "Nothing else." And nobody really knew, including him. Look at Roger, he was thirty years older and knew five times as much. And he didn't know either—all he could do was find the flaws in what everybody else said. This was too important, more important than trashing a billboard or slashing the tires on a bulldozer. This was key. He had to share this.

"Folks . . . friends. . . ." People quieted suddenly, responding to something new in his tone. They'd heard him falsely jovial, studiously "listening" when they could see he was just waiting to get his own points across, angry when people disagreed. Here was something different.

"Really, really . . ." he spoke almost too quietly to be heard, and then paused, looking at each of them in turn. "I don't know what we should do. I think I know what's right for me, but I can't speak for Benjamin or Lily or Erica or Wendy or anyone else. But there's something I need to share with you now. It's about how we feel about all this, and how that makes us treat each other.

"Can you listen?"

In his huge den, The Developer clicked off a 52-inch wall-mounted Sony 7.1 channel surround sound home entertainment center and smiled to himself. What should I call it? he wondered. Valley Stream Mall? Mall in the Glen? Woods Heart? Each of the thirty-three malls he'd built, the businesses that had made him a millionaire many times over, had names taken from nature. Made everything seem calm and welcoming.

That should have satisfied the environmentalists, he smiled to himself. But nooooooo, they were *never* happy. He'd paved over a stupid stream; somebody, somewhere, had cut down the wrong trees to make the wood; or the coffee beans in the four-dollar hazelnut lattes weren't organic enough.

And now this latest crowd. "Save the wetlands." What a joke. *He* provided jobs, kept the economy humming along, gave people a place to buy what they needed and to have a little fun. This was how modern people enjoyed themselves. Were these environmentalists against jobs and fun and relaxation, for God's sake?

And of course *they* always drove their cars to the demonstrations they loved to hold. Where did they think cars came from? Even if they rode their goddamn bikes, did they think bikes grew on trees? Actually, someone had to mine the metal, form the plastic, and make the gears and brakes in an actual *factory*. And where that factory was, there had been a forest or a meadow. Want to save the wetland? Then don't buy a bike. It was like the old joke about California—everybody wanted to be the last son of a bitch to move in.

But when *they* bought a bike, used a cell phone, took home some fair-trade coffee that, fair trade or not, had to be schlepped here from Central America, that was OK. It was only when *other* people did it, well then it was No Good and Time To Stop.

He'd beaten them before, and he was beating them now. A little cash in the right places, the right connections in the community, promises of construction work and jobs in the new mall—and everything went down smooth as silk. If some of the building materials weren't the cleanest, couldn't be helped. Absolutely guaranteed 100 percent clean was just too expensive. All of life involves a little risk. It wasn't his fault. And he always gave money to nature causes. Why, next year he might be up for a seat on the board of the Wilderness Society, he'd given them so much.

He stood up, stretched, and decided to have a nightcap, smiling to himself as he walked from the den to his beautifully appointed living room for a little thirty-year-old Irish whiskey. Life was good. Business was good. The economic downturn wouldn't last forever, and while it was happening he'd snap up some more properties for a song, and maybe take over a few failing development firms.

The simple fact was that people wanted jobs, and when they had more money, they wanted what was in the mall. *He gave people what they wanted.* Who were these environmentalists to tell people they should want something else—especially when they all enjoyed this system they bitched about so much? The market had given us progress—health care, the Internet, travel to anywhere, more food than anyone needed, entertainment. Malls were part of what made it work. When the rest of the world had malls, and people running around trying to be inventive and start new businesses the way they did here, they could live like Americans too, and everyone would be happy. Or at least a lot happier than they were now, starving to death, blowing each other up, getting nutty with religion. Capitalism was the best system people had ever come up with. Even the damn Chinese—when they let the entrepreneurs loose, their economy had taken off like a rocket. This was the only thing that worked. Everything else was a crazy pipe dream.

He hadn't come from money, and he enjoyed everything he had. This great home, the summer "cottage" by the shore, his and his wife's matching BMWs in the driveway. And he gave generously to charity—the cancer fund, the autism fund, the birth defects fund, the local children's hospital.

And the kids, the three kids. All great.

Except for Clarissa, the youngest.

He sipped his whiskey, admitting to himself that the only thing in his life that wasn't, well, pretty perfect was Clarissa. Came too early, never very strong, learned to talk late, kind of weak. She'd always been frail, slow, special. They'd spent a bundle on therapists and tutors and all sorts of doctors. Some of them had helped, but not too much, or for too long. And last month she'd had what looked like a seizure.

Worst of all, the doctors had no idea what this was. His wife had taken her for tests, and tests, and more tests. They'd say she had such-and-such syndrome, but then it turned out that she only had about half of what people with the syndrome had. And only about a hundred people in the world had that syndrome anyway, and they didn't know much about it yet, and would we like to bring her back for another thirteen tests? After the third time *that* happened, he'd put his foot down. If they didn't know what was wrong with her, they would just have to live with it and try to treat the symptoms.

"It is most likely some kind of genetic problem," one of the specialists said last year.

"From what?" asked his wife, fear and uncertainty in her voice, keeping her grief hidden. She carried the burden of all this more than The Developer did. "None of our families have any problems. Our other kids are fine."

"We really aren't sure," the doctor had answered. "Could be just normal genetic variation, an accident. Could be an extreme sensitivity to something in the environment. You'll never know, so you might as well put it out of your mind."

Good advice, The Developer had thought. In a life working so well, you were bound to have a little bad luck. Clarissa would be all right in the long run. And if not, she'd be taken care of. Anyway, there was nothing they could have done. Not for her, or for the all the other kids the specialists had mentioned. "We're seeing a lot more of this sort of thing over the last twenty years. Some people think environmental reasons. But the jury is still out on this one."

4

PASS THE TURKEY

Bright November sunshine flooded into the Bertrams' living room as Kate entered, mumbling Thanksgiving greetings to her family: parents, two brothers, and, straight out of central casting, a gentle, alcoholic uncle. Her withdrawn, downcast hellos surprised her brother Ned, who looked up from his copy of *Mother Jones*. "What's up, sis?" he asked.

"I just saw the most horrible thing. There was this truck stopped at an intersection near 54th Street. On the outside it had signs about how fur is the look that kills and animals have rights. I've seen that sort of thing before. But then there was something different. The back of the truck was open, and inside was a huge screen showing these awful film clips: cows being clubbed to death, foxes gnawing their legs off to get out of traps, chickens all stuffed together in some huge industrial henhouse. The looks in their eyes were just. . . ." Her voice trailed off.

Ned saw the tears at the corners of Kate's eyes. He ran his hand through his sandy hair in a nervous gesture, straightened his painfully thin body, and tried to comfort her the only way he knew how.

"Well, what can you expect? In this society *everything* is treated like a commodity. People's labor, fish, forests—all of it. As long as the means of production are owned by a conscienceless class of rapacious bastards, that's the way it will be. We'll only have kindness when capitalism is replaced by socialism."

Ned patted Kate on the back and tried to change the tone. "Hey Mom," he shouted playfully, "how's the turkey doing? I'm starving!"

Danny, the baby of the family but now nineteen, had been hoping in vain to soothe an upset stomach by massaging the reflexology points on his left foot. He looked much younger than his age, with innocent eyes and thick black hair reaching to his shoulders. If it were possible, he would have gotten more bored with Ned's endless Marxist sloganeering, but he'd reached his boredom limit years ago.

"I can see you're right in tune with history Ned," he chuckled. "The capitalists are rapacious, but you're going to enjoy your dead bird just like the head guys at Citibank."

Ned sighed. He knew that younger brothers were like that, but had hoped that on a family day Danny would give it a rest. "If," he answered with a fair imitation of patience, "you really care about moral values, what you have to do is change social institutions. If I don't eat meat, everyone else will, and nothing will change. Besides," he grinned with just a hint of mischief, "and don't tell my sensitive vegan sister, there's nothing quite as good as roast turkey with all the trimmings."

"I'm surprised how little you get this," Kate murmured. And when Ned glanced at her quizzically, she elaborated more firmly. "It's not about some future time when capitalism and all the other isms you talk about so endlessly are overcome. It's about what happened to me when I looked at those images. I felt something wrench me deep inside, like a cry for help at night. I wasn't thinking about society or moral values or aren't people and animals different or aren't they really the same. I just felt sick, and wanted it all to stop. And I was so ashamed for all of us, I felt a little like killing myself."

Ned had hoped to make her feel better, but the depth of her emotions scared him a little.

"Once when I was about seven," mused their already somewhat tipsy uncle Isaac, lifting his glass with one hand and pulling on his rumpled gray sweater with the other, "your grandfather and I woke up in the middle of the night because we heard something crying out. It was high-pitched, desperate, and it made us very upset. Off we went at two in the morning, searching suburban streets with a huge flashlight. We had no idea what it was. We just felt how scared and lonely it was. And we wanted to help."

His voice trailed off and his eyes returned to the glassy stare he cultivated, while his fingers tightened on the whiskey glass.

"Well," broke in Ned, "what was it?"

"Oh," said Isaac. "Puppy. Cute little puppy. We took it home, gave it some warm milk, and let it sleep on an old blanket in the kitchen. Next morning we called the ASPCA."

"Did someone lose it?" asked Danny.

"Nope . . . just abandoned. The ASPCA had to gas it, since no one would adopt. Too bad. Sweet little thing."

This was the turn Danny had waited for. "That's what I mean. Uncle and Grandpa. They're not big-deal political types like you, Ned, or big-deal thinkers like Dad, but it's the heart that matters. Grandpa and Uncle answered a cry in the dark. Kate responded to the films of the tortured animals. We don't have to have some fancy explanation or justification of *why* we feel this way. We just know we do."

Their father Joshua listened to all this, wondering if it was worth putting in his two cents. He was a medium-sized, well-put-together, 50ish philosophy professor at NYU. He wore a casual but elegant sport jacket, slacks, and knit shirt, and he held his body, and used his voice, with the self-assurance of someone who did everything very carefully. He distrusted Ned's sloganeering, Kate's warm but untutored heart, and Danny's (as he thought) hippie nonsense. He had tried for years to get them to see how, well, very *complex* these questions were. He was quite sure that unless people got beyond simpleminded slogans, there would never be much progress. "Clarity," he was fond of saying, "clarity is what we need. Only then can we make some sense of all these conflicting demands, interests, and values."

"Very nice, Danny, very nice," he offered to his son, trying to be encouraging but not succeeding very well. "But who is this 'we'? Many people see a good deal of animal suffering and do nothing. People who work in slaughterhouses, cattle ranchers, anyone connected to the fur industry. They don't care about the pain they see, or if they do, it certainly seems as if other things outweigh their feelings pretty easily."

"That's because of, to pardon my French, this fucked up culture," declared Danny, with a wry glance at Ned, who typically attributed all moral problems to "this goddamn capitalist system."

"On that we agree," Ned added. "Who works in slaughterhouses, after all? Illegal immigrants, poor women, the uneducated. And as a job it has about the worst safety and health record around. The wastes from hog farms poison the water table, meat eating contributes to global warming, which makes life harder for victims of imperialism the world over. That's my problem with the way we treat animals. But we'll never be decent to animals until we're decent to people."

Sly smile of his own. "Of course, even then we'll still have turkey for Thanksgiving. Let's face it; people just are more important than animals." He loved his younger brother, but he knew that Danny needed to toughen up if he was going to make it in the real world. All the crystals and books on shamanism weren't going to prepare Danny for a global marketplace, militaristic governments, and class struggle.

"And why is that?" Danny fumed at his older brother, who thought he knew everything but really just lived in a fantasyland of endless revolution in some indefinite future. "Because only humans are the subjects of history? Have a language that enables us to justify torturing animals in moronic experiments? Produce reality TV shows?" His tone said he held Ned personally responsible for animal labs and *Survivor.*

From the kitchen, where her hands were occupied with turkey basting, apple pie crust rolling, and potato peeling, Esther listened to her endlessly squabbling sons and sighed. She was a short woman, heavy around the hips, whose auburn hair now held generous streaks of gray. Her kind intelligent eyes looked at people carefully, studying them to see where she should bandage a wound or soothe a troubled heart. She loved her wonderful but at times simply impossible husband, her challenging but at times overwhelming work, and figured that, all in all, things had worked out really well for her. And what hadn't worked out she'd learned to accept, make do, and look on the bright side.

Except, except, while she adored her three children, the way they fought bothered her terribly. She'd been an only child, with cold, distant parents, and during those lonely, boring, stiff evenings in the living room she'd promised herself that she'd have a large family where everyone would be warm and happy together. Kate could usually manage, but Ned and Danny—oil and water, almost always, even when they were kids. Now that they were grown up, they could hardly be in the same room without one of them starting and the other one only too glad to join in.

Why couldn't they just accept each other? After all, it wasn't like either one of them was going to change the world right here in her living room. Or anywhere else, either. It was only *talk.* Ned's politics, Danny's ideas about Spirit and Life. If people could just be kind to one another, things would work out. And if they couldn't be kind, none of their fancy ideas would make any difference anyway, in her living room or anywhere else, for that matter. She kept wanting to order them to just accept each other for five minutes. But she knew they wouldn't listen.

"Now, now, Danny, don't get all upset," she joked with a little laugh as she walked into the living room. "Why are people more important than animals? Oh, I don't know. We just are. Don't tell me you'd feel just as bad running over a squirrel as over a human child. Why would you feel different? Who can tell! Dinner in about a half hour, guys."

"In other words," said Joshua gently, never one to miss an opportunity to make it all clear, stroking his salt-and-pepper beard while he waited to get their attention back, "people have intuitions that feel completely certain. The theoretical work is to explain why these are true. But the explanations will never be more certain than the intuitions themselves."

"Really?" exclaimed Kate, who loved her father dearly but thought that with all his scholarly brilliance he often missed the point. "We are *certain*," she emphasized the word in a slight parody of her father, "that people are worth more than animals. And of *course* we know that men are worth more than women, Christians than Jews and . . . need I go on? So tell me, Dad, how do you tell the difference between a really, really certain moral 'intuition' and a lot of oppressive crap?"

"Good question, very good question," Joshua answered.

"Oh, spare us the professorial condescension and just get to the point," Kate shot back.

"Ahem!" Joshua began, trying not to smile at his spunky daughter's mock insolence. "You are right. As powerful as intuitions can be, they also change over time, and will be very different for different people. So what can we do? Just try to talk to each other. Get as educated as we can. Make sure that people are allowed to talk and to be heard. Make the conversation as free and equal as possible. And then we come up with an answer. Short of a direct word from God—and even that would have to be interpreted—what else can we do? Whatever we'd end up deciding in a really free conversation is what's right."

"Ah," laughed Ned, "moral life is really one big philosophy seminar." Though he might not admit it too often, he was proud of his well-published, highly respected professor father. But he still thought academic philosophy missed the point, which was not to understand the world but to change it. "Well, pardon my skepticism, but I'd still like to know who owns the building where the seminar takes place, who's providing the food and electricity and clothes for the people doing the talking, and who gets to talk and who is left out."

"No, no, no," responded Joshua impatiently. Did his children purposefully misunderstand him? "This isn't just for college students and philosophy professors. It's for everyone. It's a conversational democracy that we all would take part in."

"What do you mean, 'everyone'?" asked Esther.

"All the rational adults," Joshua answered, more impatient. "Not kids, mental defectives, or people in comas. What do you think?"

"I *think*," Esther replied, a quiet intensity in her tone, "that before I'd sign on to this I'd like to know who sets the standards for 'defective.' Cousin Peter's daughter with Down's syndrome— would she get a chance to speak or not?"

"Well . . . well . . ." Joshua's voice trailed off. No one had ever asked him this before. And his position had seemed so indubitable.

Esther smiled sweetly at her husband, then passed around some spiced pistachios.

Danny broke the silence, his voice low and intense. "Besides Peter's daughter, what about all the other beings that speak? Go to the slaughterhouse, the animal labs, the fish covered in spilled oil. It's not hard to hear what they are saying. 'Stop it, for God's sake, stop it!'" He broke off, not wanting to start crying in front of them, who probably already thought him a complete wimp. But wherever he was, he could hear the cries, and he just couldn't stand it.

"Oh well," said Joshua, back on firmer ground, and trying to save Danny the embarrassment of getting overwhelmed by his grief. "Of course animals express certain primitive emotions and feelings. They howl when hurt, fight or grovel when threatened, and lick their babies. But they can't talk like people. They can't argue about right and wrong, justice or injustice. Only people can do that, and that's why even in Ned's far-off socialist society, only people get in on these kinds of conversations. Animals couldn't, even if we wanted them to."

"You forget," Danny countered, quiet and intense, "that for thousands of years people have been conversing with animal spirits. That's what shamans do—go into the animal realm and bring back guidance. I know philosophers like you or Marxist types like Ned think you know everything, or at least know better than all the hopelessly unenlightened masses just waiting to be instructed. But have you ever tried to listen to an eagle or a dolphin? Have you ever tried to think yourselves into their skin? When we're in spiritual harmony with life, it's easier for us to be in spiritual harmony with ourselves."

And, thought Esther, it's often easier for painfully shy Danny to pet his cat than to make new friends. But she kept quiet.

"Please," responded Ned, shaking his hand dismissively, his voice louder all the time, "don't ask us to take your marvelous indigenous peoples so seriously. It's too bad that they've been destroyed, mainly by capitalist colonialism, imperialism, and commercialism. But they have no place in a modern world where science allows us to be the masters of nature and not nature's slaves. Never mind their oppressive superstitions, what's right for a small tribe isn't going to work for a global society that uses democracy and technology. Men and women who go into trances, roll their eyes back, and tell us the latest news from Mr. Eagle and Ms. Bear are just a little too old school."

"Oh, so modernity is so great?" Danny yelled, eagerly taking the chance to be irritated, fed up with his brother's unthinking arrogance. "Global warming, destroyed wilderness, dead species, environmental illness, not to mention mental misery so profound that we're drowning in drugs. Seems to me this marvelous modernity, including all those so-called socialist countries of yours, could use a little shamanism, or something, from cultures that believed all of nature was their kin."

Esther bit her lip to keep from yelling herself, knowing that yelling at people to keep them from yelling at each other generally didn't work too well. Why couldn't they see it? They needed a little respect, a little *empathy* from each other. Then maybe they'd be able to hear each other. She'd seen them get older, grow into their

opinions, and knew that for each of them these opinions made a
kind of perfect sense. Ned had been shocked, visibly shaken, when
he had first found out about world hunger and poverty. He had seen
some rough things in the city, but when he'd done that report on
Bangladesh in ninth grade, something had shifted in him. Everywhere he looked he saw oppression and injustice. It made him miserable, and he wanted it to go away. He started reading about the
world, searching out Web sites of political groups that explained
why things were the way they were. He would question his parents,
demanding to know where they stood on this issue or that. His
own middle-class lifestyle stopped making sense to him, because
he couldn't understand why he had so much more than other people. He'd started challenging his teachers about which books they
assigned, demanding to know why there weren't more women on
the school board, more books by African American authors in the
English curriculum. Underneath it all, she knew, was a deep sorrow for all the world's pain, and his politics were the only way
he knew to deal with that. So he'd become a full-time activist,
for one cause after another, right after college, making practically
no money, so he didn't have to worry about being better off than
everyone else. She was fine with all this, and proud of his commitment. But he could be so intolerant of anybody who saw things any
other way. So self-righteous. And so downright hostile to Danny.

Ah, Danny, very different from Ned. Shy, sensitive, kept to
himself most of the time. Never had many friends. Cried a lot—
why she wasn't sure. She'd always worried about him. And then
three years ago he'd stumbled across the whole New Age thing.
Crystals, meditation, music that was all soothe and no beat, visual-
izing a peaceful place and a rosy light in your heart, wisdom over
science, love for everybody and everything—except his brother,
of course. She didn't know where this would take him, but the
practices and what he believed about them seemed to make him
less lonely, less afraid of the world. Despite all the mantras and
mandalas, he could be just like his brother when he started talking
about animals—completely sure he was right and anybody on the
other side was dead wrong.

All these arguments you have, she wanted to tell them, don't you see? These ideas you hold on to and hit each other over the head with, they are just what you use to help you sleep at night, and get you through each day, and feel connected to something larger than yourself. You need them to make you feel safe, that's why you get so crazy when someone threatens them. If you could only admit that to yourselves, you could hear each other. And accept that someone else makes sense of things and feels safe a different way. But they were too wrapped up in what they thought they couldn't do without, and with the fear and sadness covered up by all their shouting. Worst of all, they just took family for granted and didn't understand how important it was to offer some caring to their actual relatives. They'd have to want it a lot more to make it work. Instead, they acted like it would kill them to admit the other person had even a tiny bit of truth on his side.

Joshua tried to calm things down with a helpful clarification. "You know, Danny, and you too, Ned," he said, wondering if he could get the boys to read something he'd written on this, "sometimes you speak as if nature and people are two different things. Yet humans are as natural as any panda. We are all products of evolution, based in carbon, and will fall through the air if someone tosses us off the roof. But do keep in mind, Danny, what you call nature is really a social product. 'Wilderness' meant something scary in the fourteenth century, and now it's a place to escape the evils of civilization. But only," he smiled, "if you've got the right equipment. All these adventures in the forest to hear nature's voice cost a pretty penny in fancy backpacks, ultralight tents, and $200 a pair Gore-Tex-lined hiking boots. What we understand as nature just depends on where we are and what we do as a society. Nature is really something we make." He looked around to make sure they all understood how important this was.

"What nonsense," laughed Kate, wondering why really sophisticated philosophers seemed to know so little about psychology. Then she laughed again at her father's shocked expression—he had made this argument so many times in lectures, and always to good effect.

"Look, Dad," she explained. "You and mom have been married for what, thirty-two years?"

"Thirty-three," he smiled. "I always say it's the first thirty that are the hardest."

"Very funny," replied Kate. "But here's the idea. Of course you see Mom, and she sees you, through the lens of your own experience—what you want and need and feel. That's just the way people are. But does that mean that Mom is your *product*? Of course not! It just means you're in a *relationship*—you shape her, and she shapes you, you see each other through your own points of view, *and* get those points of view changed by what you experience from the other person. Danny and I aren't saying, 'Leave this totally separate thing, nature, alone,' but 'Let's try to change our relationships with all these other beings.'"

"Yes," Danny jumped in, "that's why the idea of humanity controlling nature, or, to use the word you and Ned are so fond of, 'humanizing' it, is not so appealing. What kind of relationship would you have with Mom if you just tried to 'Joshualize' her?"

"Don't think he hasn't," observed Esther. "But I've 'Estherized' him as well. That's just marriage. I've even gotten him to cook and clean up a fair amount, though that didn't come easy." To say the least, she didn't add, but thought.

"Humanizing nature . . . turning nature into people?" mumbled Isaac. "How dreadful."

"Come on, Danny," countered Ned, still a little irritated that Danny took shamanism, for God's sake, seriously. "'Humanizing' nature just means we make the world into a place where we can flourish. But so will the other species. Most of them, anyway. I don't see much of a future for the AIDS virus or Ebola if we can help it—and I don't think you do, either. Capitalism gives us the power to dominate nature, not to have to spend all our time just surviving. But under socialism, people will be kind and caring and careful. We can control nature rationally and humanely."

"*Humanely*?" Danny wasn't buying it. "Humanely? What a dismal prospect. Did you and your pals ever think maybe you have something to learn from nature? Something other than how to control it, even rationally? Did you ever think that life is a mystery, a

miracle, and that at least some of the time our job is to open ourselves up to whatever *it* has to tell *us?*"

Ned's blank stare indicated, not surprisingly, that he hadn't a
clue what Danny was talking about. So Ned shifted ground.

"Tell me this," he asked Danny and Kate, with a kind of pretend innocence that didn't fool anybody. "Who do you support
when nature messes with nature?"

"Lions eat gazelles, that's fine with me," answered Danny.

"Indeed," their father added, "animals live by nature, we live by
culture and morality."

"Not so fast," Ned pushed on. "Out in California there are millions of feral cats, just abandoned by owners or lost or whatever.
They're killing so many birds, whole species are at risk. What do
you say, Danny, should we kill the cats to save the birds? Or leave
the cats alone, and it's bye-bye birdie." He smiled broadly at his
own wit, which everyone else ignored.

"I'm not sure," Danny said slowly, and Kate could see the pain
in his eyes—for the birds, for the cats.

Joshua thought he'd help the boy out. "You know, if two people
have a fight, and are so occupied in fighting that they fall off a cliff,
and then someone says, '*Now* what should we do?'—well, by then
it's a little too late to really do anything."

His three children stared at him with a shared blank look,
wondering if the old man was losing it.

Joshua could see it wasn't as obvious as he thought. "Once
we have all these cats, allow them not to be sterilized, get care-
less with them—once we do that, or other things like that, these
kinds of conflicts are inevitable. And they happen with people too,
right Ned? Different oppressed groups against each other. Different nations. Even different parts of the same country. If you give to
one, you have to take away from the other. How do you choose?"

Kate started talking, so low the others had to strain to hear
her. "Remember what I said about how that film made me feel,
almost like killing myself? That's it, that's it." She paused, searching for the words to match the feelings that were sweeping through
her. "If we didn't look at the cats and the birds, and which ones we

should kill and which ones we should save, maybe we'd have to look at ourselves. And what it would take to change all . . . *this*." She raised an arm and gestured with her hand at the city, the country, human beings everywhere.

The three men were silent, each thinking that in their own way they had the answer. For Joshua, philosophical reflection. For Ned, political action. For Danny, spiritual love. And if they could just focus hard enough on the answer, then they wouldn't have to feel the endless misery that Kate had gestured at.

Esther wondered if any of them ever admitted, even to themselves, that they really didn't know what to do about all that suffering anyway. They wanted to help, they certainly did, but the problems were so overwhelming, and so much of what people tried only helped a little, at best. Politics, religion, science, big corporations, little ones, at least half the time they just made things worse. No, she'd stick to the way she did it, that was something you could trust.

Kate poured herself a Heineken, took a long drink, and tried again. "Let's try this another way, Ned. What makes you think that a 'humane' society would be good for animals? How many times did these social movements that you talk about endlessly do anything for people outside their own group? And how many times did they just work for themselves, quite happy to let the ones below them continue to get treated like dirt?"

"You must admit she's got a good point," observed Joshua, who liked few things in life better than a good point. "In the Socialist Party of the late nineteenth century, craft workers didn't care much for unskilled workers. Men who wanted the vote for freed slaves didn't mind that women didn't get it. Some radicals of the '60s were incredibly sexist. Even environmental groups didn't take environmental racism seriously until people of color confronted them. What makes you think a socialist movement that encompassed all of humanity would necessarily be ready to give up its

Thanksgiving turkey, its bacon and eggs, its leather belts? Not to mention its subjects for medical experiments?"

"Exactly," Danny pounced. "I can just see the slogan now: Vote socialist, support worldwide, compulsory vegetarianism. You think no one pays attention to you now? That would really finish you off."

Ned seethed at this but was (for a change) at a loss for words. Even though he knew it was true, he didn't like hearing that mass movements of the oppressed could be pretty self-serving. And even more, he didn't like thinking about how few people in the world shared his vision of democratic socialism. Despite all he knew about exploitation, politics, and economics, he often felt completely powerless. And when he looked at all the injustice in the world, it just made him crazy. There had to be an answer, there just had to be.

"Look, Dad," Kate turned to her father. "Here's what I don't get. Let's say you have this perfectly open conversation about morality and politics going. Let's say we agree that only rational, nondefective people—though in my experience I haven't met any-one without lots of defects—can take part. What will they say once they get there?"

"They'll say whatever they know, whatever they believe."

"But what will they know and believe about animals?"

"Whatever they know and believe," repeated Joshua, getting exasperated again. "What are you after?"

"Just this," Kate answered. "If democracy is one big conver-sation, it's going to be a pretty stupid conversation unless people know something about politics, right? About, oh, I don't know, tax laws, and immigration, and farm subsidies. And if I'm going to talk about animals, I need to know something about them as well. How can someone talk about animals if he's never been to a slaugh-terhouse, or sat for hours watching animals in the wild, or seen a cat give birth, or held a favorite dog in his arms while it was being put to sleep? And people don't know how smart animals are, how they can be kind to people and even to other species. A friend of mine had an autistic child who was helped by swimming with some dolphins. And the dolphins could tell which kids were strong and which were weak—and they'd swim fast with the strong ones and slow with the weak ones. Rabbits have raised orphaned rat babies. And on and on.

"Without experience, without knowledge, what will we say about animals that makes any sense?"

"Very nice and sweet," broke in Ned after a pause. As usual, his sister wasn't paying enough attention to political reality. "But look at history. Workers got rights because they fought for them. The same for women, and blacks and gays and the national liberation movements that threw out the colonialists. People change the world because they are struggling for their *own* freedom and power, not because they are trying to care for other people or for animals either."

"No, *you* look at history," said Danny, thinking once again how selective Ned's examples always were. "Ever hear of the abolitionist movement? Led by white ministers, not African slaves. And guess what, a lot of the first animal rights people were also abolitionists. The animal rights movement itself—which is pretty big and effective now—is not led by animals struggling for their freedom but by people moved by—don't take offense, Ned—*love*, not anger or self-interest. The politics of the heart is the heart of politics."

"Careful, Danny," teased his father, "you'll be doing slogans just like Ned. But I'd be cautious if I were you. To me, some of these animal rights types seem a lot more angry than loving. They might not eat veal, but they sound like they'd be all too happy to kill the local butcher. Even more important, this heart business—well, it's simply too inconsistent. People love their own children and don't care about the ones dying of starvation. Or women love women, or blacks blacks, or Jews Jews, or Palestinians Palestinians—and it's just too bad about anyone outside their group. People open their hearts—but only so far and no further. Love—yes—but for whom?"

Ned saw an opening. "And all these bleeding heart animal rights types are the same way: they love animals but don't give a shit about people. Natives get displaced by 'nature preserves' for white hunters or tourists. Peasants whose gardens get trampled by elephants they mustn't shoot because some Western conservation group says the elephants are endangered—and you can imagine how long their "Save the Elephants" routine would last if the elephants were trampling on *their* Audis. And the animal lovers are pretty selective too—save the whales, sure, but who cares about rats in the ghetto, mice in your pantry, or even bats, who are a lot more important ecologically than all the charismatic megafauna who star in nature specials and bring in the big bucks."

Esther came back in and sat down gratefully on the sofa, groaning a little to finally be off her feet. "Thank God for Aamina," she said, their sometimes cleaning lady and cook, who would finish dinner and serve it. "Charismatic megafauna? Great phrase. I suppose it means, like, big cuddly animals? Anyway . . . Ned, people are inconsistent? So what? That doesn't make them hypocrites. Who isn't a little inconsistent? You hate capitalism, yet you're licking your chops to eat this food which comes to you, duh, from a capitalist economy. Would it be better if the people who tried to save dolphins or elephants stopped caring about anything? If they turned their back on everything outside their living rooms and their bank accounts? When any of us is perfect, then we can feel smug about other people's failings. Until then, let's try to appreciate whatever good they do."

Ned knew his mother hated it when he and Danny fought. She simply didn't take ideas seriously enough to believe people should argue about them. Just because they didn't work for her, she didn't think they should really be important to anyone else. He loved his mother and her kind heart. But he knew she just wasn't able to take in the big picture and what was needed to make the big changes. Kindness really didn't make it without a long-term plan, a strategy, a sense of what would make society less oppressive. If you couldn't focus on the total shift society needed, you'd just be putting on bandages forever—and there would be more and more wounds all the time.

"But it's so . . . limited," Ned muttered. He looked up at his mother, a sudden purity in his eyes that Esther loved him for. "We're capable of so much more. I know it sounds corny, and maybe even

crazy after all the horrible communist regimes, but the old Marxist line still gets to me. A world beyond necessity, where people
can be free to be creative and engaged with the world and caring,
and where the misery and waste of capitalism are only a distant
memory." He sighed.

"I get it," Danny responded softly, looking at Ned with an
affection he rarely felt and almost never expressed. "That's what I
want too. I don't use the same words you do. And for me it includes
animals and all of nature being free. But maybe it comes to the
same thing."

"Well," suggested Joshua, very pleased that his endlessly squabbling sons had found common ground for once. "At least you both
realize you're about equally distant from what you want. And that is
terribly, terribly far. Imagine someone who saw the importance of
women's equality in the seventeenth century—there really were a
few, you know. To them it was obvious—just as obvious as socialism
to you, Ned, or animal rights to you, Danny—and yet they were
centuries away from the world being where they were." He stopped
for a second, changing his tone from that of professor to caring father.
"I know the way things are breaks your hearts." They both looked
up, startled. Once in a while Dad, despite his tendency to be long-
winded and self-satisfied, showed that he actually understood something. "But sometimes you just have to accept that this is the way the
world is, and it's not likely to change all that much very soon."

Ned said quietly, "We can still dream, and hope the dream
comes true. A world without cruelty to animals, or people, or anything else."

"Ah, Ned, life is inherently cruel," Kate reminded him. "Just
ask the lion's dinner or the trout scooped up by the bear. But it's
beautiful as well."

They all paused to let these last thoughts sink in. Perhaps a
little agreement had appeared.

Or not, for then Esther spoke up again, her voice kind but with
the kind of verbal authority that she usually left to her husband.

"Look, I've been an emergency room nurse for twenty-seven
years. And you know what I do? I just try to stop the bleeding.
After that, it's someone else's job. So I don't hold with big changes,

with perfect futures. The best I ever see are little improvements, if that.

"This year I cooked a free-range organic turkey. A few years ago, I wouldn't have even thought about it, just gotten what was on sale at the supermarket. And I would have felt hurt when Kate and Danny didn't eat it. I put love into the cooking, and I want people to feel that love. But I understand a little more now. There's a tofu and lentil dish for non-meat eaters today. You'll have to take your chances on it, but it's 100 percent vegan—and there's just as much love in it as in the turkey!

"So my darling children influenced me. And changed me. It may not be much, but it's something."

She stood up and waved them toward the table. "Now it's time to put this aside and eat! And just enjoy each other, whatever we're eating. I hope it's good," she said a little insecurely—always having more confidence in her ability to stitch up a knife wound than to cook a meal. Still, she didn't mind doing it all. In fact, she felt a little sorry for people who lived in abstract arguments about far-off social transformations and never got to work to make something for others to enjoy right now.

Kate and Danny smiled their agreement, but then exchanged disappointed glances. This could have gone somewhere, Danny thought, but we're supposed to make nice for the family on this happy holiday . . . while for the turkeys it's Auschwitz. He loved animals, he could hear them screaming for mercy; and he loved his family. How was he supposed to put the two together?

Of course Mom wants us all to get along, Kate reflected. Danny and I don't eat meat, Mom and Dad and Ned and Isaac do. Let's just accept each other. But what if one of us were a rapist? Would Mom say, "Let's all get along" then? At least a rape victim lives. The animals just die and die and die. She suddenly realized, with a guilty twinge, that she hadn't helped in the kitchen, none of them had. So busy yakking we let Mom do it. She'd make up for it after dinner, and she'd make sure the others did as well.

Ned turned to his brother, speaking softly but with a little twinkle in his eye. "I'm sorry, Danny, I know how you feel, but I intend to enjoy every bite."

"You'll eat the turkey, but you loved Gerald, didn't you," Kate wanted to say to Ned, but she held herself back. The fat tabby, who had the loudest purr of any cat she'd ever heard, used to sleep on Ned's bed. She remembered the summer Ned had had chicken pox, and a really bad flu, and then broken his ankle, and all he could do was lay around the summer cottage all day while the rest of them were out swimming at the lake. He'd had books and a TV, but it was Gerald, purring in his ear, rubbing his head against Ned's forehead, kneading on his legs, who had kept him going. How he'd cried when Gerald, cat old at nineteen, had just not gotten up one day. He'd mourned for months. "A turkey, Gerald, what's the difference?" she wanted to yell. But she didn't, and he'd have had some wise guy reply anyway. But he couldn't justify what he did to animals, that she knew.

Danny didn't take the bait. "Don't be sorry, Ned, I hope you do enjoy it. And in your enjoyment, perhaps you can feel the spirit of the bird. And maybe next year, or ten years from now, you'll find a way to take pleasure in that spirit without eating its dead body."

In the kitchen Aamina, a political refugee from a small town in Nigeria, had heard bits of their conversation. While her English still had a way to go, she had gotten the gist of it. But it made little sense to her. All this fuss about animals. What for? Where she grew up, people had chickens, and goats, and cows. They ate the eggs and were very glad to have them. And when it was time for the animals to get slaughtered, they got slaughtered. Meanwhile hungry and sick people were all around the village.

She had fled Nigeria in the aftermath of the struggle over her homeland, the Ogoni region, slowly being poisoned by oil development. As the rivers and air and land had become toxic, and the children became more and more sickened, she had determined to find a place to raise her daughter that wouldn't slowly kill her. She'd worked as a translator for one of the Western aid agencies, and gotten a cherished political refugee visa when the army, acting on behalf of Shell Oil, had attacked her village to destroy the local resistance. She thought about the people who had helped her. They just ate whatever they ate. Roasted meat, tuna salad, hard-boiled eggs, bread. Would anything change for refugees if these people had lentils and yams instead?

Yet she also had to admit that Kate and Danny had been very generous to her—helping with immigration status, with finding a place to live, with English lessons. Could it be that thinking about animals the way they did had an effect on the way they thought about people?

Would it help if the people who raped our land had cared about animals? Would they destroy the land and my people less if they didn't eat meat?

"Acch," she groaned to herself. Only Allah could know for sure. And Allah wasn't saying anything at the moment, at least not to her. It would be so much easier if people who were decent and kind about one thing were decent and kind about all things. A lot of the men who worked for the oil company were probably trying to support their families, to take care of their own children.

Soon it would be time for the long subway ride home. At least it was an early dinner and she'd be walking from the station when other people were around. She didn't like walking alone to the poor neighborhood she lived in. She was scared of getting mugged, and it was sad to look at the homeless people sleeping in alleyways. And she also hated, she just realized, seeing all the stray cats—thin and sick and scared, with a world of pain in their tiny eyes. She thought of Isaac's story.

She would eat at home. Esther always pressed a big bag of leftovers on her. The turkey had smelled lovely. Or maybe, she smiled to herself, I'll become a vegetarian and just eat lentils and tofu.

5

WHOSE WOODS ARE THESE?

The rain drummed mercilessly on the tin roof. Sarah peeked out hopefully, searching for a hint of brightening, but if she was going to be honest about it, she had to admit there wasn't any. This was the second morning she'd been here, stuck in this three-sided shelter with five double bunk beds and a few other bedraggled, soggy backpackers. New Hampshire's White Mountains had promised to be brilliant this week in October, but instead the heavens had opened and all anyone had seen were thick clouds and buckets of water emptying from the sky. She ran fingers though her close-cropped black hair, thought vaguely of brushing it, then of what a mess she must have looked, then how she didn't give a damn. She was slender and wiry, a youngish forty-five with deep gray eyes that looked carefully at the world, and hands permanently stained brown from endless digging in the soil.

"Any hope?" asked a powerfully built middle-aged man with a week-old beard, clad in well-worn, high-tech outdoor gear: micro-fiber shirt, peaked hat with built-in lamp, shorts with about eleven pockets (or so it seemed—were there more zippers and Velcro than fabric?) and boots that despite the load of scratches and mud they carried seemed like they could practically walk down the trail by themselves.

"God alone knows," Sarah answered smiling, "and she ain't saying much about it."

"God . . . she? This is some kind of joke, yes?" This from a skinny young man who had come in with a friend late in the night. Despite his late arrival, he had been up early—praying with a white Jewish prayer shawl wrapped about his shoulders, a small black head covering, and a little prayer book whose pages he turned rapidly as he quietly read Hebrew words for almost an hour.

"Joke? I suppose it might be. But it's no more a joke than God . . . *he*."

The young man stared at her—shocked? Mad? But then he laughed aloud. "Ibrahim," he called to his companion, "it's a feminist, trapped by the rain just like us patriarchal types." He laughed again. Ibrahim seemed about the same age, but where the Jewish man was slight, with pale white skin and haunted eyes, Ibrahim was built like a bull—massive shoulders and chest and full black beard. "Is she friendly?" he called out, "Or will we have to take refuge in the forest to escape the wrath of the Goddess?"

Sarah stared at the two men, caught between enjoying the banter and wondering if she was being made fun of.

"Not to worry, I don't bite . . . unless it's called for," she retorted, thinking if these were some kind of religious freaks she might embarrass them with a veiled sexual reference.

"Ah . . ." Ibrahim smiled at her, "the question is not of biting, but of God. Allah calls, and we must answer." He gestured to the surrounding forest—birch, maple, pine, an overflowing river split by the high ground the shelter was on, even the gray, almost black, sky. "Surely the creation of the heavens and the earth are greater than the creation of mankind, but most people know this not. Qu'ran 40:57."

"To say the least," murmured Sarah, thinking, What the hell?

"Most people don't know jack," said the well-equipped backpacker. "But it's not God's word they are missing out on. It's this."

He gestured like Ibrahim, taking in the drenched splendor of the forest, the stream, the sky, even the rocks, then went back to fiddling with a tiny gas stove, trying to make tea.

"Why can't they have both?" the young Jew asked, with a kind of cheerful optimism that Sarah found instantly annoying. "We are taught that after Hashem—that's one way we refer to God," he explained almost apologetically, "put Adam in the garden of Eden, he showed him everything on earth—the fields, forest, oceans, all the animals—'See my world,' Hashem told Adam, 'How beautiful it is. Care for it well, for if you misuse it, there will not be another.' So we are taught to care for this earth, knowing that really it belongs to Hashem. If we love Hashem, we must guard the garden he has given us. Oh," he added, with another apologetic half smile, "I'm Jacob, by the way."

"Sarah."

"I am Ibrahim, and in our faith we also are taught this way. We are to be modest in our desires, remember that everything on earth has its own community as we have ours, and never forget that that the earth belongs not to us, but to God."

"Great, just great," grumbled the backpacker, flicking his hands at the recalcitrant stove, "but you'll have to pardon me if I'm not thrilled. You see, I know a little bit about *faith*," spitting the word out like a curse. "For fifteen years a good Baptist, reading the Bible until I knew it by heart, praying day and night, working in youth groups—I did it all. And here's what I learned: 'God said let us make man in our image . . . and give him dominion over the earth.' Well, we've had that dominion, and nobody used the Qu'ran or the Bible or anything else from *God*," another curse, "to stop it. And now the oceans are dying, the trees are dying, a lot of the rivers are already dead. What did the popes and the priests and"—pointing at Jacob—"the rabbis have to say about it? Nothing. Useless. Worse than useless. Criminal." He paused, breathing heavily.

"Such bitterness," said Jacob sympathetically, to Sarah's surprise. Where she came from, if you talked like that the religious types would be all over you. "Why? And tell us your name, please."

"I'm Martin, and here's a bitterness story for you." He tossed the stubborn stove back on his bunk, wiped his hands on his hiking shorts, and focused angry eyes on Jacob.

"I grew up in a small town in the hills of West Virginia. We were poor, that's for sure, but we had each other, and the church. There were some farming jobs, and some people worked in a coal mine forty miles away, or for the state park in the summer. Then that mine closed, and another one opened, right over us on the hilltop."

"A mine on a hilltop? I thought mines went down, into the ground," asked Ibrahim.

"Welcome to modern coal mining," Martin declared, his dark green eyes burning, his large hands clenching into fists. "Now they put the mine at the top of the hill. And they don't go into the earth—they just *take the top off the damn mountain*. Just rip it to pieces, take the coal they want, and leave all the junk behind. Falling down the hillsides, poisoning the streams, killing the towns and the people."

"I loved our little town, and when I really needed to pray I could go into the woods, to this one spot next to a stream, where a dogwood tree always flowered white in early April. I could feel God there, more even than in church. Well, the refuse from the mine blew out the stream, polluted the water so that the trees died. There was just coal ash and dead trees. My grandfather, he was a deacon at the church, got sick from what happened to the water. And on hot, humid days the air would turn yellow, *yellow air!*—who can breathe that? My sister used to cough, and cough, and cough." His big hands twisted on each other, and suddenly he stood up.

"I went to the church leaders for help. 'We've got to fight this,' I told them. 'They are destroying God's creation, and killing the town.' The pastor, the deacons, they didn't buy any of it. They called me a tree hugger, an environmentalist—the way they used the word, it was like being called a communist or a faggot some other place. 'Pray for patience, pray for a forgiving heart, that's the Christian way. And if you are like Christ, who told us to be meek and forgiving, then you will get your reward in heaven.' *Heaven*," he made a face like someone had told him to kiss a rat, "that was going to be my *true* home. That's where me, and my sister, and my grandfather, would get our reward.

"Later I found out that the pastor was on the take and so was one of the deacons. They got some money to keep us quiet, and the pastor was getting a church in another town and a little resettlement money.

"I realized that the church was full of lies, and that I was closer to God with the dogwood tree than I'd ever been with a Bible in my hands. 'Got God?'" he laughed a little. Sarah was relieved to see him lightening up a bit. "Maybe not, but as long as there are some trees left, I'll be all right. As for the church? The world is dying and all religions care about is who is sleeping with whom, how to shut up people who disagree, and whether or not they get to keep their tax exemptions." He sat back down, not realizing he'd stood up, crossed his legs, and lit a cigarette.

"Talk about pollution," Sarah complained. "Do you mind?"

"Sorry, sorry. Been trying to quit. It's crazy, but they taste really good out here for some reason." He stubbed it out and put the butt back in the pack.

People rearranged themselves, stretching cramped muscles and peering, again, at the sky. Sarah poked through her pack to see if she had anything to wear that wasn't damp, realized she didn't, and sat back with a sigh.

"My friend, I'm sorry," offered Jacob, in a gentle tone. "And I understand where you are coming from."

"Really? You come from a town destroyed by mountaintop removal just like me?"

"Well, not that. But my family was hurt, very badly, as I was growing up. My parents were visiting relatives in Israel. They took the wrong bus, and my mother died in a bombing. My father just got depressed and would sit in the bedroom, like he was waiting for her to come back. I was sixteen—so mad I thought I would kill someone. I went to the Rabbi for help, but he had nothing to say, nothing that made sense to me. But he wasn't a real rabbi anyway, just an assimilated Reform guy who didn't keep kosher and had never really studied.

"So I tried to find something for the pain. I tried drinking and drugs, like a lot of kids I knew, but there's something wrong with my nervous system." He looked up and smiled at the irony. "They just made me sick and feel even crazier. I looked at some New Age religions, but they were all about peace and love and feeling, well, *pleasant*. The last thing I wanted to feel was pleasant. Then, in the street, I met a young Jewish guy—part of an outreach group trying to get assimilated Jews like me to take it seriously, to live a really Jewish life. He listened to my tale of woe; he was a real good listener. He told me I would never, *never*, understand God, that it was silly to even try. Could my dog understand why I did what I did? Or the fish in my fish tank? All I could do was obey, and love, and God would do the rest. I was so lost I'd thought of killing myself, or, even better, killing some Palestinians until I got killed myself, so I didn't have much to lose." Jacob reached up to straighten his yarmulke, then straightened the long curls that hung down next to his ears.

"And he was right. The more I prayed, and studied, and went to the shul three times a day, the more I felt—well, not healed, but OK. Like I had a reason for living. I spent two years at a yeshiva in Jerusalem and now I'm back in the States." He grinned. "A man with mission."

"Two men with a mission," Ibrahim grinned as well.

Silence for a moment. The rain poured down heavier than ever. Sarah didn't feel like reading anymore, and not much else was going on. Might as well let them explain all this.

"Let it out, boys," she said. "What is an Orthodox Jew and some kind of Muslim doing hiking the White Mountains together?"

Ibrahim turned to Martin, pointing the fingers of both hands at him. "You're right. Religions have been part of the problem. All of us—the Christians and Jews, the Hindus and the Muslims and the Buddhists."

"Not the indigenous," Jacob corrected. "We've got to be fair."

"You're right, brother. Absolutely. But they just got rolled over by the capitalist-embracing Protestants."

"Not to mention the industry-embracing communists," Jacob added in with a giggle. "That's a kind of a religion too."

"None of them noticed, until it was almost too late. They had other things on their minds—money and power, guns for the military, butter for the masses."

"All *human* concerns," Jacob broke in again. "All *human*. What happened to nature? They didn't care. Oh, a few offbeat types here and there—mystics, loners, spiritual freaks like Thoreau or John Muir. Even a few anticommunist *Marxists*, of all people, sounded the alarm."

"Sadly, almost no one listened," Ibrahim jumped back in, his big chest bouncing up and down in eagerness. "Some rich white men decided to save the pretty places to hunt in, or feel manly about, but that didn't keep them from chewing up everything else. But, Martin," Ibrahim leaned over and put his hand on the big backpacker's forearm, "it's not like that anymore. The traditions have changed."

"Before I went to Israel I studied with one of the top rabbis in Conservative Judaism," Jacob added, his voice almost painfully sincere. "He told us to get off our fear of paganism and face what we are doing to nature. 'Paganism isn't the problem anymore,' he told us, 'ignoring the greatest crisis of our age is.'"

"So," said Ibrahim, with quiet confidence, "now we are remembering the parts of tradition that have been forgotten, the ones that tell us about the spiritual power of nature, that all of life deserves respect and care, and that a life devoted to money, toys, and power, or even good things, if those good things are just for people at the expense of everything else, is *not* a godly life."

"Really?" asked Sarah, a world of skepticism packed into one word. "Tell that to all those folks," she gestured widely, at the world beyond the forest and the swollen stream, "getting rich as fast as they can, building the biggest armies money can buy, ripping each other to bits. Tell them."

"We intend to," Ibrahim responded softly. "That's why we're here. We've been walking the Appalachian Trail since April. Started in Georgia, only have eighty miles to go until we finish. Every time we cross a town, we get to a computer and blog—we're at JewMuslimPlanetHope . . . dot org. We want to show that if we, of all people, can cooperate in the wilderness, then everyone else can as well.

"Along the way we're taking notes on the condition of the trees and the streams. We've already got two thousand photos for forest experts to examine. We're telling people that creation is God's gift, that nature is always there to be the most perfect temple for our prayers, that the greatest thinkers of our traditions—from Muhammad, peace be upon him, to the Sufi mystics, for me, from the Baal Shem Tov to Maimonides for Jacob. From Saint Francis to Pope John Paul II to the Dalai Lama for others.

"They all taught: make peace with nature, live with it, not over it, let it return—it was John Paul who said this—to being the 'sister of humanity.'"

"How nice of the pope to say that," Sarah put in, with more acid in her tone than she'd intended. "After one thousand years of murdering every tribe who honored the earth, the church has turned green."

"Better late than never," Ibrahim offered quietly. "We *know* people of faith have been stupid, selfish, and terribly shortsighted. But it's changing. All over the world religious people are doing things—greening their churches, struggling with oil companies over global warming, protecting ancient redwoods."

"God *chose* us to bring this word, so that we would help the work along." Jacob's eyes were burning again. "While I was at the yeshiva I made friends with another student, someone who worked for an Israeli environmental group. At first I thought it was all a distraction from the true path—from Talmud studies and performing mitzvot. But he showed me—in passages from Torah and Prophets, in rulings from Mishnah and sermons from great Hasidic rabbis—that it wasn't so."

"Then he met me," Ibrahim laughed, reaching over to clop Jacob on top of his head, while Jacob cowered in mock terror. "I have dual Palestinian and American citizenship. I lived in the West Bank for three years, trying to convince people that protecting the water was as important as stopping the Jewish settlements. I helped organize a group to work on it—and we were making friends with some Jews. We actually found something both groups could agree on. Well, the Palestinian authorities didn't like that, and neither did the Israeli ones. They told me to take the next plane out of there, or they couldn't be responsible for my safety. I was making trouble. *I* was making trouble." He laughed, with a palpable sadness in back of the humor. "The Jordan River is almost a trickle now. There are mounds of refuse everywhere. Money to clean things up is being spent on gangs of armed men—Fatah, the Israeli Army, Hamas. The land is dying, and all people care about is who owns the corpse." The sadness in his voice deepened. For a moment Sarah could see the tortured land through his eyes.

Jacob continued the story. "God put us next to each other on the plane home. The flight was delayed. We had hours together. At first I thought, 'This is a terrorist who will kill me.'"

"And I thought, 'Here's another Zionist out to steal my family's land,'" Ibrahim chimed in. Sarah could tell by the speed with which they fed off each others' lines that they'd done this routine before. "But one thing led to another, and pretty soon we began to talk. About water pollution."

"Air pollution."

"Recycled materials for building in the West Bank."

"Solar power collectors for the Sinai."

"Joint ventures with Lebanon and Syria."

"Ecocamping trips for Arab and Jewish teenagers."

"Etcetera," they shouted together.

Ah youth, thought Sarah. First we discover the universe, and then we think everyone will just follow along because nobody ever thought of it before. Of course, this about religious people being environmentalists, this was new.

"And how is all this going over?" asked Martin.

"Like anything else," Ibrahim said. "Sometimes yes, sometimes no. Some of the older people just think it's a distraction. Or that we're pagans, heretics. Others don't want to give anything up. They say that God is the most important thing in their lives, but they sure do like their Visa cards.

"Or they say, 'Oh, this is important. But people are *more* important.' They are stuck in the mindset that you have to choose. We say they are wrong. You can have God and the earth, a good life, a really good life, for people and save nature. And if you don't have it for both, you won't have it for either. Ecology . . . and justice. Ecojustice!"

"Even your people are in on this," Jacob smiled at Martin.

"My people? Who the hell are they?" Martin responded roughly. Thinking that religious people could be on his side was too confusing.

"Conservative white Christians from the South," Jacob answered, missing Martin's bristly tone completely. "Evangelical Christians have challenged Detroit on fuel standards, asked their fellow Christians to think about what Jesus would drive and—get this—held big-time public press conferences with big-time Harvard scientists to ask for action on global warming. Yeah, not all of them are into it. But some are. Some. That's important."

What kind of scientist would appear in public with a bunch of Bible beaters? Sarah wondered to herself. As for God? To her it was like modern art. She looked at the paintings—some of them worth a fortune, or at least could sell for a fortune—and to her it was just a lot of random splashes of paint. God was like that too. Guys like Jacob and Ibrahim looked at the world, and it called out "GOD" to them. She looked, and didn't see it. She just saw the world. To them, she was missing something big, the most important thing. To her, they saw something that just wasn't there.

Sarah opened a side pocket of her pack and took out trail mix, offering it to the others. Martin grabbed a big handful with thanks, the others smiled but shook their heads.

"Sounds like you guys are doing great," she said slowly. "And if the pope or the Evangelicals or some Jews in Israel or Muslims in Lebanon or God knows where are working to save the planet, that's good too.

"But to tell you the truth, I'm not so sure, not so sure at all. Religion is just, well, irrational. All this about God and angels and holy books. That's no way to live in the twenty-first century. It's really just a way to control people—women by men, the poor by the rich, and everybody, *everybody*, by a class of fat, well-off, self-satisfied priests.

"This is the time of science and democracy, not of people who answer tough questions with 'Well, you just have to have faith.' I'd like to see how they would react if their car mechanic thought about their engines like that, or their brain surgeon told them he had to mess around in their brains because God told him to." She harrumphed at both of them.

"I had my own run-in with religion a few years back, when Bush was president and his idiot functionaries ran the EPA. I'm a soil scientist, and I had been studying the soils near the Great Lakes, and the effects of this chemical that's used in about sixteen different industrial processes in the Midwest. Turns out the stuff is pretty lethal—damaging the frogs and the snakes in wild areas. Might be part of the birth defects and asthma we're seeing in kids. I prepared my report, and the EPA, the *EPA*, censored it. Warned me about making my conclusions public. I quit on the spot, and I've been working for universities ever since."

"I don't get it," said Jacob. "What's this got to do with religion?"

"Bush was a *man of faith*," Sarah sneered. "All his preacher friends told him we're pretty close to the second coming anyway, there's no point in being worried about what we're doing to the earth. Heaven is where's it's at. And since the makers of that chemical were also big contributors to Bush—well, why rock the boat because of a few dead frogs, a few fish born with organs *outside* their bodies, a little more asthma? And the info on the asthma wasn't conclusive yet anyway.

"Go on, talk to *religious men*," another sneer, "about science. Talk to people who think the world is six thousand years old, or that Jesus rose from the dead. Talk to them about evidence, reasoning, scientific method. You might as well talk to that oak tree over there.

"It's people who've been trained, who know how to figure out what's *really* going on who will get the facts and turn the tide. You religious folks really want to help?" She looked hard at Jacob and Ibrahim. "Go join some environmental group that supports sound science, or tell your senator to fund more basic ecological research.

"All the rest is like waiting for Santa Claus."

Martin had finally gotten his little stove to work and was brewing tea. Sarah, thinking maybe she'd been too heavy with the youngsters, reached out to offer them more trail mix. Then Ibrahim stood up suddenly, stretching both arms behind his back. He looked at her carefully. Sarah half expected him to start screaming, but he just gave her a calm smile, with maybe a little sadness in it.

"I understand. You've been hurt, and when we get hurt, we get angry. But you are a scientist, right? Maybe you should be a little more careful about too quick a generalization." She looked up, surprised. This was not what she expected.

He went on. "You talk like scientists and religious people are two different groups, as if a person can't be both. Some of the world's leading scientists, even leading environmental scientists, are believers. I'm actually getting my doctorate in forest ecology at Yale. Jacob here," he waved toward his friend, "he's the mystic, not me. That's one reason I am a Muslim—it's a system—pure, complete. Just like science.

"But never mind about me, it's just that you're so . . . well, I don't want to be disrespectful, but you just don't know what's going on. Religious thinkers are quoting scientific accounts to let their people know how bad things are. The pope does it, and the Dalai Lama, and the Saudi minister of the environment as well.

"And even more: *you* may think that science can solve this problem by itself, but a lot of scientists don't. They've been asking religious leaders for help for twenty years now. And religious leaders have been giving it. They've had joint meetings, and made joint declarations. What Jacob said about Evangelicals and Harvard scientists holding a press conference together to change our energy policy—that wasn't a joke. That was real.

"I *know* we've had our bad times in the past—and still do in some places. There are religious folks who hate the idea of evolution—and advertise their critiques on their snazzy Web sites. They want to pick and choose what science they will use and what they won't."

"They pick and choose, all right. And what do they pick and choose for?" Martin was still bitter, everyone could feel it. "For the money, the power. Just to keep themselves taken care of—while they tell everyone else how to be holy and what to do."

"And the way they want to treat women, it's simply disgusting," added Sarah, with as much bitterness as Martin, trying to blot out the reasonable points Ibrahim had just made. "'Stay in the home, obey your husband, thanks be to God I'm not a woman, cover your face, shut your mouth, obey, obey, obey.' No wonder all these religions didn't have anything to say about what we've done to nature—for them, nature and women are the same. Not rational, not as close to God, bound by instinct and not *the Law*. Control women, control the earth."

"What can I say?" Jacob responded, a soft smile on his lips. So gentle, thought Sarah, not like any of the religious types she'd ever met. Hard to be angry with someone who was so gentle, even if you think he's dead wrong.

"What can I say?" he repeated. "It's true. There *is* a lot about power, a lot of selfishness passing itself off as holiness, and more hypocrisy than you can shake a stick at—if that's your idea of a good time." He looked up hopefully to see if anyone got the Groucho Marx reference—no one did. "And for all that, I'm sorry, truly sorry. Those of us who say we are in love with God should do better.

"But," he smiled again, with a little bit more force behind it, "are we the only ones?"

He waited.

"The only ones *what?*" Sarah asked impatiently.

"The only ones who are hypocritical, power hungry, or just in it for the money. Sexist. Of course you're right, religious people had nothing to say about dangerous pesticides for decades after they came in."

"Exactly," replied Sarah. "Too busy moaning and groaning about abortion."

"But," Jacob went on, a little faster now, "Who created those pesticides? Who thought, 'Gee, we'll take leftover nerve gas from World War II and kill all the bugs. We can sell it for a bundle and make life oh so much easier at the same time.' Who?"

"What do you mean, 'Who'?" Martin broke in. "You want their names?"

"Not the names, dopey," Sarah replied, suddenly realizing that whatever religious nonsense Jacob believed, he wasn't stupid. "He means it was people like me."

"Well, not you *personally*," Jacob said reassuringly. "You seem very nice and . . . responsible. But it was scientists and engineers. You know, the rational people, the ones who believe in evidence and sound method. Sure the religious leaders turned a blind eye, but it was science that *did* it.

"And do you think scientists are any better for women than priests? Medical treatments for menopause that cause cancer but make women more sexually available. Psychiatric diagnoses that say women are supposed to be masochists. Endless interventions into childbirth to promote the medical establishment." His voice had slowly become stronger, more powerful, filled with confidence.

"You really think scientists love nature, or women, any more than traditional religion does? I'd say a lot less. The Torah tells us to let our animals rest on the Sabbath, and that wild animals can eat from fields on the Sabbatical Year. If you hear that the Messiah has come, and you're planting a tree, you are to finish planting before you greet him. At least we have *something*, what does science have?

Cut it open, rip it to pieces, get to know it so we can sell it or make it into a weapon."

He had raised one arm and extended his fingers as if calling the heavens to witness. Sarah suddenly saw that as well as being a mystic, there was a little bit of prophet in Jacob. He didn't flinch from criticizing his own faith, but still, he was passionate about its gifts. Wasn't that what being a prophet meant? She had to answer in kind, but she had to be honest. She turned up the collar of her rain jacket, ran her fingers through her hair, and tried to focus.

"I know that lots of scientists are just in it for the money, or to come across as big shots. But a lot of them aren't. We look at the natural world—and it makes us cry sometimes, it's so beautiful, so complex, it works together so well. And there's always more to find out—worlds within worlds, infinitely big, infinitely small. Every single species is like a work of art."

"Or a miracle?" Jacob asked softly, his eyes gleaming.

"A miracle?" She thought that one over. "Why not?"

"Is this science or love? Where is all that scientific objectivity?" Ibrahim offered a mock warning.

Sarah spoke quietly, thinking that the chancellor who'd hired her to chair the Environmental Sciences Program would have a fit if he heard her talking like this. "I don't think you can understand something, really understand it, unless you love it a little. Otherwise you don't know how to pay attention to it. You need a loving eye to see clearly."

Jacob reached over as if he were going to put his hand on Sarah's arm, then seemed to remember something and drew back. He looked into her eyes. "You have your love, which is maybe just another word for faith. And we have ours. What's the difference?"

"I'll tell you what the difference is," Martin said, without hesitation. "Take a look around." He encouraged them with a palms-up, fingers-extended gesture to look. "You see," he continued, "that's *it*. That's all there is. Isn't that enough?"

"Huuunh," Ibrahim drawled. "I don't get it."

"The trees, the birds, the clouds, every single mosquito," Martin swatted at one who thought the lack of light from the heavy cloud cover meant it was evening, "even the damn rain. This is the earth we have. We don't *need* any more. No invisible spirits. No heavenly voices saying, 'Let there be light' or 'Follow my rules or you'll end up in hell.' Why do we have to add in something we can't see or touch or hear? Why aren't you satisfied with this?" There was a kind of deep pain in the back of his voice. Where's that coming from? wondered Sarah.

"I see God all the time," Ibrahim countered, with a kind of quiet confidence that Sarah envied a little. "When the birds sing, when I read the beautiful words of the Qu'ran, when I see someone touch another's face in kindness. To me, all these are God, for everything comes from him."

"Him," grumbled Sarah. "Him. Of course, *him*."

"Or her, I don't mind. The point is that I just can't see any of those things, or anything else, without seeing God as well."

"God is a force, yes, and a source of love and instruction," Jacob echoed. "But God is also the way the world is. An adverb, not just a noun. It is not just God, it is god*ly*. God is the source of life, and *godly* is the way life is."

Sarah bit her lip and waited. They were such *nice* boys, it almost seemed a shame to pull them back to reality. But she couldn't stop herself.

"Godly, is it? Done any reading about the Holocaust lately? Was God with the Nazis? Oh, I know, you'll tell me God was in the love people showed for each other, the heroism of the people who kept going, the last caring touch before the machine guns opened up."

She stopped for a moment. Jacob and Ibrahim had their heads down. Did this scare them? Or had they heard it all before?

"God in Auschwitz, or in Bhopal, when the chemical plant exploded and thousands of people died and were maimed, or in L.A. where kids grow up with stunted lungs because the air pollution is so bad? No, there is no God there, or not enough.

"Let's face it, boys, God gives you a promise. A little guarantee. And believing in God is for people who can't take life straight.

They need a little chaser to make it go down easier. For people without religion, what you see is what you get. A lot of times awful, sometimes great. Beautiful and horrible all at once. With every outcome uncertain, except the fact that we'll all die someday. With no Big Daddy coming to the rescue now or any other time; and no eternal life."

Jacob looked up, his eyes glistening with tears. "That's not the world I see, I feel. I couldn't live in such a place." He shuddered, then began again more forcefully. "And why should I? God is as real to me as my breath. God is my breath—Hashem breathed life into Adam and Adam lived, and Hashem breathed life into me and I live. Breath is my connection to God. No breath, no connection, no life. It is God that returns my soul to my body when I wake, that enables the holes in my body—sorry if I'm grossing you out, but this is one of our daily prayers—to function as they should. When God chooses, all that will stop and my neshama, my soul, will be with God."

"Or your consciousness will stop, and your body will be with the worms, who will cheerfully recycle all that energy." Sarah smiled. "What a terrific system."

Yet she knew that sometimes she envied people like Jacob. They never felt as alone as she did. When she heard a world-famous oceanographer say flatly, "Everything I studied to get my big-deal academic reputation—it's all dead or dying," she felt herself slipping down toward a paralyzing despair. If only she *could* have faith that something larger than her, some moral force and not just a physical one like gravity or evolution, was on her side. Every once in a while she really wanted to. But she couldn't.

"Still," admitted Ibrahim. "Still. It's not easy."

"Not easy?" asked Martin, a little incredulous. "I thought you guys just grabbed onto faith and never let go."

"There was a teacher at the mosque where I studied. A real holy man—kind, learned, gentle. He told great stories to the little kids, and engaged us older boys in serious conversations. When I think of what kind of Muslim I want to be, I think of him. I asked him once if he ever had doubts, if his faith ever wavered. At first he told me, off the cuff I think, 'Of course not. Allahu Akbar'—God is greater, that means, greater than we can understand, than we can ever put words to. Then I saw him think for a while. He put his hand on my shoulder, looked at me carefully. 'I'm sorry, Ibrahim, that was a thoughtless answer. You deserve better. Yes, sometimes, late at night, when I get a phone call that someone's child has died, then I doubt. I cry, and I doubt.'"

He looked around at them, his confidence suddenly gone. "When I realize how much of life we are killing—in the Sudan, in Gaza, in the oceans—my faith, too, is tested. I cry . . . and I wonder—is God really greater? My Sufi teachers, they will tell me, 'This is the mystery of faith, this you will never understand,' like Jacob's teacher told him. But sometimes I think mystery is just another word for nothingness. That there is no Allah, just nothing." He lay back onto the damp wooden floor, silent.

No one spoke. What could follow that? Sarah saw how they all had their doubts that they were scared to let out, because if they did, who knew what would happen? Jacob looked closely at his friend in surprise. He hadn't realized that Ibrahim *ever* doubted. Ibrahim closed his eyes, wondering why he had told these strangers about his greatest weakness. Or was it his greatest strength?

Then Martin broke the silence, his voice soft and wistful. "You know, I miss it, sometimes I really do. I think back to that warm, safe feeling I had Sunday morning—knowing everyone in the church, so comfortable with the music, the prayers, and with Jesus. I didn't have to be afraid, or ashamed because we were so much poorer than the people I saw on TV. It didn't matter if I wasn't the smartest kid in my class. God loved me.

"The earth is so beautiful . . . but it doesn't love me, not like Jesus. If I fall in that river," he pointed toward the fierce, unending sound of water over rock, "I know I could drown, easy. These little buggers," he swatted at another mosquito, "will suck my blood—not because they are evil, it's just . . . what they do. All of this . . . just does what it does. And most of the time, that's OK. It's just wonderful that it is. But sometimes, when I'm too lonely to sleep, I miss God. I know I'll never have him back. But I miss him."

He clasped his hands together, rubbing back and forth, then bent down to tie a shoelace that didn't need tying.

Sarah wondered—how much of what we cling to conceals our grief over what we've lost? Maybe all we should do is cry together for a few hours, or a few days; maybe that would clear things up. This big tough guy, so angry at his church, lying awake pining for the Jesus he'd never have again.

"But I don't get it." Martin had straightened up, looking at Jacob, then back to Ibrahim. "Where I come from, the faith was, well, the faith. The word of God. The true teaching. It didn't change. All the changes were from people who didn't have real faith, at least that's what I was taught. All this talk about a greener faith, and protecting the environment—that just sounds like you are using religion for a political fad."

"Yeah, some people think so," Jacob nodded. "But the truth is religion is *always* changing. We used to sacrifice animals—then the temple was destroyed and we got the world's first really portable religion. Read the early church histories, then the medieval times, then the Reformation. It's *always* changing. Always. The ones who say it's always been the same, that's just the way they handle the changes.

"Don't get me wrong—I believe God gave us the Torah and the oral law. I believe God wants me to follow his mitzvot, his rules for Jewish living. But let's face it: there's nothing that prepares us for a world where what humans do can change what's in our blood-streams and pollute mother's milk. To figure out what to do now, we need a whole lot of new thinking."

"The same goes for Islam. The word of God is perfect," said Ibrahim. "And that is what we must use. But we must use it, not just leave it on a shelf in the mosque. To use it, we must bring it to the tasks God has given us. In one age it is freedom from white European colonialists"—he shook his finger at Jacob, who just laughed—"and now it is to save the earth as a place for humans to live in."

"How can we save our faiths," Sarah could see Jacob finishing a thought both men shared, "if our faiths do not stand for life? What will we say to some fifteen-year-old who asks, '*How could you let this happen?'* There will be no faith if we cannot say, 'We have done this and this, and we will do more. And you?'"

"Well, good luck to us all," Sarah observed. But after a pause she pushed on. There was something about their comfort that bothered her. "Just as a matter of curiosity, you do know that your faiths are, well, pretty temporary, right? Eventually the sun will blow up, and it will be bye-bye earth."

Jacob was surprisingly unfazed. "I'm quite happy to leave that up to Hashem. In the meantime, I must in a few minutes say the afternoon prayers."

"And I too," murmured Ibrahim. "I will do what I have to do, *today*. God will guard my future. That's his job. This is mine."

"But *which* God is it," asked Martin, frustrated. "The God of the pastor in my little town, the conservative, unchanging God who wanted us to prepare for heaven? Or this new God who bikes to work and works for Greenpeace? How are we supposed to know which one is real?"

"Beats me," said Ibrahim. "I didn't think you believed in any case."

"I don't, I don't. But dammit, I want to know which God *not* to believe in."

"I'll give you an easy answer, or at least a simple one," Jacob offered. "The God who leads you to a decent, good life. And helps you figure out what that is."

"I guess I'll stay with the rocks and the trees," replied Martin. "I pray to them, sometimes, when I'm scared. Or I say thanks to them—for being what they are. I ask them to help me. 'Spirit of trees and sky,' I say, 'spirits of earth and eagles. Lend me your strength and your courage. I'm having a hard time.'" He seemed to have forgotten what he'd said about nature not caring about him.

"Oy," responded Jacob, with an old-time Yiddish accent, "a regeleh pagan."

"Do they answer?" asked Ibrahim with surprising intensity. "Do they help you?"

"Yes. No. Maybe." Martin laughed, clearly at himself. "Who the hell knows? How about *your* prayers? Does God answer *you*?"

Jacob and Ibrahim looked at each other, waiting for the other to speak. The tension grew.

Then they spoke at the same time: "Yes, no, maybe. Who the hell knows?" They exploded with laughter, high-fiving each other.

"I only know this, for certain—I feel better, I *am* better, when I pray," Jacob added softly. "What else do I need to know?"

OK, that will about do it for *me*, thought Sarah. I come to the mountains to be with the trees and I end up in a damn seminary. Still, she wondered, what made *her* a better person? It surely wasn't the three cups of coffee she had every day, or the time she wasted on the Net. Did she have something that helped with her loneliness? Or made her less grumpy with her assistant? Or kept her going when there wasn't any hope?

Suddenly a booming "hello" cut through the rain. A tall, thin man with an enormous backpack staggered up the hillside. He stumbled into the shelter, shedding water from his pack and his rain jacket, collapsed onto his back without even taking the pack off, and smiled. "Man, I *love* the mountains. But it's too damn wet right about now."

Richard looked around at the people in the shelter. Even with his cheerful greeting, he was a little disappointed to find other backpackers there. He came to the woods to get away—from noise, machines, and above all, from people. For all his organizing, he'd never been really good with people. He envied Fred, the minister who'd had to leave the Coalition because of family problems, whose easy humor and easier smile made everyone feel at home. Or Lily, the spiritual hippie type who'd been part of it too. He was always struck by how quiet she got when someone said something she didn't like, even something threatening. She didn't blow up at them, not like him.

So after a few months of hard-core organizing, he *had* to get away—to a place where he didn't have to convince anyone of anything, where he felt the only real peace he ever felt in life. Protecting *this* made all the meetings, arguments, and discomfort worthwhile. He was whole here—protected and loved. Maybe this was what some people felt in church. He certainly never had, but he felt it here.

"So, what's up, folks?" he asked, trying to be friendly.

"You probably won't believe it," Sarah answered. "But we're sitting around in this deluge discussing whether or not religion can help save the planet—part of the problem or part of the solution type thing. These guys, Jacob and Ibrahim, they're all gung ho for a brave new environmental religion. Me and Martin, we ain't so sure. I'm Sarah, by the way."

"And I'm Richard. Save the planet? Great . . . that's what I do for a living."

They all stared at him. Was he nuts? How could one person save a planet?

"I mean, I work for an environmental organization. We've been trying to protect a wetland near Binghamtown. Not so easy.

"But you guys," he turned to Ibrahim and Jacob with a big smile, "I'm all for that. We had a minister in our group, he was great. And he brought a bunch of people from the church. They came to all the meetings, worked hard. Talking about God's creation and stewardship, repentance—that sort of thing."

"And you?" asked Sarah. "You part of the crowd who dedicate themselves to the glory of God?"

"Me? Oh no. I'm just lookin' for help trying to save the planet— or the wetland. Ha-ha." He laughed awkwardly, shrugging out of his pack and brushing water from his thin brown hair.

"Kind of an opportunist, aren't you," suggested Sarah, not with hostility, but just curious. "I mean, you don't believe, but you welcome these people who do."

"What do I care *why* people do the work, just as long as they do," Richard answered cheerfully. "I need all, I mean *all*, the help I can get. And so do those guys." In a gesture they'd seen several times already, he pointed at the trees, boulders, and stream.

That does make a kind of sense, Sarah thought. What difference did it make, really, *why* people did what they did, as long as they did it? Some people did it for God, some for the trees. Some thought nature was sacred, and some didn't want their grandchildren growing up in a world full of poisons. As long as they got it done.

Jacob interrupted her reverie; fishing around in his backpack for something, he looked up at Richard. "You know, all this is fine. But there's more."

"More?"

"Yes. I've seen enough of the movement to know it's not just that religious people should join in—come to the groups you organize, follow orders, be sheep to your shepherd."

"I didn't mean it like that," Richard protested, blushing a little. Actually he had, and he knew he had, but he hadn't realized it was so obvious.

"Oh yes you did, and that's OK." Jacob smiled. He wasn't mad.

Where does he get his self-confidence from? Richard wondered. He couldn't figure these religious types. Some of them were just crazy. And some of them, like Fred, like this guy, just seemed so . . . together. He didn't get it.

"Here's what's more," Jacob continued. "The environmental movement doesn't just need our bodies on the line, our membership dues. In a way, it's the opposite: environmentalists need to become religious." He looked at Richard, then Martin, then Sarah, almost daring them to freak out at this outlandish claim. Ibrahim kept a poker face. He knew what was coming.

Uh-oh, thought Sarah, here it is. In the end these types always have to drag you over to their side. They're never satisfied until everybody believes what they do.

"And just which religion should we take on? Yours? Ibrahim's? The Christianity of Martin's little town?"

"Yeah, man, and besides, I mean, I just don't believe in God. You want me to fake it?" Richard added.

"Don't panic, guys, it's nothing like that." Jacob smiled his soft, warm smile. "I'm talking about values you can get anywhere, really, but which tend to come out of faith communities more than other places."

"Like what?" Sarah asked suspiciously. "You going to tell me that religious people are more moral because they believe in God and absolute morality? Puh-lease!"

"No, no," said Jacob soothingly, "nothing like that. Think of it this way: the environmental movement is against waste and pollution, too much consumption, using the wrong chemicals, nuclear power, coal power, oil power. We don't want people cutting down the forests, or putting junk in the ocean. But what are we *for?*"

"That's easy," responded Richard. "The opposite of all those things. No waste, no emissions, renewable energy, stop transporting food from thousands of miles away, use biodegradable materials, turn off the damn lights when you're not in the room."

"Don't, no, stop," Jacob interrupted. He stood up, shook his finger at everyone in turn, and repeated. "Don't, no, stop." Then he waited. "Sounds really inviting, doesn't it? Can't wait to join a movement with those slogans. Bet your meetings are, well, just a blast." He sat down, evidently pleased with himself.

Sarah wasn't buying it. "There are other things, and you know it. Local and organic food—better for the environment and taste better too. Bike riding is more fun than driving a car. If we save the forests, we have wilderness to hike in. If there's less pollution, we'll be healthier."

"Yeah, sure," admitted Jacob. "I know all that. But the vast majority of people don't hike in places like this. A healthy future is pretty abstract—important, but hard to touch right now. Besides all the nos, shouldn'ts, don'ts, and warnings, what does an environmentally friendly life offer *today?*"

Sarah, Martin, and Richard all knew there was something to say, but they couldn't think of it right at that moment.

"Religion gives us ways to live, *right now*, that can lead to happiness and be sustainable at the same time. I can see that you think I'm nuts, but hold on. Think of the Sabbath. Now Ibrahim and I rest on the Sabbath because we have been commanded to by God. It's something we *have* to do. But look—I get a day when I don't shop, or fix up my apartment, work, face my e-mail, or go to political meetings. I pray, rest, and study God's word. After I marry, it is a day I'll spend with my family, and celebrate life by making love. And hopefully get to take a nap afterward." He laughed aloud at their slightly shocked expressions. "Yeah, sex on the Sabbath, it's a grand old Jewish tradition."

"Don't you get it?" Ibrahim finally jumped in. "It's not about self-denial, it's about real, long-lasting *happiness*. A day for appreciating what we have instead of always wanting more. A taste of heaven." He looked over at Richard. "You want to save the planet, my friend? You have anything better than this to offer?"

Richard was silent.

"Mediation to understand our minds, compassion to understand and forgive others, prayer to focus our intentions—these are *spiritual* values, religious practices. They can come from other sources, yes. But the people who created them, who try to put them into their own lives, most of them are—well, you should pardon the expression—*religious*." Jacob waited a moment for that to sink in. "I rest my case. And now, I'm sorry to cut this short, but I am very late for afternoon prayers." He walked over to the eastern corner of the shelter, took out his small prayer book, and began reading in a quiet undertone.

The rest sat in silence. What about all the fanatics, think they'll be a big help for the movement? Sarah wanted to ask. But as Ibrahim rolled out his prayer mat near Jacob, it just didn't seem right to try to get in the last word. And besides, while the religious right and al-Qaeda and fanatic Hindu nationalists made her nuts, she had to admit that there were plenty of crazies who managed to be violent and repressive *without* religion.

She spoke quietly to Richard and Martin, not wanting to disturb the others' prayers. "I like those guys, I really do. But religion? I don't know. It just seems too . . . crazy to me. Always has, always will."

"A few years ago," Martin responded, his voice just above a whisper, "I was out in Montana. I mean, this is all nice, the White Mountains in the fall, but the Rockies?" He gave a low, admiring whistle. "Those are like, *really* mountains. Anyway, I got into a conversation with this old guy on the trail. And we ended up talking about how many people out there are against environmentalists, call them tree huggers, bumper stickers saying things like "Save the Loggers, Kill the Owls." And I asked him, how could people in such magnificent country be like that? You know what he told me? 'Well, son, I guess the mountains make a good man better and a bad man worse.' Just like that. Made sense to me."

You mean, thought Sarah, religion makes good people better and bad ones worse? Religion doesn't make them good or bad? That's it? That simple?

Richard lay back and closed his eyes. What a weird group. Well, at least they all cared about the earth. The earth, he thought to himself, is there any hope? He loved the mountains, but he was close to despair again. Yeah, there was some action on climate change, but for the most part things just got worse and worse. If he thought about it coldly, without emotion, there just wasn't much to hope for.

He looked over at Jacob and Ibrahim. Happy idiots, he thought to himself. All wrapped up in their make-believe world of voices from heaven. Then he thought, at least they don't seem quite as miserable as me. Maybe I should be a little like them—have some faith. He almost laughed aloud. Fat chance. Faith—either you had it or you didn't. And he didn't. Take more trips to the mountains, that would help. And maybe see a shrink for some pills. Get something real for his depression, not any make-believe spiritual fluff. In the meantime, there was still a planet to save.

6

NEED TO KNOW

The Chancellor drummed his fingers on the expensive antique wooden desk. Was he nervous—or impatient, Stephan wondered. Stephan would have thought he would be happy for once. It's not every day that the university gets a thirty-million-dollar donation, not in these times, or any times really. Thirty million and no strings attached—except one: it had to be used to set up one coherent program at the university—with research, courses, grad students, majors, and facilities. Outside of that, the donor didn't specify. Stephan had heard that as the donor handed over the check he'd laughed a little: "I guess you'll have to decide what's most important. What does the world need right now? That you can provide, of course." Then he left, waving off the Chancellor's effusive, nearly groveling gratitude. "Let's see what comes out of all this . . . say, twenty years down the pike. Then you can thank me, or not. If I'm still alive."

So here was Stephan, the first to arrive at a meeting of department heads who would all argue their case about why *their* programs should be given the money. As head of the university's Philosophy Department he knew he didn't have much of a shot, but he would give it the old college try nevertheless. He knew that the world needed some creative, visionary, critical thinking. He knew that political power, and military power, and technological power were being used by social groups who typically had the maturity of twelve-year-old boys. On a good day. People needed to learn to think—not just to build bigger machines or accumulate more data.

And Stephan knew he didn't have much time left. Those two years wasted in prison on that totally mistaken murder charge had taken away some of his best research time. But it had given him a much clearer sense of what people were really like out there beyond the ivory tower where he'd spent most of his life. A really smart black kid in a middle-class black family, he'd loved books and school, but gotten some raised eyebrows when he said he wanted to be a college professor. "You really want to go into a profession where you make less than a plumber?" his lawyer father had asked. Well, he hadn't cared at the time. It was The Truth that he was after. One course in philosophy—a pedestrian Introduction to Ethics course that totally captivated him—and he figured that's where it would be found. A skinny kid with slow reflexes, he'd always been pushed around. But he would use his mind to prove he was as tough as anyone else. Then the '60s erupted, and he got into radical political theory: a "ruthless criticism of everything existing"—he could smile at that old phrase now, but it had seemed completely right to him. Use Reason to critique economic power, and racial injustice, and American foreign policy. Down with the Old, Up with the New. Boy, he'd had some rip-roaring fights with his father over that one. Dad stood for Authority—hard work, keep your nose clean, go to church, get a good life and hold on to it. He'd expected his son to do the same, and could never accept the demonstrations, the radical demands, the shouted slogans at visiting lecturers from the State Department. When Stephan had been suspended for sitting in at the administration building to stop Dow Chemical from recruiting more chemists to make more napalm, his father hadn't spoken to him for a year. That just made him madder, and fueled his politics all the more.

Well, it had been a rough ride, but things had recovered. The DNA test had cleared his name, just as he'd known it would. He'd been in the wrong place at the wrong time, in front of people to whom all black men looked alike. Then when he wrote a book about critical theory and the prison experience, he'd become, nearly sixty, a hot academic commodity. It didn't hurt to be black, either. Institutions could improve their affirmative action count, get a well-known name, and, at his age, figure that he wouldn't be taking up a full professor's salary too much longer. His curly hair was shot with gray, his skinniness had turned to middle-age pot-belly, but he was still sharp-tongued and clear-eyed, and his mind was faster than ever.

So here he was: head of a seventeen-member philosophy department, a specialist in critiquing everything, ready to argue with the Chancellor that it was critical philosophy that needed this money.

Who else would be here?

The door to the office slammed open and Sarah walked in, apologizing for her lateness with a breathless account of how difficult it was to get a parking space near the administration building. She nervously ran her fingers through her short, black hair, put on some rimless glasses to study her notes, and settled her trim, slender body into one of the Chancellor's oversized chairs. Soon they were joined by the head of neuropsychiatry, a thin balding man in his early forties, reputed to be a top researcher on medications for depression in adolescents, who wore a black suit, white shirt, and black tie. Then it was the nice-looking, nicely dressed campus chaplain, a (so Stephan thought) blandly liberal Protestant named Fred.

"Well," began the Chancellor, "we're all here. Let's begin."

"Where's everyone else?" Stephan asked. "You know: sociology, literature, history, all the folks."

"I've narrowed down the meetings, large groups are too unruly," the Chancellor replied impatiently. "Didn't you get my memo?"

"Must have gotten lost in the e-mail," Stephan replied, a little embarrassed to be using a contemporary version of "the dog ate my homework." Truth was, he couldn't stand wasting time reading administrative e-mail, and once in a while he'd just close his eyes and hit the delete button randomly, curious to see what would happen.

"So, just us today?" He smiled at Sarah, whom he knew slightly, and the psychiatrist, whom he didn't, and Fred. "I'm Stephan," he said, reaching out to shake the psychiatrist's hand. The doctor waited a fraction of a moment before extending his arm, "Dr. Thorn . . . I mean, Harris. I'm so used to talking to patients and students." He almost smiled apologetically, but didn't.

"Well, now that we all know each other," the Chancellor broke in brusquely. "Tell me why you want the money. Oh . . . scratch that. I know why you want it. Tell me why I should give it to you."

"All right. I'll tell you." Harris started with a completely self-confident air. If he was intimidated by the Chancellor, nominally his boss, he didn't show it. He talked, moving his eyes to stare at each of the others in turn, otherwise keeping absolutely still, like someone used to being in control of every situation. Perk of being a shrink, thought Stephan. When he's with people, everyone agrees it's the other ones who are nuts.

"It is science, *science*, which sets off the modern world from the past, developed nations from undeveloped ones, rational human beings from the superstitious. With science we have tamed the oceans and the air, cured infectious diseases, and increased human longevity. We can replace a hip, operate on babies before they are born, and take pictures of stars light-years away.

"With science there is nothing, *nothing*, we can't do. If not today, then in the future.

"And now the last frontier, the cutting edge, is neuropsychiatry. Finding out why we behave the way we do, how the brain dictates the mind, how genetics determines whether we are cheerful or miserable, aggressive or painfully shy. We already know that chemical imbalance in the brain causes depression or bipolar disorder. We're beginning to diagnose these problems as young as two or three years old. We've already made a *revolution* in mental health care by replacing or supplementing long, expensive, wasteful talk therapy with medications.

"But there is still a great deal to do. We have to track down the genetic factors, and see if we can alter them with gene therapy. We have to get more reliable predictors for mental illness, and better tests for them, and more precise diagnostic categories. We have to fine-tune the meds so that even fewer people suffer from side effects.

"We can do all this: train the researchers, cooperate with the pharmaceuticals for resources, find the test subjects. And this place," he flicked his hand toward the window overlooking the quad, "will be the center. Wouldn't you like us to be known as the most important source of mental health treatments in the world? Think of the publicity. And the gratitude. Is there anything more important than finding the key to people's happiness—or, at least, the key to their unhappiness?"

He sat back with his almost smile, looked at Stephan, Sarah, and Fred as if daring them to fight against the power of science, and then turned, unblinking, to the Chancellor, who had been fiddling with his BlackBerry.

"Well, that's some sales talk. A little inflated, but that's what you get when you ask someone why you should give them money." The Chancellor wasn't impressed. But then, he had the reputation of never being impressed by anybody. Not surprising, since almost every faculty member who came to him was asking for more of something. Nobody ever came to say, "I've got enough," or, heaven forbid, "I'd like to give some back." Sarah tried to remember how this short, bald, rumpled-looking, basically unfriendly, and decidedly unpleasant man had become Chancellor of a university this big. Oh yes, he'd been in the Business School. Wrote some papers on how to control labor costs that some donors loved. That launched him, and he'd been climbing ever since, an administrator with a reputation for honesty, directness, and getting the most out of employees—or firing them.

"And you, Sarah," raising his eyebrows and his tone and turning to the ecologist. "Can you match Harris' spiel?"

Sarah hesitated, thinking of her own experience with Better-butrin, the medication she'd tried because she'd been so depressed by all the bad environmental news. Things had seemed so bleak and hopeless, she hadn't been able to work for a time. Work, hell, she'd had a hard time washing the dirty dishes that accumulated in her sink. The little round pills, a lovely pale blue, had made an almost immediate difference. Things seemed brighter, she had more energy. She cleaned the dishes, went to her office, and got to work. She stayed on them for six months, until she began to notice her mind getting more and more unsettled. She'd start off thinking about one thing—how she needed a new monitor for her computer—and then her focus would be off and running: from the monitor, to the computer, to an e-mail she needed to answer, to the person she was in contact with, to their dog, to her dog, to the dog's collar, to the dog's food, to canned dog food, to the supermarket—all in about twenty seconds. She wasn't miserable anymore, but she couldn't think straight either. She'd dropped the pills, fast. That was a month ago, and while she wasn't exactly Miss Bright Eyes now, she wasn't suicidal, and she could think about one thing for more than three seconds. Had the pills helped? Had they saved her? Her friend Helen had just shaken her head and suggested, "Maybe your depression is trying to tell you something. Take the pills, fine. But how are you going to find out what you were supposed to hear?" This hadn't made any sense to her at the time. It still didn't make much, but it did a little.

But how were people supposed to face this world without some help? Betterbutrin or a martini after work or a grande mocha from Farbucks. Everyone she knew needed something.

"I think Harris is right," Sarah began slowly, nodding her head sympathetically, leaning forward and looking from the psychiatrist to the Chancellor. Finally, Harris smiled for real. The Chancellor said nothing. And Stephan's grimace, which had been building throughout Harris' self-congratulatory self-promotion, got more pronounced.

"About science, I mean. The other work that goes on." She gestured toward Stephan and Fred, a little apologetically. "I mean, it's fine, it's good. I wouldn't want a university without it. But it never seems to get anywhere. People write books about philosophy, or about God. And then someone else writes another one. There's no improvement, is there? You can't really do it better than anyone else, can you?" She had tried to phrase it as diplomatically as possible, but wasn't it obvious? What these people did was pretty much a waste of time. Didn't they realize what was really important?

Stephan almost broke in, but a dark look from the Chancellor stopped him. Wait your turn, the look said, you'll get one.

"So Harris and I agree." Another smile from Harris. "Up to a point." End of smile. Suddenly Sarah's voice rose, a new note of authority and power ringing through it. "Right now the environmental crisis is the most important thing in the world. Will there be clean water? Clean air? Will the economy be devastated by global warming? Will agriculture collapse because of droughts, or because free ecosystem services like pollination by bees just dry up because we wreck the bee population? What can we do to change, right now, so that the future for our children and grandchildren isn't some environmental nightmare?"

Interesting, thought the Chancellor. This slip of a girl, who sometimes seemed too uptight to hold a social conversation, whom he'd made head of Environmental Studies because he thought she'd be malleable, getting so excited. Could he use this?

"The money should go to Environmental Studies. There isn't even a question," Sarah went on, leaning back in her chair and resting her interlaced hands on her abdomen. "It's science we need, that's for sure. But what *kind* of science?" She tilted her head to one side and then the other, letting them know this was the real question. "What Harris and his colleagues are doing is the old science: reduce everything to its smallest pieces, look for laws governing the small bits, explain the big in terms of the small, and above all, control, control, control. Control your mood, eradicate the disease, shape a person's very genetic structure."

"Oh, you're against control, are you?" Harris broke in, ignoring the Chancellor's glare. "Very interesting. And I suppose you could tell us how you can live without control—or why it frightens you so much."

Was this bad imitation of a shrink supposed to threaten her? Sarah wondered.

"We've *done* control. Or what we thought was control. How has it worked? We thought we would control the bugs, and the pesticides are in everyone's bloodstreams and the topsoil is losing its life. We thought we could control the temperature in cars, and the CFCs almost destroyed the ozone layer. We gave everyone control over where they would drive, we shipped food so people in Maine could have strawberries in January—and now the glaciers are melting and the droughts are killing the Midwest. You want control? Last year the governor of Alabama had a prayer service on the steps of the capitol—not for forgiveness or mercy or love, but for rain. *Rain!* We're so in control, we're out of control. Something else is needed."

"Yes, yes," the Chancellor was tapping his finger on the desk again, wishing these people wouldn't go on and on. "And that would be?"

"Holistic science, science with attention to how every part of the system connects to everything else. A science of emergent properties—understanding that some things are the way they are because of the complexity of the connections among the larger entities, not because some subatomic particle, or a molecule, or even a gene, shapes all the larger parts." Her voice rose as she spoke with growing excitement. "What are the feedback loops between the air and the different oceanic current patterns, and temperature layers of the ocean? How does a forest regenerate itself after a fire? How does the soil, that's my specialty, maintain itself throughout a year of different weather, different amounts of sun, different kinds of vegetation, the presence of different insects and worms and rodents? How does it all work together in a way that works for life? That's what we need to know. And then we start to imitate it, and use it, for us. Wetlands clean the water—can we create living ones in our parks? Plants take polluting heavy metals out of the soil—can we sow them over Superfund sites? Mangroves protect the coastlines—can we bring them back so that a rising ocean doesn't kill people every time there's a storm? Science? Of course. Science in the service of life."

"Holistic science?" fumed Harris, his lips pressed together in barely contained disdain. "Is this a university or some New Age retreat center? Just how do you think you're going to answer any of those questions without *old* science? That's how you find out what the processes are in the trees, what makes up the soil, how the pesticides affect the immune system. Labs, double-blind experiments, tests. Everything we've been doing for hundreds of years—only now we do it better." Ignorant, naive people made him lose his patience, which he always regretted later. But there was so much illness in the world, and he could have the means to make a difference, and this woman was in his way.

"No," said Sarah quietly, slowly. "Now it's different. With the environmental crisis, we have to look at the whole, not the part; the system, not the building blocks—or at least not *just* the building blocks. We have to learn how to cooperate with nature, to be its partner—not its owner or its boss."

"I simply have no idea what you are talking about. And I suspect you don't either." Harris was shifting in his seat, his studied immobility replaced by agitation. He had listened to quite enough of this nonsense. "We have *revolutionized*," his voice turned almost shrill, "medicine by seeing how genes make us what we are, and psychiatry by seeing how brain chemicals determine how we feel and behave. So call it control, as if there is something wrong with that. Then ask some mother of a child with bipolar illness if she likes seeing the symptoms controlled so her son has a life. And you know what? You like it too. That car you drove to get here—like the way you can control it? The fact that this building doesn't collapse in a thunderstorm—like that as well, I bet. There's science in every mouthful of food you eat, every Tylenol you take for PMS, and every antibiotic for your niece's ear infections. Take scientific control away, and we are slaves to bacteria and bad winters and our own screwed-up brains. Put it back, and we can live like human beings."

Harris stopped, almost out of breath, glaring at Sarah; then wondered why he had almost lost control of himself in a way that psychiatrists were never supposed to. Sarah glared back. The science Harris did was part of the problem, part of what had made things so bad. The Chancellor turned his head and stared over at Stephan, unmoved by their theatrics. And what have you got?

Stephan closed his eyes for a second. How could he reach these people, blind as they were? Small-minded professionals, each with their own little expertise. "Don't want to be slaves? I'm with you there. But who," he paused, looked at each of them turn, a little theatrically, "are we slaves to, really? We've got all this nifty technology, all these accomplishments, but for what?

"We've mechanized agriculture, but a billion people are close to starvation. We have incredible medicine, but we're losing the war on cancer. Our telephones can do everything, everything except help us have decent relationships with each other. We don't have so many of those, we're pretty lonely, and so we take your little pills, Harris—millions upon millions of us. You think that's a *brain* problem? All of a sudden eight-year-olds are getting depressed— and it's because they are hardwired wrong? What nonsense." He raised his right hand and extended his index finger from a clenched fist, punching forward to emphasize his points. "You hit someone in the head and they are going to have a headache. Problem isn't the headache, it's that he's getting hit in the head."

"Do you specialize in making no sense?" Harris had stopped trying to control his disdain.

"The fundamental structures of our culture, politics, economy, family life—they are all profoundly distorted. And science, science is up there with the media and the politicians and everyone else. Science isn't freedom, it's service to the highest bidder."

Harris turned to the Chancellor. "Do we really need this sort of thing, in a *university?*"

"Stephan, if you don't mind," the Chancellor's tone said he didn't give a crap whether Stephan minded or not, "get to the point and spare us the rhetorical flourishes."

"Let me break it down for you," Stephan replied, his confrontational manner giving way to a kind of breezy confidence. Sarah noticed he wasn't scared of either the Chancellor or Harris, the way she expected humanist types to be a little insecure around scientists and money guys.

"First, people need to eat and stay warm. If that takes all their labor, that's all they'll do. To get more—religion, philosophy, science, art—they need a surplus. They have to produce more than they need just to eat and stay warm. So some people work for everyone's food and shelter, and others do things like write philosophy or perform scientific experiments.

"The question is, *who controls the surplus*? Because *that's* who determines the shape of religion, and philosophy, and, yes, science."

He turned to Sarah. "You're the ecologist. I'm just the dumb philosopher. So tell me, why was it that scientists, the ones whose ideas are not just opinions, who make real progress, why they screwed up things so badly with CFCs? With DDT? With huge dam installations that even the people who paid for them, like the World Bank, admitted were a waste of money?"

He turned to Harris. "You're the great medical researcher. Your work sets us off from the animals and primitives. So you tell me: how could we have given women treatments for menopause that help cause breast cancer? How could *scientific*," somehow he managed to make the word into a nasty epithet and a question at the same time, "experts have told people not to worry about radioactive fallout from U.S. atomic tests in the '50s, or used black men as guinea pigs in syphilis experiments without telling them they were being used? Tell me how the drug companies and their scientific advisors produced medications without warning about side effects, and sometimes that really didn't do anything?"

He opened his arms wide and nodded encouragingly to each of them. "Tell me how all this could have happened. And then I'll give you another fifty examples, and you can explain *them*. And when you're done, maybe you'll see why my program should get the money. Only critical social theory will help us develop a vision of truly moral, truly democratic control over science and technology. Otherwise corporations and governments pay your way, and you'll study what they tell you to. You'll look at cures for cancer, not how to prevent it. You'll drug the uptight teenagers instead of looking at how this empty, media-driven, endlessly consuming culture makes people nuts." He slowed down, emphasizing each word with his extended finger again. "You'll treat the disease, not the causes, because that's where the bucks are, because that doesn't require any real social changes, and that's what people who control the funds want."

There was a pause. They all waited. The Chancellor had known that Stephan was some kind of flaming radical—time in prison, racism in the criminal justice system, all that sort of thing. But as far as he was concerned, that was just fluff. So cops were—or weren't—racist. What difference did it make? Science and technology and the fancy new medicine, *that's* where the action was—the big grants from the NIH and NSF, the big research support from Big Pharma, the tie-ins for a percentage of the profits on new techniques, the publicity in the *Times* and on CNN: "New cures from Dr. So-and-So of So-and-So University!!!" Well, he wanted So-and-So University to be his. He'd pretty much made up his mind to give the money to Harris, stuck-up jerk that he was. These meetings were just window dressing on the decision. He would fund the Institute for Mental Health and Brain Research. Science, medicine, health, progress. No one could quarrel with that.

Except idiots like Stephan.

He looked at the philosopher like a bug on a dining room table. "Are you telling me that our nation's scientific powers, our research budget, the incredible advances that we've made—that make us the envy of the world—that there is something wrong with all that? Want to give up your computer? Hmmm?"

"Do you know what a refugee from development is?" Stephan wasn't backing down. "People whose villages and ways of life were destroyed because someone put up a dam, cut down the forest, poisoned a river, or created a nature preserve on somebody's ancestral land. Do you want to know how many people have died from pollution? How many lives ruined by bad medicine? No, I don't want to give up my computer, but if that's the price of not having babies with a hundred toxic chemicals in their blood, I'll think about it.

"Science and technology married corporate power and the state. I'd like to initiate divorce proceedings. Let's see how they do in a trial separation, at least. Instead of you," pointing at Harris, "looking deeper and deeper in the brain, why don't you look at how isolated and lonely people are, how communities are destroyed, how every moment of waking time is infiltrated by media peddling junk to buy and junkier values.

"And you," to Sarah now, a little gentler, but not much, "might ask who is going to decide what changes will be made to save the environment. A bunch of experts like you? Some technocratic elite? Or democracy." He stopped, smiled just a little bit, and asked with surprising earnestness: "Remember democracy?" Stephan settled back in his chair, smothered a cough with a hand over his mouth, and waited.

"So," Harris responded slowly, his lips a thin line of distaste, "you distrust science because it has made mistakes? Well, I hate to break it to you, but scientists are human, and we don't always get it right. We misinterpret data, trust things that shouldn't be trusted, get a skewed sense of how something works. But we also improve. You don't like the fact that CFCs damaged the ozone layer? Don't blame you. But remember, it was *scientists* who figured out what was happening. Critical theory types like you didn't even know what a CFC molecule was, or even the ozone layer, probably. You just cheerfully used the air conditioning in your car. Later, yes, later, you got all excited. But in the meantime you took the benefits like everyone else. Scientists may make mistakes, but usually only scientists will be able to know that mistakes were made, or how to fix them."

"Which scientists? Paid by whom? With whose interests in mind?" Stephan snapped back, pointing his finger accusingly.

"When uneducated housewives see all the illness in their neighbor-hoods and figure out something's wrong with the water, it's true that they have to go to some researchers to find out what's doing it. But in the meantime they usually get run over by *other* research-ers in the pay of the chemical company that dumped it in the first place, or technical types working for the government who don't like the idea of some housewife telling them something isn't safe."

He suddenly changed his tone from aggressive to conciliatory. "Look, I *know* what you guys do is amazing." He fished a tiny MP3 player out of his shirt pocket. "Four hundred CDs on this—how do you do it?" His voice got sharp again. "But that doesn't mean you know what the hell is going on. Think of the fishing indus-try in Newfoundland. Two hundred years of family boats, limiting themselves on their catch, taking days off. Then a big corporation brought in the big trawlers: ships so big they could process and freeze the fish right there, so expensive they had to use them 365 days a year, so powerful it was like strip mining the ocean. Four years later, there was no more fishing. The stock was gone. Forty thousand people out of work. And you know something? Those funky fishermen, who couldn't begin to understand how to put together something like those huge trawlers, they *knew* that the fish wouldn't last with that kind of fishing. They were right, and all the guys who designed the big ships—they didn't know, or they didn't think, or they just didn't care."

Harris wanted to say something. He opened his mouth. But then he stopped. He was thinking of his brother, older by five years, his charming, handsome, brilliant, creative brother who had slowly lost touch with the real world, and come to inhabit some strange, wondrous land of princesses and dragons and sorcerers, who had stopped going to school, and going to doctors and even eating, until one day he'd climbed up on the roof and tried to fly. And snapped his neck on the sidewalk instead. Harris had loved his brother, worshipped him, been devastated as he slipped further and further away. That's why Harris had gone into medicine, and then psychiatry, and then neuro. If he could save one kid like his brother, maybe that would make up for something. It wasn't just some impersonal truth he was after—he *cared*. Did he forget that sometimes? Sure. Didn't everybody? Maybe Stephan was just asking him to remember.

Sarah started them off again, a hard edge in her voice. "Democracy, is it? Rule by *the people*? Let me get this straight. It's *the people* who'd rather vote for *American Idol* than the mayors of their own cities, who bury themselves in gadgets, who can't be bothered to carpool. All these average Joes and Janes who think being green means buying a different kind of skin cream, and wouldn't consider giving up meat for a day. You want to leave it to them? Look at what we've got for democratic leaders as it is—a bigger bunch of clowns I never saw, and I bet you haven't either. You want people to vote on the truth the way they vote on politicians? My God, a lot of them don't believe in evolution. You want them to figure out what ecological balance is?"

Now it was Stephan's turn to open his mouth, close it, suddenly, surprisingly unsure. He knew the scientific elite couldn't be trusted, that they tended to serve their paymasters, not the people's interests. But did the people even know what their interests were? He knew that sounded elitist, but . . . really. Look at what people ate and drank, how they spent their time, the illnesses they brought on themselves, and the crap, the awful crap, they allowed the government and corporations to pull on them. How could these people ever run things? But if they didn't . . . who could?

Fred cleared his throat. The other four looked over at him. "I'm just here by the courtesy of the Chancellor. Purely unofficial, though I suppose I could try to make the case about why my department should get the money." He looked for a receptive laugh, and didn't get it.

"You're only here because the Donor," with this kind of money involved, the Chancellor always made the word sound like it should begin with a capital letter, "suggested that you moderate. Don't thank me."

"Did I thank you? Don't believe I did." Hmm, thought Stephan, this guy's got more balls than I thought.

"The point," said Fred, turning away from the Chancellor and toward the other three, "or the problem, if I may, is that you all act like you are involved in a zero-sum game here. Now, that makes sense in funding, at least sometimes. But not in life. Never, never in life."

Well, at least he's not quoting the Bible, thought Sarah. "Maybe you could, uh, clarify a little?"

"It's simple, so simple that even as brilliant as all of you are, you didn't see it. And that's an interesting question in itself—why you didn't.

"You all need each other. Any one of your disciplines alone is inadequate. Isn't it obvious?"

"No."

"Not at all."

"Nope."

On this, at least, they agreed.

"You, Sarah, want a holistic science of the earth. You will still need fine-tuned instruments, experimental data, analysis of tiny mechanisms on the molecular level. You'll need the old science to do the new science.

"You, Harris, you want to cure mental illness? Of course we need to know how the brain works, but we also need to know what's shaping the brain. You know, better than me, that genes work in an *environment*, and that the environment itself can alter how genes function. You want to cure mental illness, you better have some holistic framework. Social life, values, the family, what's in the air and the water, even the choices people make *about* their brains.

"And you both need Stephan, unless you want to make more of the kinds of mistakes he's been talking about. You don't, do you?"

Silence. Was that a good sign? Fred wondered.

"You need someone to ask the critical questions: not about the results of your research, though if those end up making a *lot* of money for someone, we had better look at them carefully. It's the direction, the focus, that's up for grabs. Stephan is asking you to ask *yourselves*: who am I serving? Whose truth is this to be?

"But Stephan, you need, and I'm sure you know this, you need the scientific and technical community. We aren't going back to the caveman times, or even the eighteenth century. The problems we've created—a lot of them, maybe not all, require technical solutions.

"So it's simple. You need each other."

Silence.

"I remember," Sarah broke the quiet, "something that happened when I was just starting in soil research. I was collecting a sample from a small, wooded plot in Vermont. To check on the effects of acid rain. It was late fall, and the leaves had turned, and the sky was pure blue with just a few cirrus clouds in the east. Early morning, the last of the year's birdcalls in the air, a little breeze. My God, it was perfect, just perfect. As I bent down to the soil, I thought, 'They all work together—every molecule of rain and CO_2, the rotting leaves to replenish the soil, the worms and the bacteria that make the soil live.' And I wondered, 'Why can't we be like that? Why can't we fit in with each other, and with the world?' And I've been thinking about that ever since. That's why I do what I do. But sometimes, when I look at myself, I see I don't do a very good job. How am I going to get along with all the earth if I can't even listen openly to my colleagues?"

The Chancellor didn't know what to make of any of this. He'd just wanted a show meeting, a lot of posturing by people who loved to posture, and then he'd tell them all they'd hear his decision later on. Were they actually going to learn something from each other?

"Well, if the three of you can't decide who's right, what am I supposed to do?"

Stephan looked at him with outright distaste. "I suppose you'll do what you always do: figure out what's best for you personally, then the university, and, as an afterthought, the rest of the world."

The Chancellor blinked. For a moment he thought of what he could do to hurt Stephan. Oh, the guy had tenure, so his job was safe. But there were lots of other ways to make his work life pretty uncomfortable. But then he realized these people just weren't as smart as they thought. Time for a little lesson on the real world, he decided.

"I," he began, pointing his thumb at his chest, "know what you think of me. 'He's just a heartless, self-interested, self-promoting bureaucrat who doesn't understand a thing about real scholarship, knowledge, or morality.' Right?"

Not very convincingly, they murmured mild dissents.

"Never mind, I don't care what you think." He sniffed, under-lining the point. "You're so wrapped up in your little worlds that you never stop to think that it's me, *me*, who makes it all possible. Sarah, you worked for the government—had a little problem with political interference, if I recall. Ever get that here? Harris, you've been working on some project for three years, with no payoff. Think they'd stand for that in the private sector? And you, Stephan, where else but in a university could a blowhard like you spout your commie propaganda—I mean, where else could you do that and earn a good salary with great benefits?

"Nowhere, for all three of you.

"I know I'm charmless, and rough on people who don't pull their weight. And I often miss the finer points of all your priceless wisdom.

"But where would you be without me? You'd have to raise your own funds and deal with your own budgets, and attract students and manage the damn grounds and even hire your own secretar-ies—and fire them when they didn't work out. Up for that, are you? I doubt it.

"So have all the contempt for me you want. But remember how much you need me, at least once in a while."

Well, that's a bloody surprise, thought Sarah. And he has a point, after all. Everybody in the room had a point. But if every-body had a point, then . . . well, then she wouldn't be able to feel so, well, *superior* to the ones who weren't like her. The hard-core old-time scientists, the humanists with their endless, meaningless disagreements, the blunt bureaucrats who wielded the power. And if she couldn't feel superior to them, what did that say about her? That she was just another part of the intellectual ecosystem, an earthworm to their rotting leaves, a drop of water to their root system? Just part of this. . . .

"Oh lord," she spoke aloud, unwilling to finish the thought.

"What?" the three men all said at once.

"Sorry, I was just wondering . . . I mean, I know this is crazy . . . but is there any way we could do this together?"

"Do what together?" Harris was somewhere between confused and incredulous.

"The Institute. Could we set it up so that brain research and holistic ecology and critical theory—that they are all part of it?"

"But who would be in charge?" Harris asked quickly. "Who would allocate the funds?"

"Is that all you care about?" Stephan demanded. "Power, money, control."

"Take it easy, man," Fred said. "We all like our salaries and our research budgets, right? It's a reasonable question."

"OK, fair enough," Stephan answered. "I guess it's second nature for me to be suspicious of everyone. A few years in prison for a crime I didn't commit turned me a little negative."

Harris looked at Stephan for the first time. "You know, my brother killed himself when I was thirteen. I don't think I ever got over it. I'm carrying something too. I'm driven in my way, you in yours. Maybe if we shared all that, we could find some way to share the power and the funds both." Good God, he thought to himself. Am I back in therapy? Why had he unburdened himself to these strangers?

"If we are to work together," he went on, shaking his head a bit to clear it, "it has to be clear to me from *both* of you that you recognize the absolute necessity of the kind of work I do. That's basic."

"You're right," Stephan responded, softened by Harris' self-revelation. "It would be pretty dumb of me to just knock science all the time." He fished around in his pocket, and instead of his MP3 player he brought out an asthma inhaler. "I really wouldn't want to go through the spring without this. Even if it's the damn economic system that's making the pollution, I don't want to have to wait until after the revolution to breathe without coughing."

"I need the same thing from both of you as well," Sarah added. "Science, but holistic science. How else can we understand the deep troubles we're in now? And you, Stephan, surely you want our acknowledgment as well. If we're honest, Harris," Harris jerked his head back in surprise (did she think he'd been lying?), "you know we have to admit that scientists can be blind to what they're doing, get caught up in the money and the power. We need Stephan as much as he needs us."

Harris was silent again, but Stephan and Sarah noticed how much softer his expression was. He was thinking of a patient he'd had as an intern, a prison guard. The man was lonely, blue, everything seemed gray and purposeless. It was an open-and-shut diagnosis of depression. Harris had started him on a second-generation SSRI, Zooloft, and expected some decent results. But the guard came back, month after month, feeling the same. He had a bit more energy, and some digestive problems, but he still felt like crap about his life. One day, when Harris was talking the case over with his supervisor, he had a sudden insight: the guy worked in a dark, violent place filled with rage and despair. He wasn't too bright; was sort of unattractive; had no money, friends, or family. No *wonder* he felt lousy. The problem wasn't in his *head*, it was in his *life*. His supervisor had just smiled the faintly condescending smile of An Authority that Harris hadn't yet learned to cultivate. "Perhaps, perhaps, but we can't change his life, can we? Not our job. We just pay attention to the inside. You could, of course, recommend he get some counseling as well. Might help." The supervisor's tone made it clear he thought talking about all this was a waste of time. Get the chemistry right, and everything else would fall into place. "Maybe up the dose, or switch to Inefexlor? What do you think?"

Harris looked around. "Each of us help the other, change the insides of their heads and the outsides of their lives." He smiled at the other two, and at Fred and the Chancellor. "Wouldn't that surprise everybody?"

God almighty, thought the Chancellor, could this get any more nauseatingly warm and fuzzy? Employees were so much easier to control when they were competing with each other.

Stephan turned to the Chancellor. "Much as I hate to admit it, we need you too. You get the donations, build the buildings, find students to pay tuition. Maybe the owners of the surplus are going to skew the research their way, but there will always be somebody distributing it. It's not about not having it skewed, but about who is doing the skewing and who is getting skewed." He broke out into boyish giggles, something the serious, politically correct Stephan rarely did.

"This is great, just great." Ministerial Fred liked few things as much as people actually listening to each other. "I'll leave you with just one question, because I've got to run over to a christening.

"Whether or not there is some joint institute with these particular funds, it's pretty obvious you need each other. Those of you doing the intellectual work, and the people here," nods to the Chancellor, "and those not here," raises his hand and makes a circular gesture, "who produce food and houses and asthma inhalers so you can do what you do.

"Question is, why is it so easy to forget something so obvious? What makes us want to make ourselves look like the only game in town?"

The Chancellor started drumming his fingers on the desk again. Impatience, thought Stephan, no doubt about it. "This is certainly taking longer than I expected," the Chancellor said abruptly. "In fact, while it's not a christening I'm off to, I too have to be off. I will take this all, as they say, under advisement. And I will do something I very rarely do: think again. I'll be in touch."

"If you're willing to think again," Stephan responded, standing up and patting his pockets to make sure he had his wallet, keys, inhaler, and MP3 player, "you're willing to be objective. That's what one of my teachers used to say. There isn't anything else to it.

That's the heart of real knowledge—hard science, holistic ecology, or social theory. Simple, really."

They all shook hands and left, feeling elated and not quite knowing why.

Later that night . . .

Harris decided he still had time to stop at the lab and check on the latest results. Maybe something would show up this time. The Chancellor's little dig about the three-year wait time had rankled, even though he knew that these things just took as long as they took. That last breakthrough he'd had, that had taken even longer. But it had made him, gotten him the Big Lab. This one would come through as well, he was sure of it.

And then people would understand how *important* all this was. What a difference this kind of work made. Oh sure, Sarah's work was worthwhile, he supposed. Holistic ecology, whatever that meant. If people just stopped putting toxins in the water supply, we certainly would be better off. Call that science?

No, he knew in the end that what he did was science, and the rest? Well, not really. And without science, where would they be? Collegial cooperation, mutual respect—up to a point. But there had to be standards, and he knew what they were.

Sarah walked into the field in back of her house, far enough from the road that she could actually see the stars. It was the best thing about moving here from Detroit, the sky at night when it was clear. If you can't see the stars, someone had once said to her, you forget you're in a universe that's a lot bigger than your living room and Main Street.

She thought about her meeting that afternoon. A joint institute? Social theory, brain science, *and* ecology? Well, stranger things had happened, but it was pretty strange nonetheless. Then she thought of all the *time* it would take. Working together, doing budgets, compromising. Part of her rebelled at the thought. If it was the only way to get some of that money, all right. But really it should *all* go to her program. Not for herself. She lived in a tiny little house, drove an old car, and dressed like a bag lady half the time, people said.

No, it was the work. That was why she was alive.

Years ago, when she was fourteen, she'd almost killed herself. Cooped up in that tiny town in Georgia, watching her vicious father get drunk, beat the living hell out of her mother, and leer at her as she got older and looked more like a woman. She was great at schoolwork, especially math and science, so everyone made fun of her. "Little girlie scientist," they'd called her, as she made her way, friendless, across the cafeteria to sit alone, day after day, year after year.

So she'd thought about ending it all. Two quick slices with her father's hunting knife would have done the trick. She stole the knife one August evening when he'd passed out earlier than usual, and made her way out to the woods. She sat down by the bank of the creek, closed her eyes, and picked up the knife. Then she heard the voices—coming out of the stream, in the leaves moved by the soft evening breeze, in the insect hum. "Don't do it. Don't do it. Don't do it." Over and over, a hushed plea, almost like a gentle caress on her arms, her face. "Why not?" she'd screamed back. And then, the strangest thing—a long silence, and an even quieter murmur, "We love you." Just once, and so soft she had to strain to hear it. But it had been real—as real as anything else in her lonely, painful world.

That was it. She put the knife back in its sheath, amazed that she had ever thought to use it on herself. Now she had courage to wait out the years before she'd get out. She would study even harder, be the best student that little town had ever seen, get a scholarship to college, and never look back. And as soon as she heard of a kind of science you could do that served the earth, she knew that was for her. The earth had saved her, and she would try to save it in return.

But they were all running out of time. If things passed a certain point, it would be too late. So what if people were unhappy—there would always be more generations of them to learn not to make themselves miserable. And anyway, whatever he said, Harris' kind of science was based in control of nature. There was no love, no respect, no cooperation. That was the old way, hers was the new.

And Stephan's critical theory? Fine, figure out who the bad guys were, and deal with them. But political types had been complaining about injustice for decades, centuries—surely we knew enough about that already. It was the kind of knowledge she was getting that could save the world. She'd go to the Chancellor tomorrow, by herself, and make another pitch. She'd make him see. After all, it was the earth that was at stake.

Stephan sat in front of his computer, studying the several news sites he went through each day. New bonuses for the Wall Street crowd, a Republican congressman from Oklahoma making fun of the very idea of global warming, a wave of murders of gay people in Iraq, resistance to mountaintop removal growing in West Virginia, but the mines continuing to be built. The work was endless. If only he had more help—to keep in touch with what was happening, to analyze it, to produce material that would help people resist.

Cooperate with Sarah and Harris? OK, but only up to a point. After all, cooperate with everyone and you ended up in bed with Hitler, or Cheney, or the Iranian mullahs. You had to draw a line and know who was on the other side. Racists, exploiters, rapists, polluters—*they* were on the other side, and so were their servants in the world of science who were just out to make a buck. He'd be damned if he'd let anyone forget that, not if he could help it. There was too much to be won or lost.

Fred poured a generous spoonful of honey in his Rooibos Rose tea. Really didn't need so much sweetener, but even after a pretty good day at his job he needed a little something, well, sweet. There was so much conflict, so much unhappiness. He could see, even among these well-off, middle-class Americans, that desperate hunger for recognition and respect. Scratch any angry person arguing with someone else, and what would you find? A hurt child who just wanted Mommy's love and approval. That was three-quarters of his job, helping people see that was what they needed, and how to get it and give it back.

As for the Institute—might work, might not. In the meantime he'd let them discover for themselves the point he *hadn't* made: that besides needing each other, all three of them needed him as well. Not him personally, of course, but the kind of thinking he'd been taught, and tried to embody. Harris wanted to help people not to be unhappy—but happiness wasn't a matter of brain chemicals but *meaning*. What is a good life for a human being? Science would never answer that question. Couldn't even ask it. That's where religion, or at least spirituality, came in.

Sarah's work was great, but she hadn't a clue about how to join love of the earth with social justice. She'd abandon the people and save the trees. No hope in that. If the people felt left out, they'd never care about the trees.

And Stephan? Well, his passion for justice brought him closest to Fred. But Stephan was all about anger. He needed a little touch of spiritual love, the kind Fred got from Jesus. Whatever name was used, without that touch of love you'd just be angry all the time. Some help that would be.

But he didn't expect them to realize all this. Things would work out, or they wouldn't. Now that his wife's cancer had gone into a second remission, not much bothered him. He'd just do his part, leave the rest to God, and maybe put a little more honey in his tea. What the hell, you only live once.

The Chancellor finished his nighttime whiskey. Years ago he'd have had several throughout the evening, to calm down after a day of struggling with all the massive academic egos. But he'd seen that it just made him more depressed and anxious. So it was one a day, right before bed.

Quite interesting, that meeting today. People didn't surprise him very often, but those three had. Usually they were so petty that he had to do their organizing for them. But maybe Sarah, Harris, and Stephan would do something new, actually see the importance of someone else's point of view, work, passion.

It was possible, wasn't it?

FACE OFF

Charles looked at his watch impatiently, took another sip from his water glass, and grimaced. He adjusted his tic, which didn't need adjusting, ran his fingers though the sparse gray hair above his right ear, and then noticed, with sharp irritation, how nervous he was. What was there to be nervous about, he wondered. It's just a man having dinner with his son in a nice restaurant. Why Benjamin always had to be late, he didn't understand. But then, he was young, immature, and hopefully would soon grow out of this ridiculous nonsense about changing the world in about a hundred years with *The Party*. Where had he gotten these crazy ideas? As if Charles didn't know. That Jewish Marxist philosophy professor in college, who'd filled Benjamin's head with crazy ideas about the evils of globalization, and corporate influence, and how things happened "in the long run, slowly, surely, powerfully." As if that professor had anything more successful to offer than hardworking, risk-taking entrepreneurs and technological innovation.

And anyway, good things happened because everybody went about their own business, "slowly, surely, powerfully." Buying, selling, producing, consuming. Not letting the government make a lot of laws and interfere. That's the system they had, and they weren't going to get a better one because some snot-nosed kid like Benjamin told them what to do—blaming America first, riling up the poor people and the minorities. When the blacks wanted to get ahead, they did fine, like those two colored lawyers he'd known at Benron. They'd dressed right, talked right, and made out pretty damn well for themselves. Before it all went bust. Let blacks act like that, work hard, fit in, and there'd be no more racism. That's what the country, the world, needed—not Benjamin's pie-in-the-sky political groups.

But he hadn't seen his son since getting out of prison, and while he had sworn to forget his time there on the day he left Smithfield, it kept nagging at the back of his mind. All the pride in himself he'd generated over years of hard work, fitting in, rising up in the corporate chain—all that was stained now, marked forever by the stupid, crazy, just plain *wrong* things he had done. Lying to shareholders, hiding things from colleagues, avoiding the press until the last minute. Why?

He wanted to be able to look at his son with confidence, give him advice, help straighten him out. Pretty hard to do that as an ex-con, he thought bitterly, just a hint of self-loathing cracking through his neatly arranged facade of expensive gray suit, light blue tie, and finely tailored shirt.

Nonsense, he thought again, using a word he was very fond of. Anybody could make a mistake. And that's what he'd done. But he'd taken responsibility, paid his debt to society, and now he was back. There had already been some nibbles from a few venture capital firms with interests in high-tech energy start-ups. A man with his experience wouldn't go hungry, that was for sure. If he made one bad blunder in a lifetime of hard work and success, that didn't mean there was anything wrong with the system. He'd play by the rules this time, not even a hair out of place from start to finish, and everything would work out just fine. Even with that pathetic windbag Obama as president, this was still the greatest country on earth.

Benjamin had waited at the bus stop thirty-five minutes, patiently going over his notes from the last meeting of the new organization he was cultivating—an interfaith group trying to raise salaries for immigrant Haitian women working in nursing homes. Not a bad group of cadre, he thought. Of course a lot of them were just working off some middle-class guilt around the poor black folk, or maybe had seen overworked, criminally underpaid immigrants taking care of their own grandparents. Religious types worked hard, didn't fuss much, and did what they said they'd do. But they rarely saw the big picture, the long haul. They were too busy trying to do the right thing *today*. Still, there were a few he might be able to bring around to his way of thinking.

In the meantime, he decided, looking at his watch, he'd better start walking to the restaurant. His father would be sitting there, having arrived twenty minutes early to prove what a great person he was, and for sure not giving a thought to the slave wages the line cooks were paid, the injury rate of the people who worked in the slaughterhouses, or what the transportation of food from thousands of miles away was doing to the environment. No, dear old Dad was probably hooking up to another exploiting, immoral corporation, itching to take in some of the profits just bubbling out of the global economy.

Why was this man his father? What did they have in common? It hurt Benjamin, hurt him more than he could ever admit except on those very rare occasions when he had a few too many beers, that his own father was a dyed-in-the-wool conservative, whose biggest love seemed to be money, and who positively celebrated global capitalism—the system that Benjamin was devoting his life to ending. How could he take those things he said seriously? Benjamin saw so clearly everything that was wrong with global capitalism. How could his father, who was no fool, be so blind?

Benjamin kept himself in good shape, part of the discipline of the long-term revolutionary, so he knocked off the brisk two-mile walk to the restaurant in thirty-three minutes, making mental notes along the way about the possibility of some kind of citizens' coalition to demand more frequent and reliable bus service on this major route. A trillion dollars for cars and highways, fifteen cents for bikes and mass transit, he thought. Let the middle class drive and pollute, let the poor people, a lot of them people of color, wait at the bus stops or walk. What else is new?

The maître d' looked over Benjamin's faded chinos, stained sport jacket, and wrinkled turtleneck and for a moment thought of telling the compact, intense man that he wasn't dressed appropriately for this elegant establishment. Benjamin just stared at him, as if reading his mind, and then nodded toward his father, who was studying the menu at a prominent table. The maître d' remembered what Charles had said, and the twenty he'd discreetly passed him, and led Benjamin over.

Charles looked up, the usual conflicting rush of emotions passing though him: pride in his son, who despite all his crazy ideas had almost been valedictorian of his college class, irritation at the sloppy clothes, hope that they could communicate, loneliness for a son who could have shared his dreams, and barely controllable rage at the thought that *his* son could have turned into some kind of communist. History had proven those kinds of ideas wrong so many times. Benjamin wasn't stupid—how could he swallow, and then spout back, that crap?

Benjamin stood in front of Charles, torn between a manly handshake and an emotional hug. He didn't know why, but suddenly his eyes teared up and he realized that he'd been frightened, really frightened, of what would happen to his father in prison. A lot of those places were mainly black or Latino, and they might have taken out their legitimate class and racial hatred on Charles. But his father looked surprisingly good. Benjamin let himself feel the unexpected rush of relief and then, in a mental habit he never tried to control, quickly estimated how many starving infants could have been fed for the price of his father's immaculate suit.

"Sit down, sit down," Charles ordered, using the commanding tone he took when he didn't quite know what to do with a rush of paternal love, uncalled-for nervousness, and irritation.

"Sorry I'm late, Dad," said Benjamin, even though it was less than fifteen minutes past the hour. But he was, like his father, someone who prided himself on punctuality. Discipline was essential to a revolutionary life. "The bus simply didn't come for more than half an hour. It's kind of typical of what the city thinks of people who don't own cars."

"Well, perhaps if they worked a little harder, they'd own cars like the rest of us," answered Charles, trying to put a little light touch in his tone.

Benjamin pressed his lips together, fighting back the anger that being with Charles usually caused. But he'd promised himself not to take the bait this time. "OK. Dad, I'll pass along your suggestion to all the cleaning ladies I know. I'm sure they'll be grateful for the input."

Charles grunted in reply, making a sound halfway between a cough and a harrumph, then tried to interest Benjamin in a cocktail, which he refused. "Still pure at heart?"

"Yup, still pure. And besides, I don't make enough money in my organizing job to drink, so better not get into the habit. And you, you still get to the office earlier than anyone else and leave later?" It had been a mark of pride for his father, but a true one, that he really did give himself to his work.

"Well, at the moment I'm still considering my options, since leaving . . . you know. But I'm sure that when I get a job that's just what I will do."

They paused, studying the dinner menu. The price of a typical entrée here wouldn't feed quite as many starving kids as the price of the suit, Benjamin reflected, but it sure would help out. Still, he knew that there was no point in sharing that particular insight with his father, who would probably tell him that if the kids were starving it was their own fault. So he picked the cheapest vegetarian pasta dish, ignoring his father's raised eyebrows. The waiter brought Charles' Stoli martini and Benjamin's iced tap water, and wondered what the hell a Wall Street type and somebody who looked like a college dropout were doing having dinner together in a three-star restaurant.

"So," began Charles, thinking that if he got Benjamin talking about his life he could show him how much better things could be if he went to law school or got an MBA, "how are things?"

"They're OK, Dad, same old, same old, you know?" Benjamin had a hunch Charles would soon start in on the "Is this any way to live your life, think what you could have if you only took advantage of . . ." speech. He really wasn't in the mood for that right at the moment, for a whole bunch of reasons.

But Charles wasn't going to be put off. "Same old what?"

"Same old organizing, trying to get people to work together to change things, finding other people who think about the world the way I do, and bring them together. I've told you before, right?"

"You still think that a bunch of people on welfare, or who work for minimum wage, can run things better than the people who run them now?" Charles thought of homeless bums with their hands out, people lined up at the unemployment office; of the ones driving old dented cars, eating at McDonald's, buying huge plastic-wrapped packages of toilet paper on sale at Walmart. And then he had a sudden vision of the same people sitting around tables at the Pentagon, talking in boardrooms at General Motors and Citibank, making speeches on the floor of the Senate. "Come on, Benjamin, the poor are poor because they aren't too bright, or they're lazy, or they drink too much. Put them in charge and you'll just have a bigger mess than we have already." And a lot of that mess, he thought but didn't add, came from trying to please these people—who should have been damn grateful for *whatever* they had.

"Oh, I get it," Benjamin took the bait this time, finding it a lot easier to have another one of their mutual verbal assaults than to face his own confused mix of affection, dislike, concern, and yearning for approval. "So when Texaco pays off the Nigerian government to get an oil lease in the Ogoni Peninsula, and then completely pollutes the villages there, and some kid's father tries to stop it, and gets killed by the mercenaries Texaco hires to protect the oil facility, and his mother can't raise food anymore because their field's been covered with toxic sludge—well, that's the kid's fault, right?" He stopped, a little out of breath, only partly realizing he'd answered something his father hadn't said.

"No, that's not what I think," Charles answered slowly, taken aback by the rush of words and the emotions behind them. "I'm not saying everything every corporation does is good. How could I?" Knowing all too well what could happen, how things go wrong, he gave a sad smile to Benjamin, who was suddenly sorry that he'd made an out-of-place speech.

"No," Charles went on, "I'm just saying that with all the problems and all the mistakes, who else do you think could make all this work? Things could be a lot worse, you know? You could have Russia, run by gangsters. Or Saudi Arabia, where women are like slaves. People like you complain about oil and global warming and pollution, but dammit, the oil is there, and we find it and use it and billions of people have more than they used to have.

"Take that starving kid. Well, that's terrible, I agree. But could his mother, some peasant, could she get the oil out of the ground? And if she couldn't, how could all the people whose lives are better now because they have oil heating in the winter, or buses to get someplace instead of walking, and God knows what else, how could all that happen?"

Benjamin softened at his father's references to his own guilt, and suddenly, to his very great surprise, he wasn't exactly sure what to say. Maybe he'd been working too hard these last months. Maybe, if he had to admit it, the way the wetlands group had fallen apart had really bothered him. Maybe he was just glad, despite everything, to see his father alive and well.

"You know, Dad, sometimes I'm not sure."

An opening, thought Charles. Now, don't rush it.

"What do you mean, son?" He tried to be sympathetically paternal, wise, and understanding but worried he couldn't pull it off.

"I mean . . . I mean that sometimes late at night, when I've been working nonstop for days, weeks, feels like years, and nothing is moving, and we don't win, and people just can't get along with each other, and the other side is so much more together, then I wonder if it will ever happen."

"Did you ever think that this means it wasn't meant to happen? That this is, well, as good as it gets? That there's nothing better than what we have now?"

Charles raised his arm in an expansive gesture, taking in the elegant room, the well-dressed diners, the beautifully presented dishes being served, the sparkling crystal wineglasses filled with French merlot.

"Dad, no, no." Suddenly Benjamin had to stop himself from crying, or shouting. "I see what you think is here, but look at what you're missing." He managed himself by making his tone low and intense, but so much force poured out of his face that an older woman at a nearby table glanced over. "These vegetables are harvested by illegal immigrants living in shacks and choking on pesticides. The people who wash the dishes and clean up can barely live on their pay and have no health care. That filet mignon you ordered comes from an industrial farm that is spreading waste for miles around, taking food to feed cows that could feed people, and putting more greenhouse gases out than all the cars do.

"Sure it's pretty on the outside, some of it anyway. Sure it makes lots of nice gadgets. But it won't last. It can't. It's going to collapse because it's run by greed and power and too many people are suffering too much from it. The poor here and in the third world. Even the people who aren't poor are miserable. I mean," he paused, his voice suddenly soft and gentle, "look at you, Dad."

In a gesture that surprised them both, Benjamin reached over and touched Charles' hand. "Look at you," he repeated softly, with real caring.

Charles felt the caring, but couldn't take it for more than a moment. He moved his hand to take another sip of his martini.

"What about me? I had my problems, sure. I made a bad mistake, don't think I don't regret it. Every day." Every night, was more like it. He still had nightmares of spectacular mansions slipping into an earthquake, exploding into pieces, going up in smoke.

"But I did, as my charming cellmates put it, my *time*. And now that's over."

"No, Dad, you don't get it. *Why did you have to do what you did?*" Benjamin's intensity was back, but there was no anger in it. "You had all the money you needed. I don't cost you anything. You had the house, and the summer house, and a great car, and great clothes, and whatever else you needed. *Why?*"

Charles had no reply. He'd asked himself the same question a thousand times, at least, and never been able to answer it. And he still wanted to, sometimes desperately.

"I don't know," he almost pleaded, as simply and quietly as he could. "You tell me."

"It's the system, Dad, the system. More, more, more. More control, more power, more money, more toys. For the rich, for the middle class, even for the poor, who do it at Walmart instead of Tiffany's. We're all like addicts, crazy for the next fix, and the next, and the one after that. It's killing us, it's killing the earth, and it makes us kill each other—for oil, for land, for markets, for the next really, really, really good deal."

Charles was stunned into further silence. An addict. An *addict?* Like those pathetic hustlers who tried to clean his windshield for a buck, or who stopped him in the street with their ridiculous stories about broken cars and lost airline tickets, pleading, "Gee, if you could help me out with ten dollars and give me your address, I'll send you the money when I get back to Milwaukee." He thought of little Raoul from Smithfield, the crack dealer, who'd once gotten in his face and told him that there was nothing, *nothing* better than that first hit from the pipe. He smoothed his perfectly arranged necktie and looked for reassurance at his nine-hundred-dollar Rolex. He was no addict.

"What nonsense," he said, brushing off Benjamin's words.

"OK, Dad, whatever you say." Benjamin smiled a small, almost bitter smile, thinking that no matter what, his father would just never see it.

"But tell me, Dad, tell me, why?"

"No, Benjamin, you tell me. You call it addiction, I call it progress, change, development, innovation. Tell me what you've got that's better, that will feed more people, give us more freedom and less misery. If some people overdo it, well that's too bad, but it can't be helped. Just because some people are hideously fat, that doesn't mean there's anything wrong with eating, now does it?"

"I've told you before, Dad," Benjamin sighed, then stopped talking as the waiter brought his vegetable lasagna and his father's filet mignon. He started chewing his dish slowly, wondering how they could charge $38.50 for what was basically white flour, some not-very-fresh broccoli and carrots, and a very small amount of cheese. He tried to explain, for the nth time. "You can call it socialism, you can call it real democracy, you can call it sustainability, you can call it feminism, or whatever. But only if we deal with everything can we deal with anything. Rights for women, for the land, for animals; democratic control over industry, over science, over consumption. I know people," he thought of Lily, and of Erica, "who really care about nature, or about their communities of color, and I do too. Only for me it's all or nothing. Fix *it all*—with a group so large, committed, and powerful that nothing will stop us—or everything will stay pretty much the same, even if looks a little different."

Now it was Charles' turn to sigh. "You know your mother, toward the end, started praying again." They both looked down at their plates and chewed harder. Things had been better for both of them before she'd died of breast cancer.

"So?" Benjamin finally asked.

"So you're kind of religious yourself, you know. She thought that Jesus would come down off the cross and make her well, and you . . . you think *they*"—another expansive gesture, but this time aimed at the busboys, the dishwashers, the welfare queens—"can really make a better world than the one made by people like me.

"So, tell me, just *how* do you know this?"

When Benjamin was silent, he pushed on. "Look, son," taking Benjamin's pause as evidence that he'd struck a nerve, "I know you're a decent man." Benjamin looked up. Did he? Did his father know that? "You work hard. I don't know why you do what you do, but God knows you're not lazy. And you're smart. So much smarter than me, it isn't funny. Why, if you went to that MBA program we talked about, in no time you could be earning. . . ." Carried away with the image of his son in a blue suit walking into a huge office building, it took a few moments for Charles to notice Benjamin's amused smile.

"Dad, remember? I'm trying to end capitalism, not become a CEO."

Secretly he was glad Charles had shifted into this old, worthless gambit about going to grad school. Because, if truth be told, he had no answer to Charles' question. How did he know that "the people" could make a better world? That it wouldn't all fall into something horrible like it had in the Soviet Union? Or, with its mix of market optimism and Stalinist repression, what China had become? How did he know that the people of the U.S., or now the middle classes of India and Thailand and all the other nations, that these people wouldn't prefer to choke on their own wastes than really change society into something just and rational—or at least not so insanely self-destructive. So many times the left had risen, and then fallen. So many betrayals, miscalculations, bad decisions. Could people really rule themselves? Or would it always turn back on some elite? How did he know? He didn't.

"All right, Dad. I don't know. Maybe I'm just a believer, like Mom. And you?"

"And me what?"

"How do you know that *this*"—Benjamin's own version of Charles' expansive gesture took in the ethnic wars, the trillions of dollars for the Defense Department, the Wall Street bonuses—"is the best we can have? How do you know that having the U.S. make a war in Iraq to control the oil is really the best energy policy? Or that going to the mall is really the high point of human civilization? Or that the places, and there are some, you know, in Spain, in Scandinavia, in Bangladesh, where people have gotten together, taken some kind of collective, mutually supportive power, and made their lives a lot better—how do you know that's not what the human race should hope for, and not this globalized nightmare?"

Charles didn't answer. He was no fool. He saw the rotting inner cities, the junk that passed as technological innovation and was really a waste, the times the U.S. supported dictators. Was this the best people could do? Could we still have personal freedom and a little more . . . hell, he didn't even know what word to use . . . common sense? He didn't know any more than Benjamin did.

"Bangladesh?" he asked skeptically.

"Yeah, Bangladesh. Pretty solidly organized group of organic farmers. They save seeds, dropped all the chemical fertilizers and toxic insecticides, energized the peasants, work on some local political issues."

"And this," Charles couldn't take it seriously, "is what—thirty-five people educated at Harvard?"

"No, Dad," Benjamin smiled sweetly. He had, thought Charles, a sweet smile. Didn't come out that often, not with what he thought about most of the time. But it was sweet when it came. "No, it's over sixty thousand people."

That stopped Charles, and they both chewed in silence for awhile. After a time the waiter cleared their dishes, and they ordered dessert—Benjamin, allowing himself a rare indulgence, opted for the richest chocolate creation they had, while Charles limited himself to fruit and coffee.

Well, thought Charles to himself, this went better than usual. Advantage of meeting in a nice place like this, Benjamin a lot less likely to fly off the handle and start yelling about capitalist exploiters.

Well, thought Benjamin, he's in better shape than I expected. And at least in this overpriced dump he's a lot less likely to start yelling about crazy communists and their worthless ideas.

Well, they both thought, maybe there's hope yet. He is still pretty lost in his wrongheaded ideas, unrealistic, out of touch. But maybe I'll get him to listen to what I know and see at least a piece of the truth.

Next time.

DESPAIR: IN FOUR ACTS

Buried in the frozen landscape of despair, there is usually a seed of grief.

—Miriam Greenspan

When things are so bad you cannot even recite psalms, just sit and hold whatever it is up to God in silence.

—Rabbi Pinchas of Koretz

Act One: The Group Meeting

One by one they come, carrying their woes—in battered duffle bags, elegant black suitcases, tan canvas shopping bags from Holistic Foods and The Body's Shoppe. Each of them has a story to tell, a reason for the lines of pain on their faces, their hunched shoulders and slow, unsure steps.

They unpack their bags and set their pain near them, like protective walls to keep anyone from getting too close. They look around, taking in each other's presence. Does it make it less lonely that all these people are suffering too? Or does it just multiply the misery? Their own lives in ruins, and all this other suffering they can't do anything about.

"Let's begin," says The Teacher. "Tell us your story. We'll listen. And we'll see what comes out in answer."

Coughs, shrugs, whimpers. All of them feel beaten, angry, bored, unable to think about anything else, even when they aren't thinking about it.

The Teacher starts, almost chanting:

"Life sucks and then you die.

"The First Noble Truth of Buddhism: life is suffering.

"Job: 'Man is born to trouble as the sparks fly upward.'

"Samuel Beckett: An old man on a rocky beach, moving tiny sucking stones from one pocket to the next of his overcoat and jacket and trousers. Over and over and over again. Nothing else.

"And maybe the best, considering the source: 'I am told God loves me—and yet the reality of darkness and coldness and emptiness is so great that nothing touches my soul.' Mother Teresa.

"So, you ain't the first, nor the last. That's what they had to say. What's your story?"

"All right, I will begin." This from Jacob, fresh tears making wet lines down his cheeks, his shining prophet's eyes dulled with grief and uncomprehending loss. "I thought . . . I thought we had something, and now it's all gone. He's left me."

"Who?" The Teacher prompts. "Remember, we're not inside your head."

"Ibrahim. The last round of fighting between Hamas and Israel. The rockets from his side, the tanks and helicopters and soldiers from ours. His teacher, his gentle teacher he loved so much, gunned down by an Israeli sergeant. For no reason. None. It was too much for Ibrahim. He got more and more depressed. And he would start picking fights with me. Over nothing! Until one day he came to me, and put his hand on my arm and looked at me with that gentle sweetness he had, and I thought, 'Great, he's feeling better.' But no, he just said he loved me, and wished me well, but he couldn't think about the soil, and the trees, and the Jordan River anymore.

He was going back to Palestine, to Gaza, to work for Hamas. He would kill Jews until they left his land and let his people have a country. If he had to die, so be it.

"The research we were doing fell apart. I don't know enough to do it on my own. Nobody wants to work with me—I'm too weird"—he gestured at his long beard and side curls, the knotted strings hanging from his ritual undershirt—"only Ibrahim understood me. At the shul people just say, 'What can you expect? An Arab is an Arab—a killer.'" He starts to cry. "If we can't do it, who can? There's no hope. We have betrayed God's trust."

His gaunt body trembles, his fingers curl into impotent fists. "And even that's not the worst—the worst is, I don't know where God is anymore. I thought he had a purpose for me. I know we were just two small people in a big world. But I had faith we could make a difference, fulfilling God's plans. And now? Nothing. No fulfillment. And sometimes I think, no God."

His whole body sags like a wilted flower as the sobs shake him. Silence.

Fred stands up and starts, and stops, and then starts again.

"There isn't anything left of me. It had always seemed that God and I, well, we had our little understanding. I'd give love to the world, just as he did. And he would take care of me. Nothing fancy—a job, a little house, my wife and kids. I didn't want power or fame or more money. I knew that things were hard all over the world, that's why I spent so much time in justice work.

"Why did he have to take my family? Everyone said it was just an accident, a terrible accident. But why, why did they allow that stuff on the highways? Why weren't the safety inspections done better. Why?" His voice is getting lower and lower, clouded with grief.

"My wife's cancer was in remission. My kids were doing better. We had suffered enough, ENOUGH." Everyone starts as his quiet voice shifts to a sudden scream.

Then, in a barely audible whisper, "The things I used to say to my parishioners—'It's a mystery,' 'God is in the comfort and love people give each other,' 'We're only supposed to be on this earth for a short while, make the most of it,' even, 'I'm so sorry, would you like me to sit with you, to pray with you?' This whole *system* I had . . . it's gone. I feel like a fraud, a phony. For years I told people how to deal with their grief, and now . . . I can't."

He turns to Jacob, bitterness burning in each word. "God? I'm sorry my friend, it's just another illusion." Looking up at the sky, almost screaming, "Only you were supposed to be crucified, not any of *us*. And when they did it to you, it was quick. And three days later you came back, good as new." Quiet again, beaten. "Now it goes on forever. And no one comes out of the cave."

Silence.

The Teacher points at Lily, sitting straight backed but so emotionally folded in on herself she looks like she wants to disappear. Or as if she is half into another world already. She gestures at her pain, spread around her in a neat, feminine circle. "See the chairs, and the dining room table, and the vegetable garden, and the living room where we all made music together? See it?" A sudden burst of energy has her standing, and then she stomps down with her foot, crushing the little models into broken pieces. "It's all gone now, The Farm, all gone. Rachel sold it. We woke up one morning and she was gone. Left a note saying how it had all gotten too hard, and that her karma was taking her somewhere else. We had a month to get out, and then the developers would come.

"I just don't know what to do now. It was so . . . perfect . I mean, I know that we had our bad days, our fights about this and that—how to farm, who should do which chores, what we could and couldn't eat. These got pretty bad sometimes, and Rachel was always trying to make peace, to get us to do something else with our anger. And then one time a few of the men turned on her, called her a controlling bitch.

"But, couldn't she have done something else? It was there, and then . . . it was gone.

"Now I'll never have a safe place, never somewhere to live spiritually and try to save the earth at the same time. I'll be alone, always."

She sits back down, arranges herself neatly again, and swallows a few small sobs.

Silence.

Sarah begins slowly, looking down at her hands.

"I'm sorry for all your troubles. Especially you, Reverend. My God, I don't know how anyone could survive that. I'm all right, I mean I'm not, but it isn't as if anything happened to me personally. Or to me individually, at least." She turns up the corners of her mouth in an almost smile, just for a moment.

"It's the world, the earth, everything. So much of life is being lost. The rain forest will be gone in thirty years. Half the coral reefs are dead already. The tribes disappearing, pushed out to make room for oil wells or a huge dam. I cry all the time—on the way to work, on the way home, trying to sleep. It's just endless, and I can't think about anything else. I feel like my family is being killed, over and over."

She looks at Fred. "I'm sorry, Reverend, if that sounds stupid to you. I never was married, no kids. The earth is my family." Fred just stares at her. Not angry, not sympathetic.

Silence.

Richard stumbles in, dragging his troubles behind him in a rolling backpack with a rip on one side and a chipped wheel. He apologizes for being late. Meeting ran over. Problems with the permit for the demo. Not sure the speaker can make it. Too much to do. Sorry. Sorry.

"Well," says The Teacher, neither impatient nor patient. "Even though you're late, you still have to share your story. Let's hear it."

"Me, oh, I'm never sure what I'm doing here. But I guess . . . I mean, the work goes on, right? There's always more to do—send out e-mails, print leaflets, check on the new environmental laws, meet new people.

"But I'm just," he sits down suddenly, sighs heavily. "I'm just so *tired*. Nothing seems to work, or not for very long. I try to get people involved, rally the troops, create something—but they always fall apart. The thing is," he looks around the group, "people don't really like me. And you know something? I don't blame them. I'm boring and stiff and all I can think about is The Movement— change, action, fight back. So I'm fighting, but I'm not winning.

We're not winning. I can't get it right. I'm just a loser, a failure, at the only thing I've ever cared about. It's getting harder and harder to get up in the morning, to make the calls, find the cause, get it done. Each week . . . each day, I'm not sure I'll be able to keep on."

After the last words die out, the plaintive tone in his voice seems to echo around the circle.

"So," begins The Teacher, speaking softly but so clearly they all can hear each word. "A world of despair, in each of your broken hearts. You know it, you feel it. You're not covering it up with work or drink or denial, not expecting some shrink to take it away with the magic meds, not even feeling guilty because you're *supposed* to be chipper and actually you feel like death warmed over.

"That's a good start." She waits. Looks at each one of them.

"Great, just great," Fred's bitterness erupts. "I *know* I feel horrible. Wonderful. But is it enough, I ask myself?"

"Skip the sarcasm, it's a waste of time," The Teacher answers him—not angry, but firm, brooking no nonsense. "I don't blame you for being angry. You've got a lot to be angry about."

She pauses, then asks, her voice neutral, "Does the anger help?"

"Sometimes it's the only thing that gets me up in the morning," Richard admits. "How much I hate the people who are doing these things to other people, to the earth." Sarah nods in quiet agreement.

"Fine," says The Teacher. "And then, when you see that they are winning and you are not, what happens to the anger then?"

"Turns inward," Lily whispers. "I just hate myself for being so weak."

"So maybe that's not really the best answer you can come up with."

"What else is there?" demands Fred, wrapped in his rage like a protective blanket.

"You tell me," counters The Teacher. "All I do is bring you here."

"I don't know," whispers Lily, and they all echo her.

"So you don't know?" They all nod. "Want to find out?" They nod again. "Careful now, are you *sure* you want to find out? After all, there's something comforting about despair. It's a kind of finish, a place where you don't have to do anything, because there's no hope anyway. Could you give that up?"

Nobody says anything for a time. They know she is right. No more hope means no more disappointment. It hurt to hope, hurt like crazy—Lily's dreams for The Farm, Jacob's for his work with Ibrahim, even Fred's simple, ordinary dream that he would see his children grow up. They don't want that hope any more, or the pain that comes when everything crashes to the ground.

But they were still alive, so they had to choose.

They *had* come here, after all. So there must have been something they wanted to do with their pain besides just, well, be in pain.

"Yes, please," begs Fred. "Please. I don't want to feel like this forever." They all nod in agreement, some with more energy than others.

The Teacher looks hard at each of them, testing their resolve, inviting them to change their minds. They stare back, a little more strength in their gaze, as if hearing the others' stories had helped somehow.

"All right. I will help you. But in the end the choice is yours. There is a way out for each of you. I will tell you where to look. But even with my help," she pauses, holding their attention, "it will always be up to you."

"With God's help, and the Goddess, of course." And she laughs.

Act Two: The Search

Why had The Teacher told him to go here? Jacob wonders. It is so desolate. Shapes come into view out of a thick haze of . . . what? Fog, dust, smoke —he can't be sure. And then, over his head, he sees the sign. "Oh *no*, not here. Why do they always send us here?" *Arbeit Macht Frei. Work makes us free.* The sign over the gate that leads to hell. Auschwitz. The darkest hour of his people. Maybe the darkest of all of human history. Or, he thinks bitterly, tied for first. Yeah, tied for first at least, that's for sure.

He's read the histories and the testimonies. He's met survivors, listened to their stories. Hell, this was what Jews *did*. Find out. Remember. Never forgive, never forget. He's seen some

premonition of environmental destruction in the Final Solution—
all that denial that people could really do such things, all those
machines with no conscience, so much power and so little soul.
Even the gas that killed the Jews started out as an insecticide. Kill
one life with no feeling, any life at all, and you'll end up killing
everyone.

Doesn't he know all this?

"Go there," The Teacher had told him, "Go *there*. And see what
you find."

A man comes out of the mist, or is it smoke from burning bodies? "And you? What do you want?" in a gravelly voice tinged with
impatience. He peers at Jacob from under bushy eyebrows, the
hairs jumping in different directions, his face covered by a long
white beard, a dirty yarmulke on his head, his feet, strangely, bare,
and the rest of him cloaked in a long, torn overcoat and striped
pajama pants, the kind you've seen in all the pictures, even in the
Spielberg movie, to give you the sense of "what it was like."

"I was sent here. For help. Please."

"Ach, by that fool of a Teacher? Another one of you? All right,
all right. You all come here looking for something. Faith, hope. A
lesson—God help me—in love. It's not enough that we died here,
that we suffered—you can't imagine it in your worst nightmare, or
if you can imagine it, God help you too. That's not enough. We're
supposed to *teach* you something. As if what we went through
wasn't enough by itself. It's not enough, is it?" He coughs loudly,
spits to the side, glares at Jacob.

"I'm so alone now," Jacob begins. "I know what I have to do,
but I don't see how I can, with my friend gone. I just . . . can't." He
starts to cry.

The man answers—or is he talking to himself?—his voice flat,
unfeeling, impersonal. "I saw my father shot, in the back of the
head, as a whim by some SS guard who didn't like it when my
father looked up at the sun one fine morning in March. We froze
in the barracks all night, froze at the roll call for hours. Then the
sun came out and it was a little warmer. My father looked up just
for a second. The guard didn't like it. 'The sun is not for Jews,' he

said, took out his pistol and put a bullet in my father's brain. 'You,' he ordered me, quietly. That one always talked quiet, and God help you if you didn't hear what he told you to do. 'Clean up the mess.'"

"The mess . . . that was my *father*," the single word carrying pain from this world to the next. "I had loved him more than the world. The guard was looking at me. I picked up his body, and pieces of his head, and carried them off, saying Kaddish for him as I walked. I just tossed my father in the pit with a lot of other bodies.

"For the next month, I don't know how I lived. I got up, I worked, I ate . . . so little I was beyond hunger. But I didn't care anymore. I would just have thrown myself at a guard and hoped I could kill one before they shot me. But I felt so weak that I knew any of those monsters would have brushed me off like a flea.

"And then one day the man in the bunk next to me whispered something in my ear. I had never liked him. He was a Greek Jew, a bit of a gangster, I think. Cruel, selfish. Not a sainted Jewish victim—just an ordinary, nasty schmuck.

"What did he whisper, you want to know. Yes?" Jacob leaned forward. He did want to know. Was this what he had come for?

"Yes. Yes."

The man tossed his head from side to side, "I don't care what you want," said the gesture, "I really don't."

"He told me that as far as he was concerned I could die at any time, he'd just take the shoes off my feet before my body was cold. *But*, if I wanted to, I could help the resistance, the underground." He looks at Jacob. "Do you understand? Even there, even *there*, people would fight back. Smuggle food. Steal things. Help each other. They got a plan going. Bring in tiny bits of explosives, taken from the factory down the road, and blow up something. We had a Russian soldier who knew how to make bombs. We had the women slaves in the munitions factory getting us the powder. But we had to pass it along, pass it along. If we'd been caught—worse than death, I assure you." He smiles a bitter, unfunny smile.

"And?" asks Jacob.

"And," he is answered. Then . . . "And I worked with them. My father was dead, and I had done nothing. This man, a thief, a gangster, *before*. He was my contact. It wasn't important who he was. It was only important that . . . we do something. We had to do *something*. Or we would just lie down and die where we stood."

"And?"

"In the end we killed some guards, blew up a crematorium. And all of us were killed trying to escape. But we did something. And it didn't matter who we worked with. We were in a death camp, it didn't matter.

"Now go back to wherever you came from. Take whatever lesson you want from this." He points at the smoke, the mist, the dust, the sign. And then he disappears.

The sign over the office door says *Seth Miller—Family Therapy: All Kinds of Therapy, All Kinds of Families.* What is she doing here? Lily wonders, but this is where she has been told to go. She walks up the short flight of steps, opens the door, hears wind chimes on the door frame tinkle quietly, and sits down on a saggy black couch. She lifts her index finger toward her mouth, then remembers her mother's "Lily, for God's sake, stop biting your nails. You look like a fool," drops her hand into her lap—and then takes a quick, compulsive nibble of the already well-worn nail.

The walls of the waiting room are covered with posters of mothers. From Manhattan and somewhere in Africa, Rio and Glasgow. Mothers with one kid or a dozen, of all ages. Some smiling, some, from the third world, looking like they'd been ground down into the dirt for years.

"What's the point, what's the point?" Lily mumbles to herself. So mothers had children. Did that mean something?

"What's the point of what?" A conspicuously fat man wearing a brown suit and striped bow tie, absurdly paired with fancy-looking Asics running shoes, comes through a door at the end of the waiting room. Lily can't tell if he is forty or sixty, something about his face keeps shifting in the light. Were those shadows? Or lines around his eyes and mouth?

"Excuse me," she says. "Are you Dr. Miller?"

"I'm Miller, all right, without the doctor. Just a humble coun-selor with a bush-league master's. And a few other things, it turns out. I repeat myself: what's the point of what?"

"I'm sorry, I didn't mean to be rude."

"Never mind that. And your answer is?"

"The point of these pictures. What are they trying to say?

"What do they say to you?"

Oh God, thinks Lily, a *therapist*. Questions answered with questions. Then, at long last, the diagnosis. And the bill.

"They say that women have children and love them. Not like my family." She thinks of the coldness of her house, the money without care, how only nature gave her comfort.

"Really," says Miller. "Really? Perhaps look once again."

Lily looks again; her mouth drops open in shock. The pictures have changed. Instead of the reassurance of mother-child love, they are now images of horror and loss. Here a father rapes his nine-year-old daughter, there a mother stands in front of a bombed-out apartment building, tears streaming down her face and two small bundles wrapped in white sheets in her arms. Here a woman with a monstrously thin infant extends her hand to beg. And then a whole series of courtrooms, legal offices, mediation centers—where rageful men and sullen women glare at each other and their chil-dren sit in the corners in anguished silence.

"Family life, ain't it grand?" asks Miller. A single tear drops from Lily's left eye, runs down her cheek, and drops onto her bit-ten nail.

"Come in, my dear, come in. The waiting room is just, well, a warm-up. No doubt The Teacher would say it was kind of a sick joke, but she never did have much of a sense of humor."

They go into the inner office, and Lily seats herself in a large black recliner, doing her best to keep it upright even while it seems to want to lean back.

"Why are you here?" she is asked.

"Because I lost my family . . . my new family, I mean. My old family? They were just never there for me anyway. But my new family, in a place called The Farm. I thought I would find a new way of life there, someplace safe to change the world and myself. But it turned out to be just like my old family. Fights, and then it all fell apart."

"So, in *this* world, in *this* body, you want a place of safety?"

Lily just looks at him. Isn't that what everyone wants?

"I repeat myself: in this world, in this body, you want a place of safety?"

"Yes. Please. Can you help me find it?"

"Is that why you've come here? Is that what you think I do?"

"Well, The Teacher sent me to you. Why else?"

"Indeed. Why else." Miller strokes his chin, a faraway look in his eyes. "All right, my dear, let's take a little trip."

"Where?"

"You'll see. Or maybe you won't. Well . . . we'll see whether or not you see." Miller chortles at his own wit, while Lily just clasps her hands, wondering what in the world is going on.

Miller takes Lily's hand in one of his, raises his other one over his head with his index finger pointed at the ceiling, and begins making circles in the air. Lily stares at his hand, suddenly trans-fixed by the rapid circular movements of the finger, until the room blurs, vibrates, grows suddenly insubstantial, and is gone.

They are someplace very different—the savannah in Africa. Lily gasps and cries aloud, terrified by the shift. "Don't worry, my dear. This is all perfectly safe. Did you really think you were in an office? This place is no more real than anything else. Of course, no less real either." Miller laughs again. Lily's eyes get wider and wider, she grasps Miller's hands as tightly as she can.

"Oh, never mind all that," Miller tells her. "Look!" A pride of lions is resting at a water hole. Suddenly two of the females, luxuri-ously muscled tawny beasts whose every movement is colored by power and threat, move off to hunt a nearby herd of antelope. They circle until they pick out a slightly lame midsized prey. In moments they bring him down, break his neck, and, after some choice bites for themselves, drag the carcass back to the pride for their cubs.

Miller raises his hand again, makes the circles again, and sud-denly they are underwater, strangely able to breathe. Lily sees a huge gray beluga, nursing her young. After the baby is finished, the two of them are suddenly attacked by sharks. The mother is kept occupied while her infant is torn to pieces.

They shift again and again, to see delicate bushes destroyed by grazing elephants, caterpillars eaten from the inside by wasp lar-vae, AIDS patients coughing out their last hours in hospices, whole forests incinerated by volcanoes, a small fish swallowed—in one quick gulp—by a larger one, and—strangest of all—the last of the dinosaurs, weak and dying in a strangely colder world.

And then they are back in Miller's office, in the waiting room. Lily feels like she has wakened from a crazy dream. She is breath-less, trembling, confused, frightened—and also, she doesn't know why, exhilarated. The pictures on the wall are back to mothers and children, only now they include animals as well as people: wolf mothers and wolf cubs, eagles and their chicks, otters and ants and giraffes, next to images of Eskimos and Ecuadorians and Hungarians.

Lily doesn't even try to make sense of how the pictures change, or how she could possibly have seen what she has seen. She follows Miller back into his inner office, sits down in the black chair, and this time lets it lean her back.

"Nu?" asks Miller. "Did you see?"

Lily has nothing to say. She saw, yes. But what?

"It's so simple, it's always been right in front of you." Miller speaks emphatically, his arm sweeping around in an expansive ges-ture. "But you didn't *want* to see it." Then he holds one hand still, palm facing up in a "what do you expect?" gesture. "I know," his voice turns gentle, almost in a whisper, "I know. I didn't want to see it either.

"There's no safe place. No. Where. We are born to die and decay. Every mountain will be laid low, every whale and wildebeest will live only five or ten or a hundred years—the blink of an eye. This is *life*—not a playground, a fairyland, or a heaven where we go on and on and on and on. It's temporary. After a time, a long time of course, but in time, the earth itself will cease to exist. You don't like it? I don't blame you. You want to cry about it? So cry, cry your heart out. I cry all the time. You want to find someplace where it's *different*? Good luck.

"You think you love the earth? Love it as it is."

"Love it as it is, as it is, as it issssssss . . ." Miller's last words echo in Lily's head as, once again, the walls of his office blur, vibrate, grow suddenly insubstantial, and are gone. This time he doesn't come with her.

"God is dead. God is dead. God is dead." The phrase is repeated over and over. Where is it coming from? Fred wonders. It is sung to a strangely beautiful melody, like something written by Bach and arranged by John Williams, by musicians he can't see. A bright sun illuminates carefully tended lush flowerbeds on either side of the small road on which he walks. There is a sweet freshness to the air.

For some reason he is not fearful or confused. Since his family has died he simply does not care enough about his own life to be afraid, and he is not interested enough in anything to be bothered when things don't make sense. The Teacher had been clear. "You don't believe in God anymore? Fine. Go see what it's like without him. Or her. As the case may be." She'd laughed that annoying smart-ass laugh of hers, and done something with her fingers, and then he was walking down this road.

Suddenly the road turns a corner and other people appear, walking with him, humming along with the music which, oddly, doesn't get louder or quieter no matter how far he walks. Well-built old houses line the road, and in back of them Fred sees soaring trees, different-colored birds swooping low in search of food and then rising on thermal currents to soar high above the tallest branches. In the far distance a range of snow-covered mountains sets the horizon, and before that is a gently meandering river, its banks lined with wildflowers. A breeze ruffles his hair, keeping him at a perfect temperature in the bright sunshine. Smells of roses and lilacs fill his nostrils. With the music; the weather; the views; the pleasant, smiling, friendly (but oddly silent) people, it is just about perfect.

If this is a world without God, that's fine with me, thinks Fred.
I've had enough promises: incarnation, resurrection, communion.
It's all lies.

He turns to a pretty blond women dressed in black slacks and
a thin cotton sweater, her hair cut short to frame a round, pleasant
face, her eyes kind and distant at the same time, "Where are you
going?"

"Going? I'm not going anywhere," she answers, her smile
unchanging.

"But you're walking along here, where do you want to get to?"

"I don't want to get anywhere. I'm fine where I am."

"But where are we?"

"We're here. And we always will be. Where else could we be?
There isn't anywhere else to be, is there?" She broadens her smile,
speeds up a bit, and then gradually fades into nothingness.

Fred turns to another person and has exactly the same
exchange, and the same result. And another. And another.

They are walking along a perfect road in a perfect world, and
they are not going anywhere, he muses. All right. I'll buy that.

And why would you need God in such a world? If it's perfect,
there is no need for God to come and save you. Or comfort you.
There's no pain, no one walks in the valley of death, so who needs
a shepherd?

"All right, you get the point. Or at least half the point. Good
for you." Fred notices, again without shock or fear, since he still
really doesn't care, that he is now inside one of the houses that line
the road. A thin woman who looks to be in her sixties, wearing a
nondescript black dress, small glasses with silver metal frames, and
a large dragonfly-shaped hair clip gathering a full head of gray and
black hair into a ponytail, is speaking to him.

"And you are?"

"Yes, I am. And so are you. And so is God. Or not. That last
one is up to you."

"How can it be up to me?"

"This is simple, but people have been complicating it for a long
time. We bring God into existence by our hope, our *faith*, that life

can be better, that we can be better, that we can *get* somewhere. These people—they have no God, thus they have no place to get to. Your family died, were killed really, I am sorry about that. You don't care anymore. You don't have any place to get to either. So for you, God is dead."

"Look, either there is God or there isn't. It can't be up to me. It just seems to me now that there isn't. But that's not my choice, that's just the way things are. So much pain, so much loss—no God."

"You think God is like that couch?" She points a finger and a rather ugly red couch appears, then disappears, then appears again. "Either it's here or it isn't? Somebody makes it, you buy it at the showroom, then they deliver it to your living room, and," she sings out the phrase, "*ta da*, it's here! Then it gets worn out and you sell it for peanuts and then, *ta da*, it's not here. You think God is like that?"

Fred frowned. He didn't want to think of the God he no longer believed in as being like a couch, but he didn't want the God he no longer believed in to just be a figment of his imagination, either. He suddenly realized he had a terrible headache.

"My head hurts, and I'm having a hard time understanding you. What are you saying?"

"Four words. Write them down on your hand to help you remember. *God is a relationship.* That's it. Pretty simple. If you have a relationship with something, anything, that calls you to life, that asks you to *move* from where you are to someplace better, that calls you to love your neighbor, or pray for rain, or get down on your knees and wail because your family died, or that commands you to get up, get up, get up—you're still alive, don't throw away this gift—if you have that relationship, you have God. Whether it's the God of the Qu'ran or the Bible, or the Buddhist precepts, or someone who tells us that rocks are sacred, or even someone who says he sees a promised land where people love each other, doesn't matter."

"But . . . is God *real*? Did he create the universe? Is Jesus his son? And if he is real, how can he allow all this pain?"

"Not important and I don't know, and vice versa. Not important, because whether or not God is real or just a figment of our overheated frontal lobes, we still have to decide how we will live. God is only real if you hear the call. You think there are teachers without students, that you could be a minister if nobody listened to you? God isn't God without you. You want to move in her direction—or you want to stay in one place, forever, like those nice folks out there?" She pointed out the window at the people who kept walking but were clearly not going anywhere.

"But people who want money, or power, or to pick someone up in a bar, they want to move too. What's the difference?"

"You know the difference. Just like you know the difference between people who are truly called by God and people who are drawn to money or power or sex and *call* it God. Look at how they talk, how they live, how they love, laugh, grieve.

"Besides, and much more important, the question isn't about them. It's about you. Do *you* want that relationship . . . or not?"

"I don't know anymore. I always thought I did. Now I don't. At least, I don't think I do."

"Well, I'll tell you what. You sit here and think about it for awhile. You'll have plenty of time, not like in the real world." And she disappears.

So Fred sits and thinks. As always now, his mind goes back to the day he lost everything. And his daughter's ravaged face on the hospital bed, her small hand clutching his but becoming weaker and weaker until he couldn't feel the pressure on his fingers anymore, and then, it seemed like hours later, but it couldn't have been, could it? someone from the hospital prying his fingers off his daughter, or what was now his daughter's corpse. He thinks of his empty bed, the hole in his heart where his wife had been for nineteen years. He thinks of the silence that greets him when he comes home at night, dragging himself through the front door as he'd dragged himself to work.

And he starts to cry. Oh, he had cried before, but not like this. Not holding any of it back, scared to upset anyone or act too crazy. His stiff upper lip dissolves into unrestrained misery, rage at his fate, at the truck driver and manufacturer, or that awful chemical, and most of all, most of all, at God.

On and on he cries, minutes, hours, days, weeks, years. He ages, and cries, grows old, and weeps, for as there is no measure of his loss, there is no measure of his grief.

Until one day he stops. He has cried enough. And a small voice within him says, "There is work to be done."

"No," he almost shrieks in reply, "my wife, my children."

"I know, they are dead. And you? Are you alive? This is a gift, this life. That's all I can ever really promise you, that you have this gift. Do you want to throw it away? Do you want to lose more than you have lost already?"

Fred pleads with the voice. "If you are real, give me a sign. Let me know. I need to know that something out there is on my side."

"Take a look around, that's all you need to know."

"At what? What do you mean?"

Silence. But then, like a huge movie screen suddenly unfolding in front of his face, Fred sees images—of his wife and children, of hawks streaking toward mice in open fields, of trout leaping for flies in shadowed lakes at dawn, of rock-solid maples turning red and orange in October, of mango trees heavy with fruit in August, of a hundred, a thousand sunsets in orange and pink and purple, of the blue earth spinning in space seen from the moon, and the full moon over jagged mountains seen from earth, of people, all over the blue world, getting up in the morning, going to work, kissing their children, burying their dead, rebuilding bombed-out villages, pushing their parents in wheelchairs, and asking each other forgiveness for the pain they have caused.

"This is all you need, or at any rate it's all I'm giving you. Faith is not a dream of something else, it is your trust in this life.

"Take it . . . or leave it.

"As for your family? They were precious, but they were not the only thing you received. You will always remember them with love. Now it's time to forget."

Fred stands up and walks toward the door. And then he is gone.

Sarah feels like she simply doesn't have enough energy to move another inch. She sits down, slumping against a tree stump, in the middle of an endless field of tree stumps. About a half a mile away she can see the huge bulldozers dragging the chains that will rip even the stumps out of the earth, destroying what little vegetation is left of this brutally clear-cut forest.

Why in God's name has The Teacher sent her here? Another forest eaten by the monster. Pile it on, she thinks, pile it on. Dead trees, dead rivers, dead species. And let's not forget the displaced tribes, the sickened children. And for those of you, she says to an imaginary audience, for those of you who are not tree huggers like me, let's add in the victims of war and terrorism, needless poverty and calculated abuse.

There is no end to it.

Suddenly, right in front of her face, she sees a hummingbird. Its feathers are a brilliant mix of green and blue, and the breathlessly fast motions of the bird's wings keep it, miraculously, exactly in the same place, six inches from her nose.

There are no hummingbirds in these kinds of forests, she thinks. But then, the forest isn't here anymore. She cocks her head, studying the bird, her scientist's eyes trying to figure out what type of hummingbird it is, searching her memory for usual habitat, mating patterns, range of nesting locations.

In an exact mimicry of Sarah, the hummingbird tips its body slightly to the side as well. And then it begins to speak.

"Do you know that hummingbirds weigh about as much as a penny, that we can fly sixty miles an hour and migrate five hundred miles without stopping, and when we are in love, our hearts beat two hundred times a second? Amazing, right?"

Sarah can only nod. What else could you do with a talking hummingbird?

"So ask yourself this," the bird goes on. "Suppose I couldn't talk, couldn't understand you, couldn't see how lousy you feel. Yeah, I know, this is pretty damn strange, like a dream, or something that happens after you take acid, or while you're going nuts. But forget all that, am I or am I not pretty incredible even *without* being a talking bird?"

Again, Sarah can only nod.

"Now you talk," demands the bird. "Say it."

"Yes, oh yes. Even when they don't talk, hummingbirds are incredible. But hummingbirds are under attack. Predators from invasive species, chemicals in their natural food, new viruses from global warming. It's not clear how long they'll last."

"What, you're telling me something I don't know? It's rough out here, that's for sure." The bird turns to look at the bulldozers, then faces Sarah again.

"But that's *not* what we were talking about. I didn't ask you for another long, gloomy song. I asked you: aren't I amazing? And you agreed. Now hold that thought, tight, without anything else, until I come back."

The bird flies off, so fast it's almost like a disappearing act, but Sarah manages to follow its rapid, jerky motion as it aims itself off toward some bushes to her right. She straightens up against the tree trunk and tries to follow the bird's instructions. Amazing, amazing, amazing . . . yes . . . amazing. Strangely, she doesn't follow her usual train of thought from how amazing, to how threatened, to how everything is being lost. She just stays with amazing.

Hours later, a smile on her face, she greets the returning bird. "A*ha*," the bird observes. "You look a lot better—heart rate down, breathing up, immune system improved, posture straighter. Guess what, you're not so depressed. And, guess what, *I'm still an endangered species*." The bird flies closer, so close his wings almost brush against Sarah's nose. "Want to hear a secret, want to hear a secret, want to hear a secret?" The bird chants it like a mantra, or a prayer, or an advertising jingle.

"Yes, yes, yes, yes, yes." Sarah takes up the tune in reply.

"WE . . . ARE . . . ALL . . . ENDANGERED!!!! All of us. All the time. That's just the way it is around here." The bird spins around and around, so fast and so close to Sarah's face that she instinctively jerks her head back. "That's just life, sweetie." The hummingbird chortles, then giggles, then starts to laugh, almost hysterically, thinks Sarah. Spinning around and around, it begins to change shape, and becomes a squirrel, an owl, a dolphin, a praying mantis, an architect, a nursing mother, an ibex, a grieving soil ecologist, a litter of kittens, an indigenous shaman from Borneo fighting to protect his land, a golden retriever, a soldier in Iraq—American or al-Qaeda Sarah can't tell—a nine-year-old picking over the garbage dumps in Rio, an old woman with Alzheimer's abandoned in a back bedroom, one of the last of an endangered species of whale/fox/osprey/hummingbird . . . until it gets smaller and smaller, and then, with a slight hissing sound, it disappears altogether.

Life, thinks Sarah. Life, life, life. That's all there is.

Enough, enough, enough.

Enough. And so she returns.

Richard is lost in the forest. Strange, he thinks, the forest is the one place he almost always feels at home. It is people who make him feel lost, no matter how much effort he puts into getting them to take up the cause and fight the fight. He remembers a story. Deep in the wilds of Ecuador an anthropologist is studying the language of a tribe in the rain forest. To find their word for "wilderness," he asks one of them, "Suppose you were in the forest, and you were lost. What would you call the place you were in?" The native looked at him, uncomprehending. "If I was in the forest, I wouldn't be lost."

Well, thinks Richard, I'm in the damn forest, and I'm sure lost.

He can't even remember what The Teacher told him to find. Home, was that it? How can he find home in the wilderness? Oh, he loved the woods, all right. But wasn't home supposed to have *people* in it? Outside of his sister, he'd never felt comfortable with anybody. After she'd died, and his parents had split up, and his mother had gotten really depressed, there wasn't anything that even looked like home. So mainly he'd hung out in the woods, and when he got old enough to figure out what was what, decided to try to save what had saved him. If people didn't care about him, it didn't matter.

But home, *home*, where was it, what could it be?

The forest thins a bit, and Richard sees a man walking toward him. There is something familiar about him—the worn jeans, the brown flannel shirt, red checked bandana across his forehead, scruffy beard, tousled black hair with a bit of gray at the temples. Richard is sure he knows this guy, but for the moment he can't place him.

The man stops in front of Richard, looks him up and down without speaking, and extends his hand in greeting. They shake hands.

"Can you tell me where I am?" Richard asks, a note of fear in his voice.

"Can *I* tell *you* where *you* are?" the stranger repeats, emphasizing the words to make it sound ridiculous.

"Look," says Richard, "I'm lost. Can't you help me?"

"Can't you help yourself?"

"I've tried. I've tried. Over and over, but nothing works." Suddenly Richard isn't talking about the forest, but about his life. How his organizing efforts haven't born fruit, how they all fall apart, how he never feels like anything he does works, how he wants to give up.

"I see, I see," the man murmurs. "Take another look at the forest, and maybe you'll see something now."

Richard does, and the strangest thing happens. His face is on every tree trunk. He looks back at the man, and suddenly realizes why the man looks so familiar—the pants, the shirt, the bandana, the beard—they are all his. The man is him.

"Why. . . . How . . . ?"

"Simple," comes the answer. "*Your* work, *your* hope, *your* effort—it's one big you. When it's all desperation, of course things don't come out right. And when it's all desperation, and it doesn't work, of course you feel like giving up.

"If you can't see something else but your own pain and need, you'll be in this forest forever. Or you'll just leave the forest, and stop caring."

"But what else am I supposed to see?" Richard demands. He truly doesn't understand. "I'm here for the woods, the wildlife, what else is there?"

"Figure it out. Or die. Even if you are alive." The man walks off at a fast pace. Richard calls after him to wait, stop, help him understand. But he just keeps walking until he disappears in the woods

Too deep for me, Richard thinks. At least right now. But I'll keep looking. There must be an answer out here somewhere. And if I can't figure it out, well, then there was a job at his cousin's Lexus dealership. He'd give organizing a rest for awhile. He couldn't be blamed if nothing he did worked. He was tired of trying, tired of explaining to people what needed to be done, tired of waiting for them to come around to seeing it his way. Tired, tired, tired. Let somebody else carry the load. He would just stop thinking about the world and take care of himself, make a little money for a change, get a decent car and a nice apartment, maybe have some time for a social life. He deserved it.

Act Three: The Return

They are back. Some of them, anyway. On the beach there are gentle waves, and small, multicolored stones. It reminds Sarah of an island in Greece where by some fluke of geology the entire beach was covered with brightly colored rocks, so filled with splashes of color that anyone might have thought they'd been made by people. All the tourists, herself included, had prowled the beach with their heads down, stuffing amazing stone after amazing stone into their pockets and backpacks.

The Teacher stands next to a large fire made of driftwood, warming her hands and nodding for them to join her.

They come: Sarah, Lily, Fred, Jacob.

"Where's Richard?" asks Lily, concerned. She'd never really liked Richard—he was, well, just too hard, too (she hated the word, but it fit) pushy. But still she worries about him.

"Oh, he's not coming back here," The Teacher answers, a reassuring smile on her face. "But he's all right. I mean, he isn't all right, but it's not because something happened to him. It's just that who he is, is not all right—not for himself, I mean. If he wants to, he can come here. Anytime."

"And now what?" asks Fred.

"Now what? You tell me."

They look at each other, trying to fight through the silence. Then, with strained, halting words, as if she is practicing a new language, Lily begins.

"I learned, I think I learned, anyway, that there is no safety. No. Place. And that dream I had, that I could find somewhere perfectly safe to be and love the earth at the same time, I see now, that was always impossible. I love the earth because it's beautiful, and it holds me, holds all of us, really. But what I love is fragile, and temporary. And *not safe*. And other people? I can't make them safe, either. Yet all those families I saw, they weren't safe, but they had some love in them anyway. And because I know that—it's really funny when you think about it—I don't have to be so scared: of what's happening now, of the future. Even," her sudden smile is quite beautiful, "of people yelling at me. I'll be able to listen to them, and respond, because I'll know it's just part of . . . well . . . life."

"Very good, Lily, very good," The Teacher says softly. "Just remember: even though none of us can be really safe, there's no need to take foolish chances. You know what I mean: wear a sweater, take an umbrella it case it rains, don't make friends with abusive men, and above all—take your vitamins." She says this with such deadpan seriousness that Lily doesn't know how to reply, then they all burst into laughter, Lily included. It feels good to laugh, it really does. She hasn't been able to laugh for a long time. None of them have. Even Fred has a smile on his face.

"Keep in touch. Or not," says The Teacher. She waves her hand casually, and Lily disappears.

She turns to Jacob. "And you?"

"I can't wait for a special friend. Things are just too bad. People in the Holocaust . . . they couldn't pick and choose their comrades. I can't either. I figured something else out as well, and this is so two opposite things at once it sounds crazy. On the one hand," he raises his right hand and extends his fingers, shaking them a bit as he does so, "it doesn't matter what I feel. So I'm different from other environmentalists or other Orthodox Jews, if that makes me scared and a little lonely, it's not really important. I can talk to people and listen, learn from them and work with them, even if I'm scared and lonely.

"And even if what I'm trying to do for the earth all feels hopeless, well that's not really so important either. I mean, what was more hopeless than Auschwitz? But we remember what they did, and it comforts us. They couldn't know if anything they tried would make this much," he holds his thumb and index finger a quarter inch apart, "difference. But that didn't stop them.

"And so everything, I feel, really isn't important. And yet," he raises his other hand and extends the fingers, "at the same time, my love for God's creation, for my tradition, and my grief for all that's been lost . . . I need to listen to what those feelings are telling me, and to honor the messages. And do something.

"Both at once, you know what I mean?"

"Indeed I do," The Teacher answered. "And besides, given who you are, I suspect you'll find some other friends, maybe where you least expect to. Life is full of surprises, not all of them terrible. Goodbye, Jacob." She waves again, and, like Lily, Jacob disappears.

"I guess I'll go next," says Sarah, first looking at Fred with wordless sympathy. "All these years—being smart, being a top student, doing research—as much as I loved the natural world, I thought I could stand apart. I could understand everything, and make it heal the way I wanted.

"Now I see that I can't. *We are all endangered.*" She giggles. "Hell of a message to get from a tiny turquoise bird, don't you think?" The Teacher waits calmly. Fred looks up with interest, realizing that he wasn't the only one who'd had a pretty strange experience. "And it's the people too. They are as endangered as any bird. Even if we're doing it to ourselves."

"So?" asks The Teacher. "What does that tell you?"

"Just do the work. Love the beauty, cry for the dead, and do the work. Love, work. Work, love. And listen to what other people are saying—because after all, they are just as endangered as I am. Like it or not, we're all in this together. Maybe I need them as much as they need me—or maybe just a little bit, anyway.

"If I can keep all this in mind, I don't have to be so afraid of what's coming next. It," she raises both arms over her head and opens her arms in an expansive gesture to the sky, as if she could embrace the whole world, "was never going to be *forever* anyway. Maybe it's enough that it ever was."

She walks over to The Teacher with words of gratitude, kisses her on the cheek, waves at Fred, steps over an imaginary rock into an imaginary abyss—and is gone.

"And then there was one," The Teacher whispers to herself.

"Leaves me, I guess," says Fred with a small, but real, smile. The Teacher just looks at him. "I'm not a bad guy, I don't think." The Teacher nods. No argument from her. "But somehow all those years of work for other people—supporting people in my congregation, organizing for political refugees from El Salvador, or victims of environmental racism in Dallas—all those years I didn't think it would be me. I was safe, I was the helper, not the one who needed help.

"I had chosen God, and God would protect me, and give me strength, and let me do his work. It was a beautiful friendship. But now I know the truth."

"Ah," nods The Teacher, "the truth, nothing like it."

"The truth is that God didn't make any special promise to me that I'd be spared. I'm just as vulnerable as everyone else. Oh, I know I'm a middle-class American, so I'm a lot less likely to get arrested by the secret police or starve to death or die in a hurricane. But I can still be hurt in a thousand ways. I understand something about pain now, and hopelessness, and the rage that can't go anywhere. I understand a little bit what all the victims of injustice I've been talking about for years feel like. I'll be better at what I do—a little less entitled and quietly arrogant, a better listener.

"Does all that insight make their deaths worth it?" He looks at the sky and shakes his fist, and yells a rebellious "*No, no, a thousand times no.*"

"But," his voice and his fist drop down, "what can you do?"

"You can do a lot," answers The Teacher, "if you want to."

"Yes, and I do. I still want to move, with love, toward something better. I still care, even if my heart has been shattered. So I must still believe in God."

"Heart has to break," The Teacher is whispering again, "that's how the light gets in."

"Well, I guess I will have plenty of light," Fred responds, "because I know I'll always be broken. And when I meet my Maker, we'll have some words to share. But right now, it's time to move."

He nods at The Teacher, crouches down into a low squat, and then, to her great surprise and no small delight, leaps straight up into the air . . . and is gone.

Act Four: Are Human Beings Worth It?

Back here, The Teacher is a man, a college professor, who writes papers on, of all things, environmental ethics, and once in a while is asked to give a talk somewhere. He is a decent speaker, but has a terrible habit of waiting until the last minute to prepare.

Preparing for this particular talk was very hard. He was tired of giving pat answers to difficult questions, tired of acting like he wasn't a part of the problems he was writing about, tired of having to pretend he wasn't emotionally involved in the fate of the earth, or that any real answer had to avoid something spiritual, or that sometimes he didn't feel downright lousy about being part of the human race.

So here he is at a conference on humanity and sustainability, or something like that, talking about, well, whatever the formal title, he is really talking about the value, the worth, of human beings, and how to face the shame, guilt, and despair we feel when we look at ourselves.

I had a devil of a time, he begins, *figuring out what to write for this talk*. At first, it seemed so easy: describe what we are doing to nature, including to ourselves, and see if in my own small way, my own miniscule way, really, I could encourage us to stop it. After all, once you have read about the continent-sized mess of plastic junk called the Great Pacific Garbage Patch, or find out that babies are born with a hundred toxic chemicals in their blood, after that, well, you don't need much more, do you? Perhaps all that's really needed—or justified anyway—is a blank piece of paper, with or without a long scream.

But the conference organizers would be upset if that is all I came with; and my department chair would surely wonder why I missed class if all I did was scream. Though when you think about it, if that is what is most appropriate, why wouldn't it be acceptable? Or, perhaps it is part of the problem that it is not acceptable to scream, when that is what is most called for.

The other thing that kept giving me pause, that always gives me pause, is that even though being preachy and self-righteous has, shall I say, a certain appeal, it is kind of hard to pull off. At least when, even though I live pretty close to the conference, I drove here, thus making my own contribution to things like global warming.

So if by getting "us" to stop it I really meant "get other people to stop it while I continue to live in the same old way," that seemed not really very morally authentic. And if by getting "us" to stop it I included myself, then I might start by not coming here at all. But what kind of conference paper would it be that I wrote not to present at the conference? There would be a certain rough justice in it, no doubt, a kind of logic that a time of things like the Great Pacific Garbage Patch might warrant, but in terms of actually communicating something it surely wouldn't have worked at all. Then again, I could have walked. But that would have taken a fairly long time, and interfered with my other responsibilities (as professor, father, husband, etc.). And, to be honest, it also might have interfered with some of my pleasures as well—walking my dog, listening to Beethoven, playing Half-Life 2. But probably my pleasures aren't that important morally, not with everything that is at stake.

You see why I was having so much trouble.

It got so bad, I couldn't sleep. So last night (very early morning, really) I called a rabbi friend of mine. He has insomnia all the time, because he worries a lot—about what God could be doing when the world is in such rough shape, and whether or not the people

who are putting it in such rough shape have any right to ask that
question. Things like that.

"Come right over," he said. "Maybe I can help."

Rabbi Solomon's study was brightly lit for 4:45 a.m., overflowing with books, magazines, and newspapers, an enormous bulletin board covering an entire wall. On one side were sayings from
the Talmud, and Levinas and Martin Buber—about how saving
one person is like saving the world, how a person's face calls to
us morally before we know anything about them, and how we can
treat other people like objects or like, well, people. These quota-
tions indicated how much effort many, many human beings have
expended trying to understand what it means to be a decent person, to be thoughtful, compassionate, empathic, loving.

On the other side of the bulletin board were a hundred news
clippings from the *Times* and *Newsweek* and dozens of Web sites, all
of which indicated in excruciating detail the ways in which human
beings were quite busy treating each other like objects, not noticing each others' faces, and not even saving one person. Story after
story made you wonder why on earth people existed at all. Murders
and rapes and tortures, repressive governments killing dissidents,
drones killing civilians, terrorists terrorizing the innocent, drug
lords (this one even I had a hard time believing) killing twenty people at a drug rehab, the unbelievably rich happily coexisting with
the desperately poor. And throughout it all, the desperate plight of
the environment—poisoned rivers, polluted seas, carcinogens in
building materials, genetically engineered flies with eyes all over
their bodies, and lots of coal. Rabbi Solomon lived with the contrast between these different sides of the bulletin board. It was in
the struggle between the two, he often said, that he found God.

I told him my problem. "Ah," he murmured, stroking his beard
pensively, "I think I see what you are going through. It's not totally
unlike the Problem of Evil, but of course it is we human beings who
are, you might say, on trial."

"Where is our pride when we examine our history?" he mumbled to himself. "Endless centuries of war, cruelty, and waste."
Then he looked up at me and smiled quietly: "What's the one thing

all religions, and almost all secular philosophers, agree on?" I was used to Solomon suddenly posing a seemingly unrelated question. He was a master of rhetorical misdirection. But given the time of night and the fact that I was really nervous about having a paper for this conference, I gave him some offhand truism about the Golden Rule, compassion, and moral universality. He dismissed these clichés with a wave of his hand. "No, no," and he smiled at me, a little sadly. "They all agree that *they* have the moral answer, that *they* know what they are talking about, that *they* know about wisdom and goodness." He closed his eyes. "They all agree on that, and yet look how they live."

He was quiet for some time, for so long I began to wonder if he had dozed off, but then he jumped up with the rabbinic eagerness of someone in search of exactly the right text, and started looking for a particular book. Moments later he waved it triumphantly over his head. "The little-known midrash—you know the term, right? Sort of an imaginative spiritual story—of Rabbi Leopold Brower, who worried about the same sorts of things as this conference of yours—that and the rules over blessings. Just listen to this." And he began to read:

THE FISH, THE TRIAL, AND THE DEFENSE ATTORNEY:
AN ENVIRONMENTAL MIDRASH

Once upon a time there was a fish. After all, why not a fish? And the fish put human beings on trial. For the fish was fed up—with the oil slicks that killed the seabirds, the underwater noises that confused the whales, the ten million sharks killed each year (while people talked about how dangerous sharks were), coral dying from global warming, and species after species of fish just, well, fished out. The great fish contacted some brethren on land (never mind how he contacted them, he just did) and found out that things were even worse there. Dying forests, mice created to get cancer, frogs born with their organs outside their bodies. All from what human beings were doing.

So the fish gathered lots of other animals together and charged the human race with ecocide. They pulled in some Great Man, whether it was a professor or a doctor or an industrialist or a president, I'm not sure (probably not a housewife, I shouldn't think, but who knows?) and listed all of humanity's crimes against nature. Starting thousands of years ago with the salination of Babylonia's fields from overirrigation, to native peoples killing large animals in North America, to European deforestation, Indian deforestation, Latin American deforestation, African . . . well, you get the idea.

And then down to the worst charge of all—"Which is," said the Fish, "that now you cannot plead ignorance any more. You know what is going on. From little kids with their Earth Day field trips to the businessmen to the scholars to the politicians to the plain citizens. You know, and you're not doing much about it. A little, but not much. You will not change your ways because you just want what you want—money, power, pleasure, your precious family welfare, your truly gross national products. And whatever happens to us (here he gestured to a fox serving as judge, assorted small mammals in the jury, a few representative plants, dolphins, the odd microbe, and so forth)—you don't care.

"So I accuse you—of willful blindness, of inexcusable negligence and shortsightedness, of forfeiting your right to survive. Take your higher intelligence, your spiritual aspirations, your art and religions and political systems, and go into oblivion. You are an evolutionary experiment that has turned the whole earth into one despairing killing field. Go, and slaughter us no more."

The representative man sat there and took it, head bowed, tears running down his face, hands trembling. When it was his turn to reply, there was little he could say except an endless round of excuses—struggle for survival, love of family outweighs other factors, importance of national pride, addiction to consumption, shortsighted confidence in technical powers, rough childhood leads to authoritarian personality types—and an even more endless round of apologies. "We have sinned, we have done wrong. Please forgive us. You have all been so generous to us, given us so much beauty and so many resources. And we have been such fools. But we are learning. There are environmental organizations, laws, international environmental treaties. We're working on global warming. Please give us another chance."

"Sit down, you idiot, and stop apologizing," hissed a thin, narrow-faced, gravelly voiced man in a black suit who, the court realized, was listed as "associate counsel." "You don't win criminal cases by whining about how sorry you are. You win by making your accusers into the accused."

"Ahem," he began slowly, clearing his throat as he rose. "Of course, of course," he appealed to them in a mild, almost ingratiating tone, "we have done all these things to the earth community. In a sense, we are guilty as charged." Murmurs of assent run throughout the courtroom, along with a few mutters of "Execute him," and "Let them die."

"But if we are guilty, what are you? Are you not as guilty as we . . . if not more?"

"Preposterous," muttered much of the jury, except perhaps the microbes, rats, and mosquitoes, who sensed where this might be heading.

"Explain yourself," commanded the judge.

"All our technology and science—where do you think they came from? They came because you were killing us! We saw our children die of starvation and our women in childbirth, a third of Europe fell from one stinking germ in the Black Plague. You ravaged our gardens and infected our wounds.

"You're not really upset because we kill so many of you." His voice had turned rich with sneering sarcasm. "You're just mad because we are so much better at it."

After a stunned pause, a series of shouts and denunciations rang out in the courtroom. "Nonsense," "Madness," "You're the one on trial here, not us!"

"Very clever," responded the fish, "but you know that this is not what it is about. Of course we are all engaged in the struggle to survive. But it is a balance, a cycle. We kill and eat. We are killed and we are eaten. Our wastes are someone else's food. Our dead bodies are someone else's homes. We kill within reason, within natural law. We don't kill to create empires. We don't have to prove our manhood by shooting wolves from helicopters or get insanely wealthy by slaughtering ten million chickens a year. We do what comes naturally. And it worked. Until you came along."

"Baloney," replied the associate counsel. "Whatever do you think you mean? It makes no sense to say that you 'all' get nourished, because so many of you are dying every second. How many organisms are consumed in one instant on the earth? How many salmon did you rip to pieces last year, Mr. Bear? How many caterpillars were eaten from the inside out by your larvae, Ms. Wasp?"

The whole courtroom seemed on the verge of chaos, as the mosquitoes and bats, salmon and bears, caterpillars and wasps starting shouting at, and then threatening, each other.

"Quiet," barked the fox, showing his teeth and swishing his tail angrily. "Do you purposefully misunderstand?" he said to the human. "Or is this some cheap courtroom trick you learned in Philadelphia? It is not the individual that is the key in an ecosystem, it is the species. The 'all' that gets nourished is 'all the species,' not each individual one of us. It is a complete, a total, a perfect system."

"Then," the man's voice rising in theatrical triumph, "I accuse the sys tem. This thing you call evolution, or life, or nature—how many species has it killed? Of all the types of life that ever lived, how many are gone forever? We humans are killers, there is no doubt. But nothing the human race has ever done, nothing it ever will do, can compare with what life does on its own. 'All the species nourished?' Tell that to the dinosaurs. It is not human beings who consign you to death, it is the nature of existence itself. Life . . . is simply death.

"I rest my case."

A horrified silence spread over the courtroom. No one, from the jabbering monkeys to the wise and placid whales, had anything to say.

"Oh Philip," called a gentle, laughing female voice from the back of the room. "Well done. But you know of course you don't mean it. It is all a lot of talk."

Philip, the look of glee fading from his face, turned and faced the woman. "Mother, what exactly are you doing here?"

"What a show!" she replied. "I wouldn't miss it for the world. But here's the point. Life is a beautiful, creative, and destructive process. But there is no Designer behind the scenes who is responsible for what it does, so you can't 'accuse' it of anything, least of all being murderous. It would be like asking your kitchen cabinet to vote for mayor. The same thing with all these folks. Although they are all quite, quite brilliant at being themselves (ever tried to use human intelligence to be a bat or a squid?), they are practically no good at morality. Except for a few very basic examples, and none that involve conversation, or reasons, they simply are not part of the moral universe.

"So you see, the point is that since we alone have a moral intelligence, we alone can be asked about our behavior. And when we are asked, all these generalizations about how evolution kills species or bats eat mosquitoes are quite beside the point. It would be like saying it is all right for me to spit up on the table because my infant does it.

"And so the question for human beings is, do we meet our own moral standards? Are we wasteful or careful? Generous or stingy? Mature—or grasping, quarrelsome, addicted teenagers?

"Only we can answer those questions. And only our proper shame, our reasonable guilt, and the final realization that waste, stinginess, violence, and compulsive pleasures won't make us happy, will ever lead us to anything else. For it won't be a court of animals that condemns us, but ourselves. Either in one giant cataclysm or in a long, slow apocalypse of pollution, war, emotional depression, and spiritual suicide.

"Come on, Philip, and Mr. Defendant, let these folks get back to making honey, eating rabbits, and growing leaves. And let us get on with trying, bit by bit, to become more human."

The people left. Everyone else left as well, feeling a strange combination of comforting satisfaction and cold doubt.

Only two dolphins remained.

"Very eloquent, that woman," said one.

"Indeed," said the other. "But did you notice how she made the whole thing about them? Their future, their moral development? Their guilt and their hope?"

"Oh well, they always do that. That is as far as they've come."

"Can they do any better?"

"God alone knows."

And then suddenly, magically (it's a midrash, after all), they were transported to the warm waters between Spain and Morocco.

"Isn't it nice to be back?"

"Better than ever."

"Now . . . where were we? . . . Ah, I remember: who's for lunch?"

"That's it?" I asked Solomon.

"Of course that's it," he replied. "What else should there be?"

"But what does it add up to?" I persisted, still somewhat desperate, though a little tired, considering it was about 5:30 in the morning.

"What does it add up to? Didn't you get the point?" He demanded.

"I guess not," I mumbled.

"Look. You go to your conference, you read the midrash. You'll say something, and someone else, they'll also say something. That is what conferences are for. And books too. And that is OK. And if it all helps a few people to be a little kinder, a little more responsible—well, that's fine. Maybe somebody will join Greenpeace; maybe you'll ride your bike more often. Excellent. But do you really think they will do those things because you made a good argument? Is that what they need to hear—more brilliant points from you? Do you think," he asked, scratching the faded numbers on his wrist, "that we could have argued Hitler out of killing my family? No, my friend, I don't know *how* it works, but I do know that it *doesn't* work like that. It is something else we listen to, if we are really listening, some other kind of voice that touches us. The change you want—it isn't because we hear a really good argument, even one with a really good footnote." We both laughed, me a little ruefully. I have been known to say that anyone can write a book, but a good footnote is something special.

"Now I must go to pray to the one who created all this. He may know what you're supposed to say, but he's not telling. He's leaving that up to you." He chuckled and ushered me out the door.

Dawn was just beginning, a faint pink reflection in the eastern sky. I was struck by how beautiful it was and, not for the first time, what a miracle it is that we live in a world with colors. After all, we probably could have managed with just black and white and gray. Purple irises, red cardinals, yellow-striped angelfish—are just something that got tossed in as extras.

It was then that I remembered something else, something which seemed to fit with the midrash, though it really was totally different. It was a character from Dostoevsky's novel *The Brothers Karamazov*, a beloved spiritual teacher, talking about his own moments of spiritual awakening from a dissolute and violent life. "This earth," he taught, "could be a paradise. We could wake up tomorrow and it would all be perfect. We could be truly happy, and truly loving. If only we wanted it badly enough and really believed. A paradise."

In other words (like the rabbi said, there are always other words), it does not have to be like this. We know enough to do better.

So in the end, it is not a scream I am offering you, it is a kind of prayer. And if that is not right for academia, well maybe that is also part of the problem.

Rebenu shel olam is a Hebrew term for God, usually translated as "master of the universe." Some read it as "master of the mysteries." Is there a greater mystery than the human heart? As a source of pain, it confounds our understanding. And yet sometimes it turns to something beautiful, filled with so much love it makes us weep with joy.

Let our hearts ask, "*Rebenu shel olam,* what have we done, and what are we doing?" Let us question ourselves as much as we question the mystery, or other people, and listen for answers with humility and care, and there is a chance we will get somewhere, and then the dolphins would say, "Look, they are doing better." So my prayer is that we ask about ourselves in that way. Whether we are addressing God, or Goddess, or the great mystery and miracle that there is life and we are part of it, let us ask, "*Rebenu shel olam,* in God's name what have we done, and what are we doing?"

If that is how we ask, and how we listen for an answer, surely, surely, we can hear something that will help us change our ways.

FEELING LEFT OUT?

Those were Samuel's stories. My first reaction was, not bad, as such things go. I mean, they weren't really *philosophy*, but they did touch on some good points along the way. If he hadn't put in all those details about this one's unhappy childhood and that one's neurosis, he would have had a lot more room for serious arguments.

But the more I thought about the stories, the more I began to wonder if I wasn't missing the point, or a whole lot of points. So I did something a little out of character—I asked for help. I wanted to see if other people—people different from me in lots of ways—could see some things I hadn't.

I started with Elizabeth, a therapist who is a good friend of my wife. I'd helped her son get into college, so she owed me a favor. Liz is in her late fifties, a tall, slender woman with a beautiful head of straight, silvery gray hair, deep gray eyes, and a wise smile, who looks the very image of a shrink. She always wears long, flowing skirts, and earth-toned tunics, and necklaces with spiritual jewelry. I imagine that if Lily got it together later in life, she'd look like Liz.

Liz had been one of the heavy-duty radical feminists in the 1970s, the kind who would talk about patriarchy in every other sentence and say that this time they were "going all the way, no turning back," meaning male power was going to be overthrown once and for all. Over the years, some of her politics had taken a spiritual turn, so now she talked about the Great Mother, and how women's wisdom could save the planet, along with how violence against women was the norm of male society. For her, women's power meant that love and intuition would take the place of political domination and detached science, and we'd stop raping the earth and start loving our Real Selves, not our programmed consumerist selves. Liz was pretty smart, but she didn't talk a lot about day-to-day political issues. She would just look at you, with a lot of focus and empathy, and tell you to try to get in touch with your True Self. Once in a while you could hear her muttering under her breath how the kind of work women did—mothering, caregiving, looking after grandpa and the new baby and the sick—got no respect, but that every stupid thing men did was honored.

That's the sort of person Liz was.

So I gave her a copy of the stories and asked her to tell me what she thought. About two weeks later she called me.

"Well, I've read them all, some of them twice. He's searching for something about communication, and listening, I can see. That guy Richard, he seems to be onto something at the end of chapter 3, something about the relation between lack of certainty and fear, and coming across like you're sure you're right when deep down you're terribly afraid because you know you aren't. It was just touched on in chapters 6 and 7, but not nearly enough. Too bad that wasn't developed more.

"And the character Lily, she seems to know a little bit about talking to people, and listening, even to people she thinks are wrong.

"But the rest of them? Dearie me, they are so—you might not like this—but it's so obvious. They are so *male*. 'Listen to *me*, I'm right, you're wrong, believe what I believe.' Win the point, win the argument, win *something*. There's so little empathy in the stories, so little attempt to understand the other person. That *is* the way men talk. And it's one reason the world is in such bad shape. Where's the search for common ground? For mutual understanding? For something besides 'who is right'? Where's a woman's voice?"

I was a little surprised to hear this. There had been some moments of empathy and mutuality in the stories, after all. And didn't they all point in that direction even if they didn't say so directly? Had she really read them—or did something set her off and she was just seeing what she always saw? But I didn't say that, I just pointed out a few things.

"Look, Liz, isn't it true that women, when they get involved in political or moral arguments, are as male as you say men are? I mean, think of Hillary Clinton, right-wing personalities like Ann Coulter and Laura Ingraham—the women who write for a liberal paper like *The Nation* or a conservative one like *Commentary*. And when different types of feminists go at each other, they don't sound any more conciliatory or empathic than men do."

"Of course, women can adopt a male style," she answered impatiently, as if this was so obvious it didn't need to be said. "Women can be contract killers, bomber pilots, and CEOs. Just like men. Rah. But that's not what I'm talking about."

I tried again: "Well, maybe women who are just in the family, or among friends, can be more empathic than men. But once it's politics, all that changes, and gender doesn't really matter anymore."

"There is no place," she replied, a little coldly, "where gender doesn't matter. Not in this world. And probably not in the next as well. If you really want to understand what I'm saying, we can try this again some other time. But I've got a client now. Take care, Roger."

I put down the phone, thinking, well, it's no surprise. She's a therapist and not a political theorist. Her position was really weak. Too much of a generalization about women, too little knowledge of how women actually functioned in political life.

A few hours later, though, I had a nagging doubt. Had I really listened to her? Or had I just done what I always do when someone says something I don't like—ask critical questions designed not to learn something but to prove them wrong? Was that just what she was talking about?

Next time I see her, I'll ask again.

Then there was Joseph. He was a professor. In his early sixties. Very accomplished in nineteenth-century religious history. We'd become unlikely friends after being on the same panel at a conference on disability issues. We were both fathers of disabled daughters, so despite the fact that I'm so far to the left that I occasionally fall off the planet and Joseph is a not particularly moderate conservative Republican, we were able to share our experiences about doctor's appointments, unusual treatments that don't work, the effects of our daughters on our marriages, and how we feel about other people's more or less normal children. Acquaintances who knew us both could never figure out what two such different people were doing together, having dinner in some conference hotel, laughing like hell at a joke about how we handled our daughters' menstrual cycles.

We never, almost never, anyway, talked about politics or moral issues beyond the basics. We could agree on honesty, love, respect, and vague human rights. But when it came to abortion, corporate power, American foreign policy (certainly not *that* one), single-payer health insurance, or how important it is to resist human-caused climate change, we were worlds apart. Not to mention gay marriage.

So I asked Joseph. After all, the whole point of the stories was to see how people who were very far apart politically and morally could talk to each other. I thought Samuel had done a good job on that, but I wasn't sure.

We met for our once-a-year dinner at the big conference of professors of religious studies. After a little small talk, I looked at him expectantly. "Well?"

"Well . . ." he hesitated, which was unusual. Joseph was a wiry little guy with a sharp tongue and no dearth of opinions. If you asked him what he thought, he usually gave it to you straight. And fast.

"Well, you know how we've managed this friendship by pretty much avoiding politics, right?"

I agreed with him. We'd figured out early what we could share, and even learn from each other. And what there just was no point in going into. We'd gotten good at treasuring the positive, and just forgetting about the rest. After all, it wasn't like we *had* to agree on abortion rights or the American invasion of Iraq.

"So, I don't want you to take this the wrong way," he was still speaking slowly, buttering a dinner roll, "but since you're asking me, I've got to say that this is, well, pretty much one-sided. And it certainly isn't my side. The conservative religious people are a joke—a murderer and a Muslim fanatic. Then there's the mall developer with no conscience, an uptight scientist, and—did I miss anyone else? Oh yeah, a white-collar criminal. On the other hand, there is a whole rainbow of different liberals and radicals. Environmentalists who think we should work for the trees, and ones who are sympathetic to socialism, and some who want to fight violently for the cause. But is there a serious voice who says that a lot, a whole lot, of environmental rhetoric is overblown, and that a lot of the so-called science that environmental groups claim is more opinion than fact, and that environmentalists want more money for their organizations and that's what leads to their 'help, the sky is falling' rhetoric? Is there a serious voice defending this country as the greatest country on earth and the free market as part of what makes it great? Or who says that without religion you just can't have a moral society?"

He waited to see if I'd challenge him, drank some wine, then went on when I didn't.

"No, there isn't. So maybe this is a book just for liberals. But any self-respecting conservative would feel he'd just been parodied, marginalized, and treated like dirt."

I could see Joseph was upset. He was usually a pretty restrained, unflappable type, except when he lost it talking about insurance bureaucrats who gave him a hard time about his daughter's medical expenses. But this book had, well, *bothered* him. I wasn't sure why, but I didn't want to go into it any more. I told him not to worry about it and offered to buy him the fanciest dessert on the menu to repay him for reading the stories.

The real truth was that I couldn't take a lot of Joseph's political opinions seriously myself. Doubting the basic premises of environmentalism? Not seeing American imperialism as the threat that it was? Thinking of religion—*religion?*—with the clergy sex abuse and fanaticism and misogyny that it carried along with it, as some kind of guarantee of morality?

I just couldn't. There were limits.

Maybe that's what had happened to Samuel as well. Maybe Samuel, who was clearly on the liberal to even radical side, just couldn't take conservative beliefs seriously enough not to caricature people who held them. Maybe there was just an inevitable cutoff point that you can't overcome. I've always prided myself on being open to my students and undogmatic in class, but was I? Did I really make my conservative students feel they were as favored as the few student radicals who showed up?

If there was a way out, maybe it could only be for people like me and Joseph to become friends for years before we could cautiously, tenderly, talk about the things that divided us. Maybe you couldn't do it without some kind of personal bond, like the pro-choice and pro-life women who'd had conversations in Boston, and who had become friends despite their differences, but only after meeting together for a long time.

Maybe seeing some of the truth of somebody's ideas, even if you thought they were dead wrong, had something to do with seeing the truth of them as a person—as someone who was kind, and funny, and gentle to his disabled daughter as well as conservative. I knew Joseph, so I could trust him as a human being, and that would make it at least possible to think again about his wrongheaded ideas. I could trust that they were as important to him as mine were to me, that they helped him understand the world, connected him to people he loved, helped him get through the night. I could take him seriously, give him a kind of intellectual empathy, just like I could sympathize with what he went through as a father. And, I was pretty sure, he would eventually be able to give that to me as well.

I wasn't in the mood that night, but I know, as our friendship develops, at some time we will listen to each other. But without the personal bond? I didn't see how there could even be a chance. How could I trust, or value, people I didn't know? People whose ideas were dangerous and destructive? I could never love them as I loved Joseph. Was there some other way?

I also thought that maybe, just maybe, Joseph hadn't read the stories so carefully. I'd look again at the arguments Samuel gave the conservatives—could be they weren't so bad after all.

Finally, I tried Aamina, who works doing child care and some housecleaning for my brother's family. Aamina has been studying English for years, ever since she got here as a political refugee from a predominantly Muslim country in Africa. She had tried to organize a shelter for women who had been abused by their husbands. Some of the local religious authorities hadn't liked the idea, and she'd had to leave. In the middle of the night. In the trunk of a car underneath boxes of rags that the driver had told people were being sold in the capital.

An international women's organization had paid for her trip out, and somebody's connections to someone else had gotten her refugee status. She was smart, but not very educated. So she wasn't one of these refugees who could barely speak English but was teaching physics or doing eye surgery. She was a domestic helper, and felt pretty good about it, even though she missed her mother and her sisters.

I'd always had fun chatting with Aamina and occasionally would help with her English studies. So I thought it would be interesting to get her take on these stories. She might not get a lot of the cultural and historical references, but that would make her response pretty interesting in itself.

At first she demurred. Her English wasn't good enough. She was too ignorant to comment on someone who was a writer

(Aamina hadn't had enough education to hold writers in contempt). So I reassured her that her opinion was as good as anyone else's. In a way, that was what the book was about. That upped her confidence. And since I was her employer's brother, she probably didn't want to say no to me in any case.

Six weeks later I cornered her in the kitchen. Told her to sit down, I'd finish the dishes if she gave me her response to the stories.

"I really don't know what to say," she began. "I liked the stories. I liked the way they listened to each other and tried to keep talking even though they disagreed." I was a little surprised, comparing her response to Liz'. "And?" I pushed.

"And I don't know. I would like to educate myself more before I could figure out what I think about all these things. I told you, I don't know enough. But . . ."

"But what?" I prompted.

"But I can tell you one thing."

"And that is?"

"It is wonderful," here you could see the sincerity brimming out of her dark brown eyes. She reached out to touch my arm to emphasize her point, and then stopped herself from breaking decorum in such an obvious way.

"It is wonderful," she repeated, "to live in a place where people with such differences can talk at all. Where I come from, they don't talk so much. If you say the wrong thing, if you disagree with the wrong person, they just shoot you. Or rape you first and then shoot you. What a privilege, what a . . . gift you have here."

She looked up at me, smiling. And then her expression turned sad. "What a gift, but I wonder how many people know they have it. And now I have more work to do. Thank you for helping me."

"And you me," I answered, struck by what she had said. All Liz could see was the disagreement, the hostility. Joseph had seen his point of view marginalized. Aamina saw something else. Civility, a tradition of political discourse, real inquiry into different views. Or, if not fully real, at least something not usually terminated by a bullet in the back of the head. I thought again how limited we all were by what we took for granted. She also had pled ignorance. An easy way not so say something that might offend me? Or the kind of response too few of us ever offer? How often do any of us—how often do I—admit that we don't really know enough to offer a useful opinion?

And then I turned it around, a habit reading the stories had reinforced. Maybe Aamina was impressed by something that was just part of the illusions that run things around here. Sure we get to talk all we want, because it doesn't make any difference what we say. The people with real power do what they want, and the rest of us can write books, like this one, and complain and criticize, and no one cares. In other countries power is more fragile, unstable. What you say matters. So the violence comes a lot quicker.

Somewhere between all these views, I thought, between Joseph and Liz and Aamina and a dozen others I couldn't even think of, that's where the truth is.

How could I ever find that?

THE END?

So that's it. Or at least I thought that was it until last week, when I got a call from Aamina.

"Roger," she said, in a soft, hesitant voice, not sure if it was her place to speak but nevertheless having something to say. "I've been still wondering about those stories, that book you loaned me. And . . ."

"And?" I prompted. I was delighted that someone out of academia would take this kind of thing seriously enough to think twice about it.

"And what I don't understand is this word 'spiritual' that you use at the beginning. I understand 'nonviolent' because I knew about Gandhi before I came here, and since then I've learned about Martin Luther King Jr. But this idea of spiritual, we don't use it where I come from. Is it the same as religion, or is it just trying to be a good person, or is it something else?"

I had to teach a class then, and I promised I would get back to her with an answer soon. And I will, I'm sure.

In the meantime, I've realized she was completely right. What was that word doing here?

A few days ago I think I saw the answer, or at least the beginnings of one. I was driving home from work, listening to a famous conservative talk show host. I listen to these talk shows all the time, "to know what the enemy is thinking," I laughingly explain to friends. As I heard his views on health care, environmentalism, and immigration, I could feel my mind jumping around in two directions at the same time.

One direction was old, familiar, safe: "What an idiot, a dupe, or just an out-and-out tool of the rich and powerful. And the people who listen to him, how can they be so ignorant, misguided, and out of touch?" That was the old way to think, and it still has a big appeal for me.

But there was another response—a second one, going on, strangely enough, at the same time. "I'm sure most of what he says is wrong, and that won't change. But wait a minute, what he said there, and there—well, could be some truth in that, maybe not a lot, but some. And now, this point about immigration (or Democrats in Congress, or whatever), well, that's simply true. Why didn't I see that? Or if I did, why didn't I make a point of acknowledging it, instead of stomping on it just because it came from him?"

Between those two responses lies a choice: a choice to overcome my arrogance, and all the desperation and grief for the world underneath that arrogance. A choice to get over my desire to be right at all times and at all costs, and the emotional insecurity that lies under that desire. A willingness to put away my culturally male desire for victory; and my philosophical training, which taught me to go in for the quick kill in verbal encounters; and my adolescent tendency to want to stick it to somebody by showing them they don't know what they are talking about. And perhaps above all an opportunity to admit to myself how unsure I am of what needs to be done to protect the earth and make people more kind and more sane.

To live out the second response, I would have to listen with a fresh mind and be willing to admit how little—after all these years!—I know. I would have to feel that even in the turmoil of moral conflict and political struggle I could take a chance, trust that something in the universe would hold me safe so that I could at least listen to this other person I so wanted to despise. I could respect those I oppose to the point of trying, really trying, to understand what they are saying and the deep sense it makes to them. I wouldn't have to abandon my basic values and what I think is true, dissolve into a soft pudding of bland tolerance, or act as if everyone's point of view is equally valid. I wouldn't be called to surrender my convictions. No, I would simply learn to live them out in a way that allowed me to listen—honestly engaging with these other voices instead of trying to shut them out or shut them down.

What would help me choose the second option? Well, here's where "spiritual" comes in. Because I can't do it by myself. At least, I can't do it as my usual, ordinary Roger. The simple truth is that all the forces of fear and habit and my own despair are too strong to overcome without help from something else. You might say the help would come from prayer, or meditation, or a desperate desire to be a nicer rather than a meaner person, or a deep willingness to overcome my ego and transform myself into the compassionate and wise teacher I've often claimed I want to be. You can say the support has to come from a power greater than my individual self— God's grace, the Force of Spirit, an impersonal enlightenment. Or you could just say it would come from moral goodness, a slowly developing emotional maturity, or a quiet mental spaciousness that allows me to sit with things that bother me.

I describe what helps me as progress on a spiritual path—a long process of trying to move toward compassion, humility, self-awareness, and nonviolence; making myself (with great difficulty and many setbacks) a fundamentally different person—or perhaps just taking something that I've always had and making it an ever-larger part of my daily life. You can describe spiritual paths with religious words or with secular ones—I'm not sure it's all that important which. Patience, humility, devotion to the Lord, listening to your inner voice, imitating Christ or Moses or the Buddha, empowerment from the Goddess, overcoming attachments, finding a place of true balance, loving wisdom—yes, even the original meaning of "philosophy" fits in here as well. All these phrases and metaphors—they are all hopes that something can help us move beyond the limits that enslave us now; that something can make us, in some mysterious way, more whole, and can connect us to other people in a way that's good for all of us.

And that's what the word spiritual is doing here.

I'd like to say that reading Samuel's stories really helped me change, helped my spiritual development. And sometimes I think it's true. Other times I think the whole experience was like a dream: vivid, powerful, deeply moving—and soon forgotten. Probably it's somewhere in between. Maybe it's too soon to tell. I guess I'll just have to find out.

NOTES

I can't be certain where Samuel got his ideas for the stories, or his information either, for that matter. He was well read in philosophy, history, current events, and different religions but didn't have much sense of scholarly responsibility in the footnote area. So I've done some research to try to give the reader a way to pursue these ideas in more detail—and with less fictional shadings.

Introduction

bigger than the United States. The Pacific Garbage Patch is "The World's Largest Dump," *Discover*, July 10, 2008, http://discovermagazine .com/2008/jul/10-the-worlds-largest-dump. You may Google the Garbage Patch and find that it is "merely" the size of Texas—which is what it was when it first got wide publicity. It has grown since then. Body burden: "Body Burden—The Pollution in Newborns," Environmental Working Group Web site, July 2005, http://www.ewg.org/reports/bodyburden2/ execsumm.php.

I had my reasons. Some of these can be found in my *A Greener Faith: Religious Environmentalism and Our Planet's Future* (New York: Oxford University Press, 2006) and *A Spirituality of Resistance: Finding a Peaceful Heart and Protecting the Earth* (Lanham, Md.: Rowman & Littlefield, 2002).

blessing and what is the curse. Samuel had clearly read the Bible, carefully.

Probably he had this passage in mind, in which Moses summarizes God's law (again) in Deuteronomy 30:19: "This day I call heaven and earth as witnesses against you that I have set before you life and death, blessings and curses."

and the other thing you. This position is essential to the account of our moral interdependence in Alasdair MacIntyre, *Dependent Rational Animals: Why Human Beings Need the Virtues* (Chicago: Open Court, 2001). The ability and willingness to have an open-ended and ongoing conversation is also brilliantly represented as essential to moral life in Rowan Williams, *Dostoevsky: Language, Faith, and Fiction* (Waco, Tex.: Baylor University Press, 2008).

you get the idea. Interestingly, moral theory seems to combine two seemingly opposing tasks. On the one hand, we are charged to think ourselves out of our self-interested point of view so that we can understand and follow universal rules (as in Kant) or take everyone's happiness as seriously as our own (utilitarianism). On the other, we are directed inward—to reflect on our own emotional condition (as in feminist empathy or care ethics) or what would lead to a truly good life for ourselves (virtue theory). In all cases, however, the possibility can arise that our beliefs and values are distorted by our social situation.

Professional peacemakers do the same. Professional peacemakers engage with warring communities and try to get them to peaceful coexistence. Two interesting accounts of this are John Paul Lederach, *The Journey toward Reconciliation* (Scottdale, Penn.: Herald Press, 1999); and Michael Henderson, *No Enemy to Conquer: Forgiveness in an Unforgiving World* (Waco, Tex.: Baylor University Press, 2009). Carol Gilligan helped initiate a continuing discussion in ethical theory by arguing that women employ a culturally distinct form of moral reasoning based in empathy and communication rather than universal rules: *In a Different Voice: Psychological Theory and Women's Development* (Cambridge, Mass.: Harvard University Press, 1993). The idea that democracy is about communication rather than individual rights and the vote is developed brilliantly in Jeffrey Stout, *Democracy and Tradition* (Princeton: Princeton University Press, 2005). The ideal of the beloved community can be found in any history of the civil rights movement, and any study of Gandhi will describe his attitude toward external or internal opponents.

Chapter 1

and it was all my own fault. Astute readers will notice that Samuel has lifted the essential story line of Leo Tolstoy's *The Death of Ivan Ilyich*, in which a shallow, selfish, careerist bureaucrat is morally remade by illness. In Tolstoy's version the protagonist dies. I've often wondered what would have happened if he'd made a miraculous recovery.

to obey their husbands. This is a common theme in some fundamentalist Christian circles, for which feminist ideas of gender equality are the source of terrible social ills. For a detailed and clear-eyed account of this aspect of contemporary Christianity, see Kathryn Joyce, *Quiverfull: Inside the Christian Patriarchy Movement* (Boston: Beacon Press, 2009).

the natural law for all peoples. This is an essential belief of the most aggressive forms of contemporary Islam. The basic claim is that Sharia law is as theologically and morally right for human beings as, say, strictures on health derived from medicine. To resist this law is thus a betrayal of one's own interests, and the effort to impose it is one of service, not conquest. See Michael Scheuer, *Through our Enemies' Eyes: Osama bin Laden, Radical Islam, and the Future of America* (Washington, D.C.: Potomac Books, 2007).

and you call us terrorists. Whatever else one may say about al-Qaeda, and one may say a great deal, they are not lacking for extensive justifications of their actions. These are illuminating in many ways. See Raymond Ibrahim, ed., *The Al-Qaeda Reader* (New York: Broadway, 2007).

I blew him away. Jamaal's story parallels that of Ali in the classic film *Battle of Algiers* (1966). As the anticolonial forces develop power in the Arab quarter, they first warn, and then execute, drug dealers.

do whatever we want. Expressed in a wide variety of ways, the essential idea is the liberal claim that political freedom and equality grant each of us an opportunity to pursue our personal philosophical, religious, aesthetic (etc.) interests, especially since with the decline of the social status of religion there is no commonly accepted understanding of what the goal of a human life should be. John Rawls has described this as the absence of shared "comprehensive [philosophical, religious] doctrines" in modern societies. In John Rawls, *Political Liberalism* (New York: Columbia University Press, 1993). Richard Rorty has made the same point repeatedly by saying that individual pursuits of artistic excellence, extreme athleticism, meditative bliss, or anything else are an essentially personal matter separate from political control or moral evaluation. In Richard Rorty, *Contingency, Irony, and Solidarity* (New York: Cambridge University Press, 1993).

This is your secular freedom? Many religious or "communitarian" critics of secular society make the argument that without shared values, preferably religious ones, human beings become confused, depressed, morally out of control, etc. For a position that combines both the religious and the communitarian with a serious critique of the weaknesses of liberal society and politics, see Stanley Hauerwas, *The Hauerwas Reader* (Durham, N.C.: Duke University Press, 2002).

U.S. government to Zimbabwe. Samuel had clearly done his homework here. For details on what this looks like in a foreign country, where a combination of powerful multinational corporations, the local political elite, and U.S. governmental support combined to seriously exploit the local population in India's Maharashtra state, see Arundhati Roy, *Power Politics* (Boston: South End Press, 2002).

Buddhists came to teach here. As unlikely as it sounds, there have been a number of projects in which Buddhist meditation is taught in prisons. *The Dhamma Brothers* (2008) (http://www.dhammabrothers.com/) is a fascinating movie about a project in a Georgia prison, which was not limited to a few hours of weekly instruction but led to a ten-day, ten-hour-a-day meditation retreat. For a print account, see Jenny Phillips, *Letters from the Dhamma Brothers* (Onalaska, Wash.: Pariyatti Publishing, 2008).

My anger is a bigger poison. The *Dhammapada* is a collection of early Buddhist teaching, often attributed to the Buddha himself. In its first verse we find, "If a man speaks or acts with an evil thought, pain follows him, as the wheel follows the foot of the ox that draws the carriage."

used to cure the hides. This kind of story, sadly, is a common one in the "toxics" movement in the U.S. and around the world. The films *A Civil Action* (1998) and *Erin Brockovich* (2000) brought such local disasters to popular awareness. Lois Gibbs, an "ordinary" (extraordinary) citizen who faced a toxic neighborhood in Love Canal in New York State, helped found a national organization to confront comparable situations: the Center for Health, Environment, and Justice (http://www.chej.org/about.htm).

Then I found Earth First! For an insider account of the formation and activities of Earth First!, see Judi Bari, *Timber Wars* (Monroe, Maine: Common Courage Press, 1994). For a variety of intelligent philosophical perspectives on the strengths and weaknesses of direct action in environmental politics, see Peter List, ed., *Radical Environmentalism: Philosophy and Tactics* (Florence, Ky.: Wadsworth, 1993). Christopher Manes describes the formation and cultural values of the movement in *Green Rage: Radical Environmentalism and the Unmaking of Civilization* (Boston: Back Bay Books, 1991).

Chapter 2

I'm ready to do some protecting. This religious commitment to environmentalism is described in my books noted above. There is also an intriguing film, *Renewal* (2008), which contains short segments on nine different religious communities taking action (http://www.renewalproject.net/).

you **are the endangered species**. With the concept of environmental racism (and environmental justice, which is what you get when you don't have environmental racism anymore), the environmental movement morphed into a comprehensive confrontation with virtually all aspects of contemporary social and political issues. Since there are interconnections among the economy, consumption, poverty, militarism, human rights, health care, gender, race, and all aspects of environmental practices, virtually nothing is left out. For readers unfamiliar with the concept, a good starting point is

Robert D. Bullard, ed., *The Quest for Environmental Justice: Human Rights and the Politics of Pollution* (San Francisco: Sierra Club Books, 2005). Many religious groups use the term "ecojustice" and have task forces working on it.

But that's not why I'm doing it. I don't know if Samuel was aware of the extensive writings on the philosophical question of whether or not nature has "intrinsic" value or if only people deserve, in and of themselves, moral consideration. Out of the seeming intractability of this question, a position known as "environmental pragmatism" has arisen, arguing that we can put off the theoretical disagreements and that both sides can work together on shared issues of environmental concern. The reasons for one's activism are unimportant compared to the activism itself. See Andrew Light and Eric Katz, eds., *Environmental Pragmatism* (New York: Routledge, 1996).

land got moved somewhere else. This has been a common practice from the nineteenth-century creation of national parks in the U.S. to worldwide conservation efforts today. See Mark Dowie, *Conservation Refugees* (Cambridge, Mass.: MIT Press, 2009).

I value you as well. There are many philosophical attempts to support the claim that animals, plants, and ecosystems possess inherent moral value and should be taken seriously as beings meriting some kind of moral concern. A very clear version is found in Holmes Rolston III, "Environmental Ethics: Duties To and In the Natural World," in *Environmental Ethics*, ed. Michael Boylan (Upper Saddle River, N.J.: Prentice Hall, 2001).

suck power all the time. So-called "standby power" is omnipresent in American households and now in many other places in the world. It includes TVs or other appliances which can be turned on by remote controls, the ubiquitous clocks on microwaves or DVD players, etc., and it accounts, in the U.S. alone, for 5–10 percent of domestic energy use—more than the total combined energy consumption of Greece and Vietnam.

It's some particular group. Here Samuel is invoking the political perspective of what is sometimes called "social ecology"—a perspective which includes ecofeminism, socialist or Marxist ecology, etc. The general idea here is that humanity's treatment of the natural world is largely a product of humanity's treatment of itself, and that this relation must be understood in fairly conventional terms of collective forms of domination, oppression, and exploitation. The journal *Capitalism Nature Socialism* has been exploring this perspective for many years.

Chapter 3

unity among the oppressed. This is the role of the communist in Lenin's classic pamphlet "What Is to Be Done?" Central to Lenin's position was the idea that without the leadership of the party, different segments of the working class would remain separated by their own limited interests.

they were just *part* of nature. The Australian rain forest activist John Seed, on engaging in civil disobedience to obstruct the clearing of a major area of forest: "I knew then that I was no longer acting on behalf of myself or my human ideas, but on behalf of the Earth . . . on behalf of my larger self, that I was literally part of the rainforest defending herself." John Seed, *Thinking Like a Mountain* (Philadelphia: New Society Publishers, 1988), 6.

they have to come first. On the one hand, it would seem natural that our moral responsibility to our family outweighs those to strangers. On the other, we might wonder by just how much it outweighs. In what I call the Godfather defense, people sometimes say that they are justified in all sorts of horrible actions because they are "just putting food on my family's table." Clearly, there is a limit; just how much of a limit is a matter of great moral import.

and tired to think straight. Interestingly, this matches my experiences of small-group politics in 1970s Boston.

It's a simple, iron law. Sociologist Robert Michels, *Political Parties: A Socio-logical Study of the Oligarchical Tendencies of Modern Democracy* (New York: Free Press, 1966), invoked what he called the "iron law of oligarchy" to help explain the collapse of the Second International of Socialist Parties. The idea is applicable to any structured group in which leaders have interests different from those of the rank and file: for instance, because they get money, power, prestige, etc. by being leaders of the group. I have examined the historical examples Roger is describing in *History and Subjectivity: The Transformation of Marxist Theory* (Philadelphia: Temple University Press, 1986) and *Marxism 1844–1990: Origins, Betrayal, Rebirth* (New York: Routledge, 1992).

this huge recession we're having. Well before the recession, counterattacks on feminism were manifest in a number of ways. See Susan Faludi, *Backlash: The Undeclared War on American Women* (New York: Anchor, 1992).

But it's just not possible. Perhaps the best way to understand the point being made here is that current forms of injustice and irrationality depend not just on the inculcation of false beliefs (about the economy or foreign policy, for example) but also on the creation of personality structures. Competitiveness, consumerism, hyperindividualism, fear of responsibility, deference to authority—all these make cooperative political action toward social change extremely difficult. See the essays by Max Horkheimer, Theodor Adorno, Herbert Marcuse, and especially Wilhelm Reich in Roger S. Gottlieb, ed., *An Anthology of Western Marxism: From Lukács and Gramsci to Socialist-Feminism* (New York: Oxford University Press, 1990).

Some people think environmental reasons. There is in fact a great deal of evidence that environmental causes are at the heart of a devastating rise in chronic illness among America's children, nearly one-third of whom suffer from a variety of serious ailments. For details, see Philip Shabecoff and Alice Shabecoff, *Poisoned Profits: The Toxic Assault on Our Children* (New York: Random House, 2009).

Chapter 4

Her voice trailed off. This is actually a scene from a movie called *The Witness* (2000), a short and deceptively simple documentary about how working-class building contractor Eddie Lama became a vigorous advocate of animal rights. Lama outfitted the truck and stopped at intersections in Manhattan. The film shows the often intense reactions of passersby.

a little like killing myself. When my daughter, Anna Gottlieb, saw *The Witness*, this was her reaction.

way we treat animals. Most environmental organizations have Web site pages with this information. For one example, see this National Resources Defense Council report on factory farm lagoons, where wastes are improperly stored: http://www.nrdc.org/water/pollution/cesspools/cessinx.asp. For a book on this topic, see Christina Johnson, *Factory Farming* (London: Blackwell, 1991).

than the intuitions themselves. The idea that one task of moral theory is to balance highly general principles with particular and powerfully felt moral intuitions is known as "reflective equilibrium." It stems from the work of political philosopher John Rawls.

free conversation is what's right. This position has been developed over the last thirty years both by Jürgen Habermas and by proponents of "deliberative democracy." See, for example, Jürgen Habermas, *The Theory of Communicative Action*, trans. Thomas McCarthy (Cambridge: Polity, 1984–1987); and Amy Gutmann and Dennis Thompson, *Democracy and Disagreement* (Cambridge, Mass.: Harvard University Press, 1996).

if we wanted them to. A powerful criticism of the idea that animals can communicate in a way relevant to moral discussion is developed by Steven Vogel, *Against Nature: The Concept of Nature in Critical Theory* (Albany: State University of New York Press, 1996), chapter 6.

and bring back guidance. This is a key element in any form of shamanism. For a philosophical account that describes the human-nature relationship in a way somewhat less dependent on a non-Western culture, see David Abram, *The Spell of the Sensuous* (New York: Pantheon, 1998), especially the brilliant first chapter. For a perspective directly adapted to environmental issues, see Joanna Macy, *World as Lover, World as Self* (Berkeley, Calif.: Parallax, 1991).

really something we make. See Vogel, *Against Nature*, as well as many authors with a "postmodern" perspective. I have addressed both sides of this argument in some detail in *Spirituality of Resistance*, chapter 4.

get treated like dirt. Competition among oppressed groups is addressed by any serious history of progressive political movements. I have examined its impact on political struggles in *History and Subjectivity*. For an account of the emergence of awareness of and response to environmental racism, see Luke Cole and Sheila Foster, *From the Ground Up: Environmental Racism and the Rise of the Environmental Justice Movement* (New York: NYU Press, 2001).

know something about them as well. For a wonderful introduction to interspecies communication, see Jim Nollman, *The Charged Border: Where Whales and Humans Meet* (New York: Henry Holt, 1999). There are incredible stories of the amazing things animals can do in Eugene Linden, *The Octopus and the Orangutan: New Tales of Animal Intrigue, Intelligence, and Ingenuity* (New York: Plume, 2003).

for white hunters or tourists. For a history and critique of Western attitudes and practices in wildlife conservation, see Raymond Bonner, *At the Hand of Man: Peril and Hope for Africa's Wildlife* (New York: Knopf, 1993).

a free-range organic turkey. The value of the "free-range" designation is itself rather questionable. It may mean no more than that the turkey has some extremely limited access to the outdoors. See, e.g., the "all-creatures" Web site, http://all-creatures.org/anex/turkey-fr-01.html.

poisoned by oil development. For a quick overview of this struggle, see "Fact Sheet on the Ogoni Struggle," on the Ending Corporate Governance Web site, at http://www.ratical.org/corporations/OgoniFactS.html. Essentially, oil development has turned a highly fertile area into a ravaged landscape colored by death, where church sermons implore God to keep oil from being discovered nearby.

Chapter 5

there will not be another. Besides my *A Greener Faith: Religious Environmentalism and Our Planet's Future* (New York: Oxford University Press, 2006), evidence of the remarkable growth and scope of religious environmentalism can be found in the following books, which I edited: *The Oxford Handbook of Religion and Ecology* (New York: Oxford University Press, 2006); *This Sacred Earth: Religion, Nature, Environment*, 2nd ed. (New York: Routledge, 2003); and *Religion and the Environment*, vols. 1–4 (London: Routledge, 2010). There is also the *Encyclopedia of Religion and Nature*, ed. Bron Taylor (London: Continuum, 2006), filled with a wide range of intelligent and readable articles. For those who like the Web more than the page, see Forum on Religion and Ecology (http://fore.research.yale.edu/religion/) and Alliance of Religions and Conservation (http://www.arcworld.org/).

Worse than useless. Criminal. Many years ago historian Lynn White helped shape the conversation on Western, and in particular Christian, responsibility for environmental destruction, calling Christianity history's "most anthropocentric religion." Lynn Townsend White Jr., "The Historical

Roots of Our Ecologic Crisis," *Science* 155, no. 3767 (March 10, 1967): 1203–7. Reprinted in Gottlieb, ed., *This Sacred Earth*.

killing the towns and the people. Mountaintop removal is without doubt one of the great environmental crimes in the contemporary U.S. See the Web site of the Mountaintop Removal Clearinghouse, http://mtrinfo. wordpress.com.

the industry-embracing communists. Communist governments typically sacrificed environmental concerns, if they were aware of them at all, to military power and economic growth. Much of the Soviet Union and eastern Europe had disastrous environmental situations. See Fred Singleton, ed., *Environmental Problems in the Soviet Union and Eastern Europe* (Boulder, Colo.: Lynne Rienner Publishers, 1987). Contemporary China, which might in some sense be called communist (though as a friend once remarked, it is really a kind of Market Stalinism), has environmental problems so severe that they threaten to counterbalance the country's recent economic expansion. See, e.g., Jacques Leslie, "The Last Empire: China's Pollution Problem Goes Global," *Mother Jones*, December 2007, http://motherjones.com/environment/2007/12/last-empire-chinas-pollution-problem-goes-global.

Paganism isn't the problem anymore. Samuel is probably thinking of Ismar Schorch, for many years chancellor of Conservative Judaism's rabbinical training program, who wrote something very much like this in an article, "Tending to Our Cosmic Oasis," *Melton Journal* (Spring 1991).

Ecology . . . and justice. Ecojustice! This term has become the fundamental one for many religious environmental organizations. It suggests an alternative to any attempt to force a choice between humans and nature and stresses the inevitable links between reckless or unjust exploitation of either nature or people. For one example, see the National Council of Churches of Christ working group on ecojustice, http://nccecojustice .org/.

She just saw the world. This ingenious way of trying to explain the difference between theists and atheists first came to my attention in John Wisdom's beautiful article, "Gods," in his *Other Minds* (London: Blackwell, 1952).

the EPA, the *EPA*, censored it. Sadly, this sort of thing was common for many years. See this book coauthored by the head of the Sierra Club: Carl Pope and Paul Rauber, *Strategic Ignorance: Why the Bush Administration Is Recklessly Destroying a Century of Environmental Progress* (San Francisco: Sierra Club Books, 2004). Many groups of scientists publicly protested this kind of interference with their work.

leading environmental scientists, are believers. There are far too many examples of this claim to list here, but they range from Nobel Prize in Physics winners to the head of the National Human Genome Project.

it was people like me. Here is a solid account of the pesticide problem: Marvin J. Levine, *Pesticides: A Toxic Time Bomb in Our Midst* (Santa Barbara, Calif.: Greenwood Press, 2007).

a loving eye to see clearly. Years ago, feminist philosopher Marilyn Frye coined this phrase in *The Politics of Reality: Essays in Feminist Theory* (Freedom, Calif.: Crossing Press, 1983). Similar ideas about the preconditions for truly understanding living organisms can be found in the work and reflections of Nobel Prize–winning plant geneticist Barbara McClintock. For a description of McClintock's work, see Evelyn Fox Keller's aptly titled *A Feeling for the Organism: The Life and Work of Barbara McClintock* (New York: W. H. Freeman, 1984).

it's all dead or dying. At a conference I attended I heard a similarly highly regarded scientist, an oceanographer, say the same thing.

and a bad man worse. I encountered a version of this anecdote in a talk by leading environmental philosopher Holmes Rolston III.

Chapter 6

criticism of everything existing. Samuel probably got this phrase from the youthful Marx's 1843 letter in which he called for a *"ruthless criticism* of all that exists, ruthless both in the sense of not being afraid of the results it arrives at and in the sense of being just as little afraid of conflict with the powers that be." Marx to Arnold Ruge, September 1843, Letters from the Deutsch-Französische Jahrbücher, Marxists.org Web site, http://www.marxists.org/archive/marx/works/1843/letters/43_09.htm (emphasis in original).

better than anyone else, can you? This is the common idea that science is distinguished by its capacity to identify the actual nature of reality, producing truths which increase in scope and adequacy as research progresses, while other fields—philosophy and theology being two key examples—simply change. The question of the purpose of fields like religious studies or moral theory is itself old and complex. Throughout the history of philosophy, for example, many philosophers have claimed that while in the past other thinkers had been unsuccessful at coming to meaningful, rational conclusions, they now had a method which changed all that. Typically they were subjected to the exact same kind of criticism a few decades later. There is no space here to delve into this issue with any real seriousness. However, in terms of whether or not a field like philosophy is of any value, we might simply ask this: even if science is the one true source of rational knowledge, how do we know which fields are science and which aren't? This doesn't seem like a scientific question (since scientists, after all, don't study science but things like chemicals and atoms), and if it isn't a scientific question, what kind of a question is it?

Science in the service of life. The idea of a "new" holistic science, one predicated on cooperation, respect, or even reverence for nature rather than control of it, has many sources. The Frankfurt School of critical theory criticized the tendency to identify instrumental reason—the ability to accomplish a pregiven end or goal—with reason in general. Herbert Marcuse, in particular, posed the idea that there might be a science in the service of some other end than domination. Martin Heidegger connected Western science to a long tradition of Western philosophy which objectified Being as something to be simply used in human projects. More recently, feminist writers Carolyn Merchant and Susan Griffin contrasted culturally feminine forms of appreciation for the earth with the modern scientific project of control expressed in thinkers like Francis Bacon. Rachel Carson put it simply and powerfully: "The control of nature is a phrase conceived in arrogance, born of the Neanderthal age of biology and the convenience of man." *Silent Spring* (Boston: Houghton Mifflin, 1962), 297. The links between scientific research and economic, political, and military power are explored in many places. See Sheldon Krimsky, *Science in the Private Interest: Has the Lure of Profits Corrupted Biomedical Research?* (Lanham, Md.: Rowman & Littlefield, 2004). In relation to cancer research, see Devra Davis, *The Secret History of the War on Cancer* (New York: Basic Books, 2007).

like the World Bank. The case of dams and the World Bank is particularly instructive. Even after an internal study by the Bank itself showed that huge dams typically have negative human, ecological, and economic effects, the policy of funding dam projects continued.

housewife telling them something isn't safe. This is a familiar pattern in the antitoxics movement in the U.S.

or they just didn't care. The Newfoundland story is an example of the devastation that has been wrought in the world's fisheries. We now have a situation in which close to three-quarters of the world's food fishes have been greatly depleted or pretty nearly fished out. It is about as clear a case of the combination of scientific/technical expertise (huge trawlers; following schools of fish with sonar; catching, treating, and packaging fish all in one vessel) with an overall irrationality as can be imagined. See "Canadian Fisheries Collapse," Greenpeace Web site, http://archive.greenpeace.org/comms/cbio/cancod.html.

like the only game in town. This question leads us out of the realm of intellectual reality and into that of emotional insecurity, an insecurity that sustains and is sustained by a cultural climate of competition for scarce economic and psychological (love, praise, status, etc.) resources. It also raises the issue of how spiritual self-awareness and self-acceptance might make it easier to accept the reality of our physical and intellectual interdependence.

Chapter 7

"Bangladesh?" he asked skeptically. The organization is called Nayakrishi Andolon. It is discussed in Bill McKibben's book *Deep Economy* (New York: Macmillan, 2007), 200–209; and is described in a research paper by the international development research center (http://www.idrc.ca/en/ev-85301-201-1-DO_TOPIC.html).

Chapter 8

saying Kaddish for him as I walked. Kaddish is the traditional Jewish prayer for the dead.

in a death camp, it didn't matter. Samuel is using the actual story of the inmate uprising in Auschwitz. The woman slave was Rosa Robota, who was caught and hung. The Russian prisoner was named Borodin. Generally not well known, there was armed Jewish resistance to the Nazis in the ghettos, the camps, and the forests. For one of the many accounts of this resistance, see Yuri Suhl, *They Fought Back: The Story of Jewish Resistance in Nazi Europe* (New York: Schocken Books, 1975).

God is dead. Samuel's literary nod to the philosopher Friedrich Nietzsche, who coined this phrase.

God is a relationship. From Søren Kierkegaard to Martin Buber and Emmanuel Levinas, this is a familiar, if typically marginalized, understanding of religious life. Most people seem to prefer to think that God really is like the couch.

it disappears altogether. As I read this, I couldn't help wondering if Samuel had been influenced a bit by the classic Hindu text The Bhagavad Gita. In a conversation between the human Arjuna and the Lord Krishna, Krishna manifests himself in countless different guises (chapter 11). There is a similar vision toward the end of Herman Hesse's profound study of spiritual life, *Siddhartha*.

what is most called for. The radical psychiatrist R. D. Laing raised a similar possibility at the beginning of his visionary book *The Politics of Experience* (New York: Pantheon, 1983).

an environmental midrash. This was Samuel at his most playful—for I'd published a shorter version of this midrash under my own name as "A Real Coda to an Imaginary Trial," *Conservation Biology* 20, no. 6 (2006): 1574–75.

could be a paradise. Fyodor Dostoevsky, *The Brothers Karamazov*, trans. A. R. MacAndrew (New York: Bantam, 2003), 383.

Chapter 9

That *is* the way men talk. A great deal has been written on the differences between male and female communicative styles. The overall idea is that a culturally male style is more individualistic, competitive, aggressive, and problem solving, while a culturally female style tends toward openness, relationality, affiliation, and empathy. See, for example, Deborah Tannen, *You Just Don't Understand: Women and Men in Conversation* (New York: Harper, 2001).

Friends despite their differences. For a discussion of this experience, see "Talking with the Enemy," Public Conversations Web site, http://www.publicconversations.org/dialogue/policy/abortion.

ACKNOWLEDGMENTS

Many people were kind enough to read drafts of this book and tell me what they thought, encourage me that it was worthwhile, and make very helpful suggestions. I am indebted to them all: Miriam Greenspan, John Sanbonmatsu, Seamus Carey, Nick Baker, Svetlana Nikitina, Sid Brown, Mordechai Liebling, Constance Clark, Anne Mackin, Andrew Bingham, Anthony Weston, Vincent Pawlowski, David Barnhill, Seth Karstaedt, Candace Chouinard, Kristin Boudreau.

To the folks who told me, "This isn't bad, Roger, but you should try to make it more like Dostoevsky," I can only say I'm still working on that one.

My deep gratitude also to Carey Newman, head of Baylor University Press, for initial interest in a Quite Different type of book, and for unflinching criticism delivered with a gentle touch. It has been a real pleasure to work with Baylor University Press on this project.

Above all, my appreciation for those people, now and over the long centuries, who have tried to combine understanding the world with loving it.

And to my friends the trees.